The Indispensable Guide
for Smaller Churches

The
Indispensable Guide
for Smaller Churches

David R. Ray

The Pilgrim Press
Cleveland

The Pilgrim Press, 700 Prospect Avenue East, Cleveland, Ohio 44115-1100
pilgrimpress.com
© 2003 David R. Ray

Grateful acknowledgement for permission to reprint from the following: Excerpt from "Choruses from 'The Rock'" in *Collected Poems 1909–1962* by T.S. Eliot, copyright 1936 by Harcourt, Inc., copyright © 1964, 1963 by T.S. Eliot, reprinted by permission of the publisher. • Excerpts from "Little Gidding - V" in *Four Quartets*, copyright 1942 by T.S. Eliot and renewed 1970 by Esme Valerie Eliot, reprinted by permission of Harcourt, Inc. • Nancy T. Foltz, *Religious Education in the Small Membership Church*, published by Religious Education Press. • From *Traveling Mercies* by Anne Lamott, copyright © 1999 by Anne Lamott. Used by permission of Pantheon Books, a division of Random House, Inc. • Reprinted with permission from Peter L. Benson and Carolyn H. Eklin, *Effective Christian Education: A National Study of Protestant Congregations—A Summary Report on Faith, Loyalty, and Congregational Life* (Minneapolis, MN: Search Institute). © Search Institute, 1990. <www.search-institute.org>. • Reprinted from *Developing Your Small Church's Potential* by Carl S. Dudley and Douglas Alan Walrath, copyright © 1988 by Judson Press. Used by permission of Judson Press, 800-4-JUDSON, www.judsonpress.com. • *Looking in the Mirror: Self-appraisal in the Local Church*, Lyle E. Schaller (Nashville, Tenn.: Abingdon, 1984). Used by permission. • *Meeting the Moment: Leadership and Well-Being in Ministry*, G. Douglass Lewis (Nashville, Tenn.: Abingdon, 1997). Used by permission. • Arlin J. Rothauge, *Sizing Up the Congregation for New Member Ministry* (New York: Episcopal Church Center, 1989). Used by permission. • Cris Williamson, "Song of the Soul," (Marcola, Oreg.: Bird Ankles Music, 1973). Used by permission. • Douglas A. Walrath, "Types of Small Congregations and Their Implications for Planning," *Small Churches Are Beautiful*, ed. Jackson W. Carroll (San Francisco: Harper & Row, 1977). Used by permission of author.

06 05 04 03   5 4 3 2 1

Library of Congress Cataloging-in-Publication Data

Ray, David R., 1942-
    The indispensable guide for smaller churches / David R. Ray.
        p.   cm.
    Includes bibliographical references and index.
    ISBN 0-8298-1507-4 (pbk. : alk. paper)
    1. Small churches.   I. Title.

BV637.8 .R388   2002
254—dc21   2002042541

Contents

Preface

I love the church. I do not want to write about the church as a
problem, a source of conflict, a place of controversies, but as the
Body of Christ for us here and now.
                                   —Henri J. M. Nouwen, *Sabbatical Journey*

THANK YOU FOR PICKING UP THIS BOOK. I invite you to join me in
thinking what we have not thought before, in understanding smaller
churches in new ways, and in exploring how we might invest our
talents and resources in their greater faithfulness. It will assist you in
thinking deeply, creatively, and concretely about that which God loves
deeply, which has been crucial in history, and which the future will
depend on—smaller communities of faith. It will provide you with
thorough understanding, genuine handles, tools, and strategies that
fit and work.

Is this book intended for you? If you are interested in the subject of
smaller churches, then it's for you. If you are a pastor of a smaller
church or are considering providing pastoral leadership for smaller
congregations, then this book is especially for you. If you are a layperson (and thus the lifeblood of a smaller church), then this is defi-
nitely for you and those like you. If you are in a larger church and
would like your church to feel and act like the best of a smaller church,
then this is also for you. If you're in the seminary world, then this
book can be used as a text in many courses and schools. For denominational people who work with smaller churches, this can be a helpful resource for your ministry. In fact, this book is for anyone who
wonders about God's church in God's future.

Walker Percy's novel, *The Moviegoer*, speaks of the deepest of life's meanings. The main character, Binx Bolling, says:

> What is the nature of the search? you ask. Really it is very simple at least for a fellow like me; so simple that it is easily overlooked. The search is what anyone would undertake if he were not sunk in the everydayness of his own life. . . . To become aware of the possibility of the search is to be on to something. Not to be on to something is to be in despair.[1]

It's in the search for spiritual meaning, greater faithfulness, and addressing the needs of others that churches find their zest for life and hope for tomorrow. Many churches, including smaller ones, have ceased searching and have sunk into the everydayness of their own lives or are drowning in difficulty and despair. Each of the four churches I've pastored awakened to the possibility of the search. As we searched, we found what we were "on to," what enlivened our worship, what permeated our common life, what led us to our mission—in short, that which was our *raison d'être*. Being on to something true and vital is the hope of the church and makes all the difference in preventing everydayness and despair.

In the following pages, I will share with you what a variety of faithful and effective churches—especially smaller ones—and I are on to. I will introduce you to a score of churches from coast to coast; I will help you better understand smaller churches in all their considerable complexity and uniqueness; I will help you discern their theological validity; and I will help you envision how they can be a precursor of and paradigm for the future and not an anachronism from the past.

I've been committed to smaller churches since I was in seminary in 1968. Over the past thirty years, I've been pastor of four, very different, smaller churches, from coast to coast and from very rural to urban. The only qualities they shared were their size, their denomination, and the fact that they were all in serious decline. The Trinitarian Congregational Church of Warwick, Massachusetts, was a hill-town, blue-collar church of fourteen or so mostly older folks plus a few children, whose church was two rooms in an old colonial house. The

Shrewsbury Community Church in Shrewsbury, Vermont, was the troubled remnant of a three-church merger in the mountains above Rutland, Vermont. The United Church of Christ in Emmetsburg, Iowa, was on the brink of closing in the Catholic, Lutheran, Methodist, shrinking-county-seat town in Palo Alto County, Iowa. The First Congregational Church of San Rafael, California, just north of San Francisco, is in a quite beautiful, very secular and urbane environment. It was once much larger and is a highly educated congregation.

These very dissimilar congregations actually have one very important trait in common—their size. These smaller churches each grew in every way and were vibrant and highly faithful, even as they retained the positive qualities of a smaller congregation.

Throughout my ministry, I've "moonlighted" with other callings while being a pastor. I've been part of three United Church of Christ regional staffs, taught at six seminaries, written three other books about smaller churches, been a program resource and consultant for a dozen denominations from coast to coast, and worked as a pastoral counselor and director of two social service agencies. Since 1971, I've been on to two things—I am called to bring life and direction to some of God's smaller churches and these smaller churches share two fundamental and defining characteristics:

- They are the right size to be and do all that God created congregations to be and do.
- Because of the power and consequences of numbers, smaller churches are fundamentally different than other sized churches.

These two fundamental and defining characteristics have been missed or dismissed by many in the church world.

What makes this book indispensable is its comprehensive, personal, and time-tested approach to the subject of smaller churches. While smaller churches seem simple to understand, they aren't. There's much to comprehend, and there are many pitfalls to trip the novice and the nonobservant. Just as a traveler buys a guide prepared by those who have gone before to assist in charting the journey, a guide that provides essential history and information, identifies the highlights, and suggests what should not be missed, this is a comprehensive guide for those who journey in the complex and intriguing world of smaller churches.

The title of this book uses the word "smaller," not "small." In a bigger-is-better world, many church people are embarrassed or ashamed to identify their church as "small." To many, small means failure, inadequacy, immaturity, or a stage that precedes legitimacy. One thing I'm on to is that smaller churches won't fulfill what they can be as long as they deny or are ashamed of what they are. So I use the word "smaller" because it is more gentle and acceptable to many with whom I want to communicate.

The title also uses the word "churches." "Church" is the organized community in which I live and work and know and write about. However, much in this book is relevant for those in faith communities other than Christian churches and for those in other kinds of smaller groups, such as schools and social and work groups. I have also drawn on and utilized material from a wide variety of resources outside the church world.

This book is not a recycling of what I've written before. *Small Churches Are the Right Size* was a comprehensive book for the 1980s. *The Big Small Church Book* took small churches into the new century. Building on the cumulative foundation of that earlier work, this book takes smaller churches further into the new century. I've sought out the experiences of many smaller churches, which addresses the reality of both urban and rural smaller churches.

The reader will find here a theology that defines the crucial role of smaller faith communities in a world grown too large, too fast, and too impersonal. There are enough theoretical tools to help the practitioner craft a ministry that specifically fits her or his setting and congregation. In addition to new approaches to worship, education, care giving, and mission, the reader will find substantive chapters on morale and self-esteem, finances in smaller churches, and attracting and keeping new people. The questions for thought and discussion at the end of each chapter make this a useful study book for groups of laity and pastors' groups. Finally, I will look deeply into my crystal ball to try to see what the next thirty years holds for smaller churches.

This book is both an anthology of timeless truth and a timely book that draws on the best of current thinking. Some of the best old and tested wisdom is here along with that which is fresh and new. In the spirit of a good anthology, I've provided a composite of the profound and the anecdotal, the historical and the futuristic, the theoretical and the pragmatic, the challenging and the reassuring.

When is a church small or smaller? The most common criteria is that it has less than one hundred attending worship. By this standard, two-thirds of the Protestant churches in the United States are smaller churches. In Chapter 4, I name and describe thirty qualities characteristic of a smaller church. These are qualities that can result in greater faithfulness and effectiveness. Larger churches can strategize ways to realize many of these qualities, thus helping their larger church feel and act like a smaller one. In the Roman Catholic Church, there is a growing movement of over 37,000 "small Christian communities." There are millions of intentional small gatherings of the faithful throughout the world. A case can be made that smaller faith communities are the wave of the future.

This book is dedicated to two groups of people. First, I'm profoundly grateful to the people of the four churches who have called me "Pastor" over the last thirty years. They have been good to me, taught me much, and followed me far. I'm particularly grateful to the people of First Congregational Church in San Rafael, California, who have journeyed with me on an extraordinarily fruitful nine-year adventure and granted me time to write this book.

Second, this book is dedicated to you, the readers. Unless people like you catch the vision of what's possible and needed and provide the required leadership, thousands of smaller churches will close just when our society needs their genuine community and opportunity for belonging.

Our family was vacationing at our old farmhouse off the coast of Maine. As we prepared for the visit of a large family, our plumbing completely stopped up. Our regular plumber was busy, so we called Jim, a young plumber who had just moved to the island. He came at eight the next morning, went to work, and solved our main problem, plus a few others. Impressed by his knowledge and skill, I asked whether he had been raised in a plumber's family, gone to vocational school, or apprenticed with a master plumber. He said: "Well, my two brothers are plumbers and my father and my grandfather were plumbers. And I studied plumbing in school and worked with another plumber." Then, with the utmost seriousness, he put his hand to his chest and said: "But you have to have a fire in your heart for it!" For smaller churches to have the future to which God is calling them, thousands of people like you and me are needed who have both a fire in their heart for them and the insights and tools to lead them effectively.

T. S. Eliot sets the stage for the exploration of our subject:

> With the drawing of this Love and the voice of this Calling
> We shall not cease from exploration
> And the end of all our exploring
> Will be to arrive where we started
> And know the place for the first time. . . .
> Quick now, here, now, always—
> A condition of complete simplicity
> (Costing not less than everything)
> And all shall be well and
> All manner of thing shall be well
> When the tongues of flame are in-folded
> Into the crowned knot of fire
> And the fire and the rose are one[2]

Introduction

Anne Lamott illustrates in her popular book, *Traveling Mercies: Some Thoughts on Faith*, the extraordinary potential for smaller faith communities to bring transformation to even the most troubled life. St. Andrew Presbyterian was literally a lifesaver for her, as such churches have been for many. Welcome to the possibilities of Spirit-filled smaller churches.

> If I happened to be there between eleven and one on Sundays, I could hear gospel music coming from a church right across the street. It was called St. Andrew Presbyterian, and it looked homely and impoverished, a ramshackle building with a cross on top, sitting on a small parcel of land with a few skinny pine trees. But the music wafting out was so pretty that I would stop and listen. I knew a lot of the hymns from the times I'd gone to church with my grandparents and from the albums we'd had of spirituals. Finally, I began stopping in at St. Andrew from time to time, standing in the doorway to listen to the songs. I couldn't believe how run-down it was, with terrible linoleum that was brown and over shined, and plastic stained-glass windows. But it had a choir of five black women and one rather Amish-looking white man making all that glorious noise, and a congregation of thirty people or so, radiating kindness and warmth. During the time when people hugged and greeted each other, various people would come back to where I stood to shake my hand or try to hug me; I was as frozen and stiff as Richard Nixon. After this, Scripture was read, and then the minister named James Noel who was as tall and handsome as Marvin Gaye would preach, and it would be all about social injustice—and Jesus, which would be enough to send me running back to the sanctuary of the flea market. . . .

I went back to St. Andrew about once a month. No one tried to con me into sitting down or staying. I always left before the sermon. I loved singing, even about Jesus, but I just didn't want to be preached at about him. To me, Jesus made about as much sense as Scientology or dowsing. But the church smelled wonderful, like the air had nourishment in it, or like it was composed of these people's exhalations, of warmth and faith and peace. There were always children running around or being embraced. . . . And every other week they brought huge tubs of great food for the homeless families living at the shelter near the canal to the north. I loved this. But it was the singing that pulled me in and split me wide open.

I could sing better here than I ever had before. As part of these people, even though I stayed in the doorway, I did not recognize my voice or know where it was coming from, but sometimes I felt I could sing forever.

Eventually, a few months after I started coming, I took a seat in one of the folding chairs, off by myself. Then the singing enveloped me. It was furry and resonant, coming from everyone's heart. There was no sense of performance or judgment, only that the music was breath and food.

Something inside me that was stiff and rotting would feel soft and tender. Somehow the singing wore down all the boundaries and distinctions that kept me so isolated. Sitting there, standing with them to sing, sometimes so shaky and sick that I felt bigger than myself, like I was being taken care of, tricked into coming back to life. But I had to leave before the sermon.

[Lamott then tells of getting pregnant, having an abortion, resorting to drug and alcohol abuse, getting sick, and then mysteriously experiencing Jesus' presence in her darkest time. She and her young son, Sam, became regulars at St. Andrew. She then continues writing about her church.]

Then there would be thousands of slides of Sam and me at St. Andrew. I think we have missed church ten times in twelve years. Sam would be snuggled in people's arms in the earlier shots, shyly trying to wriggle free of hugs in the later ones. There would be different pastors along the way, none of them exactly right for us until a few years ago when a tall African-American woman named Veronica came to lead us. She has huge gentle doctor hands, with dimples where the knuckles should be, like a baby's fists. She stepped into us, the wonderful old worn pair of pants that is St. Andrew, and they fit. She sings to us sometimes from the pulpit and tells us stories of when she was a child. She told us this story just the other day: When she was about seven, her best friend got lost one day. The little girl ran up and down the streets of the big town where they lived, but she couldn't find a single landmark. She was frightened. Finally a policeman stopped to help her. He put her in the passenger seat of his car, and they drove around until she finally saw her church. She pointed it out to the policeman, and then she told him firmly, "You can let me out now. This is my church, and I can always find my way home from here."

And that is why I have stayed so close to mine—because no matter how bad I am feeling, how lost or lonely or frightened, when I see the faces of the people at my church, and hear their tawny voices, I can always find my way home.[1]

Church is not, first of all, about the institution. It is about the people. It's about their redemption and their finding a home and a people with whom to live faithfully. Lamott's life-saving love affair with St. Andrew Church was dramatic but not atypical. Each of us came into or stayed in the church through our need. If we are fortunate, we find there—in the music, the words, the sights and smells and hugs, and especially the people—a welcoming, hospitable place where we belong. The church is about and for the people.

St. Andrew Church was especially the right size for Lamott. There she was noticed and not overwhelmed. Noticed, she was reached out to and included—at her own pace. There was a niche waiting that she fit into perfectly when she was able to stop running. Smaller churches are the right size to be a nursery for the newborn, a haven for the pilgrim, an oasis for the parched, a hospital for the sinner, a contact group for the change agent, and a hospice for the dying.

Carl Dudley knows that numbers are crucial and that large size is not the answer. He got it just right with this classic statement:

In small churches, more people know more people, and know more about more people, than in most larger congregations. . . . When compared to other kinds of caring groups, the small church is much larger than it "ought to be." When church size is measured by human relationships, the small church is the largest expression of the Christian faith![2]

The Christian faith is a relational or communal faith where people join together in faithful praise and response. It has been this way throughout its history.

The History of Smaller Churches

Throughout Christian history, smaller churches have been the norm and larger ones an anomaly, if not an aberration. For the first three hundred or so years of church history, most Christian congregations were house churches. These house churches were not led by professionals with theological degrees but by those members of the church who were identified and called forth to utilize their unique spiritual gifts for pastoral leadership, alongside others in the church who used their differing gifts for faithful living.

After the Christian church was adopted and sanctioned by the Roman Empire, it became more and more institutionalized. While a few larger churches developed at the geographical crossroads, the norm remained small, intimate congregations meeting in homes, public rooms, and small buildings. Ministry gradually became more and more institutionalized as training programs became requirements and pastoral leaders were more formally credentialed. While isolated cathedral churches were established and prospered, there was nothing like what we've come to call "mega churches" until the last third of the twentieth century. Throughout church history, all but a few churches have been human-scale groupings in which every person mattered.

Key participants in the settling of North America were the farmer-preachers in the South and the circuit riders who traveled west with the settlers, attending to spiritual needs and establishing churches at the center of fledgling communities. Historians Robert Lynn and James Fraser report that, at the time of the American Revolution, no hierarchical distinction was made between larger and smaller churches. A study of Yale graduates from 1702 to 1775 shows that seventy-nine percent of those who were ministers served one parish all their lives. At that time, God called a person to a lifelong commitment to a particular people, churches "settled" their new pastor for life, and the size of the congregation was largely incidental.[3]

Lyman Beecher was quite happy with his small congregation in the mid-1800s:

> There are more Christians. No sectarians; I believe not one. Comparatively few infidels. The people are peaceable. Not a lawyer in the whole country. Industrious, hospitable; in the habit of being influenced by their minister.[4]

At the time of the Civil War, the average Protestant church had less than one hundred members. But times were changing. It was not uncommon for a wealthy, larger congregation to lure a pastor away from a poorer, smaller congregation. After the 1820s, the word "profession" came to represent a status level rather than what one professed.

Beecher was the father of a precocious clan that included Harriet Beecher Stowe, Catharine Beecher, and Henry Ward Beecher. Henry began his ministry in the poor town of Lawrenceberg, Indiana, and graduated after two years to a larger and richer church in Indianapolis. After seven years, he moved up to the fashionable suburb of Brooklyn Heights, New York, where he established the famous Plymouth Church. Soon, ferries called "Beecher Boats" brought hoards of worshipers from Manhattan to Brooklyn Heights. In this new spirit, when largest meant best, new, larger churches like Plymouth sprouted up across the country, offering something for everyone: anonymity, a relaxed standard of membership, and prestige.[5] Successful became synonymous with faithful. A symbol of the time (which still adorns the front wall of many churches) was the attendance board that recorded and promoted the hoped-for increases in attendance.

By the turn of the century, the majority of churches in the United States still had less than 150 members. As the ideal of the larger church took hold in the early decades of the twentieth century, counter reactions emerged. One was the Rural Church Movement between 1900 and 1920, which raised consciousness and morale and produced a wonderful body of literature. It was followed by the Town and Country Movement. Many seminaries had town and country departments through the middle of the twentieth century.

After World War II, the population shift from rural to urban areas increased. The parallel rise of denominationalism resulted in pressure on congregations to expand to support the institutional costs of both the congregation and the denomination. Again, there was a counter reaction. E. Franklin Frazier commented on the development of one of these, the storefront church:

> The "storefront" church represents an attempt on the part of the migrants [immigrants], especially from the rural areas of the South, to re-establish a type of church in the urban environment to which they were accustomed. They want a church, first of all, in which they are known as people. In the large city church they lose their identity completely and . . . neither the church members nor the pastor know them personally.[6]

Related to these in size and style were mission-driven churches like the East Harlem Protestant Parish in New York City and the Church of the Savior in Washington, DC. In rural and small-town areas, smaller churches carried on, adapting as needed.

As businesses, corporations, schools, and governments have consolidated in the interest of efficiency, economics, and prestige, so have churches. Five years before George Orwell wrote his anti-utopian novel *1984*, a Congregational minister from Wisconsin wrote a *Christian Century* article that took a futuristic look at what churches would be like in 1984. He predicted there would be no room or desire in the future for smaller churches. He envisioned vast, multiservice, something-for-everyone, ecclesiastical complexes that hundreds, if not thousands, of people would come to from miles around. He foresaw:

> Small, struggling, separatist churches are no longer necessary or right. These groups can be combined to form larger churches. . . . Even in the open country, churches can be combined and fine buildings erected, comparable to our consolidated schools. There will be no need for the one- or two-room country church when buses and cars can take the membership to a thrilling and busy and beautiful consolidated church in which generous and far-reaching fellowship may be enjoyed with a staff of competent leaders.[7]

With few exceptions, his 1984 church did not come to pass. Many, many people still feel more at home in small and modest-sized organizations, including churches. The human potential movement of the 1960s and 1970s, the explosion of twelve-step programs in the 1980s and 1990s, and the profusion of new, little churches are testaments to people's need to relate on a personal level.

Another movement began in the mid-1970s that is still alive and fruitful. In 1973, British economist E. F. Schumacher published his landmark book, *Small Is Beautiful*, a book and idea that changed thinking throughout society, including the church. In June 1975, a collection of church leaders came together to identify issues and to plan for a collection of papers that would be the basis of a Lilly Foundation-funded symposium at the Hartford Seminary Foundation. In January 1976, I attended the symposium, and my commitment to smaller churches was cemented. The book *Small Churches Are Beautiful*, edited by Jackson Carroll, is the collection of papers presented at the symposium.

That was the beginning of the Small Church Movement. Carl Dudley's remarkable book, *Making the Small Church Effective*, which described the style and substance of smaller churches, was published in 1978. Four years later, Lyle Schaller published *The Small Church Is Different!* and I published *Small Churches Are the Right Size*. The titles of these two books illustrate the most important things to know about smaller churches—they are different from other-sized churches, and they are the right size to be and do all that God calls a church to be and do. In a bigger-is-better world, the Small Church Movement is alive and well and building on this foundation. Today, new, smaller churches are springing up and taking root throughout the nation and around the world.

Sizeism

Ours remains a prejudiced and discriminating world. When one race or ethnic group sees another as inferior and acts accordingly, we call it "racism." If one gender takes a chauvinistic approach to another, we call it "sexism." When older people are ridiculed and dismissed, we call it "ageism." Over twenty years ago, I called our society's obsession with size and giantism (biggest tomato, muscles, sex organ, sky-scraper, salary, children, audience, house, town-state-nation, fish) "sizeism." North American advertising uses size to create big sales: Big Mac, Whopper, Jumbo Cakes, Green Giant, king-size, super-longs, extra-large, the largest airline and biggest fleet, the widest beach and biggest bank, the biggest sale, and the most for your money. Sizeism is very real and very prevalent.

One of the most interesting and revealing ways to understand a society is to examine its language. *Roget's International Thesaurus* reveals much about our view of "big" and "small." Following are typical, synonyms for the two terms:

BIG	small
GREAT	little
GRAND	slight
CONSIDERABLE	puny
SUBSTANTIAL	poky
LARGE-SCALE	piddling
MAN-SIZED	dinky
AMPLE	cramped
EXTENSIVE	limited
EXPANSIVE	one-horse
COMPREHENSIVE	pint-sized
SPACIOUS	teeny
GENEROUS	teeny-weeny
STALWART	little bitsy
IMPOSING	dwarf
WELL-FED	pygmy
MASSIVE	undersized

IMMENSE	stunted
VAST	runty
ENORMOUS	scrubby
TREMENDOUS	feeble
PRODIGIOUS	infinitesimal
STUPENDOUS	indiscernible
MIGHTY	insignificant
COLOSSAL	inconsequential
FULL-SIZED	pittance
LIFE-SIZED	partial
NOTEWORTHY	no account
POWERFUL	feeble

And the list goes on and on. The linguistic bias based on size is real and powerful. Is it any wonder that smaller churches tend to feel that they don't measure up, that they are limited, illegitimate, failing, of no account? Low self-esteem and weak morale are the most problematic issues plaguing smaller churches. Sizeism is alive, real, and acutely destructive.

It's a tragedy that the ecclesiastical world perpetuates and promotes the secular myth of bigger-is-better. There are books about the biggest churches and the biggest Sunday schools. Awards are given to the church that gave the most money or received the most new members. Denominational executives warn young clergy that they should never make a horizontal move (go to a church of the same size as their current one). Rather, they should always go bigger or their peers and superiors will think they've reached their level of competence. Not only will pastors get a larger salary if they graduate to a bigger church, they will have more prestige and feel more successful. Several years ago, a Baptist bureaucrat wrote that there are five reasons for small churches—an inadequate program, an inadequate field (or population from which to draw), inadequate evangelism, inadequate vision,

and inadequate personalities. No wonder smaller churches feel defi-
cient and put down! Yet new ones still pop up, and people drive past
larger ones to get to smaller ones.

Influenced by elements of sizeism, denominations still pressure
smaller churches to close because they are considered inefficient without looking to see if they are faithful and effective or have the potential to be so. Rather than asking if a church is big enough, it would be
better to ask three better questions—one theological, one spiritual,
and one practical:

- Theological: What is the will of God and does the church still
  have a God-given reason for being?
- Spiritual: Does the church or a significant number of its members still have the will to live?
- Practical: How can a way be found for the church to live?

I served a small Iowa church for four years. When I left, it was
healthy, vital, and viable. When it was counseled to close three years
later, I suspect that these questions were not asked and answered.

As the twenty-first century is firmly established, will the bulk of
smaller churches wither and die or flourish in fruitfulness? Kennon L.
Callahan, widely noted for his book and program *Twelve Keys to an
Effective Church*, writes in his later book, *Small, Strong Congregations*:

> The twenty-first century is the century of small, strong congregations.
> In the future, there will be many mega-congregations. There will be
> even more small, strong congregations. We are seeing the emergence
> of a vast movement of small, strong congregations across the planet.[8]

I share Callahan's belief that the hunger for face-to-face communities
of meaning will be even greater as our culture becomes more impersonal and superficial.

What will we see in years to come? Some smaller churches will
close in the face of despair or adversity or because someone else gave
up on them. Most will carry on, struggling, succeeding, touching lives,
making a difference. Many will thrive as beacons of hope and oases of

life, living as sources of spiritual health, committed to a life-saving mission. I hope the following will help revive some that are moving toward closure, sustain those that are keeping on keeping on, and provide additional nurture for those bearing abundant fruit.

Questions

1. Reflecting on Anne Lamott's account of her love affair with St. Andrew, how did your first memorable church attract and hold you?
2. What examples of sizeism do you see or experience?

Suggestion

Reproduce the lists of synonyms for BIG and small. Ask your people to read the list responsively, with two-thirds standing and exclaiming the synonyms for BIG and one-third sitting and meekly uttering the synonyms for small. Then talk together about the reality and effects of sizeism in our culture and churches.

chapter one

A Smaller Church Odyssey

Odyssey: . . . long wandering or voyage . . . or spiritual wandering
or quest.
> —Webster's Ninth New Collegiate Dictionary

For thus says the Lord: sing aloud with gladness . . . proclaim and
give praise, and say, Save, O Lord, your people, the remnant of
Israel. See, I am going to bring them from the land of the north, and
gather them from the farthest parts of the earth, among them the
blind and the lame, those with child and those in labor, together, *a
great company* . . .
> —Jeremiah 31:7–8

I LIVE AND WORK ON THE NORTH COAST OF CALIFORNIA. The place
where I have time and space to write is Vinalhaven, Maine, an island
fourteen miles out to sea in Penobscot Bay. In between are many thousands of smaller churches. While my previous writing has grown primarily out of my own ministry, in my own setting, and with my own
people, I wanted this guide to smaller churches to include illustrations and insight from other widely distributed, diverse, and representative congregations and communities.

Knowledgeable people helped me identify some smaller churches
that are "great companies" to provide an itinerary for my coast-to-
coast odyssey. My intention was to visit a diverse group of smaller
churches that had discovered how to be highly faithful and effective and how to use their size to their advantage. I suspected that
there would be several characteristics or common denominators

among these healthy churches that other smaller churches might find instructive. I was not disappointed.

On June 4, 2001, with a hand-built sea kayak on my Saturn roof, bicycle on the back, and car stuffed with a small library and a summer's worth of supplies, I kissed my wife goodbye and turned down Highway 101. Ahead of me on my zigzagging odyssey were: Vernal, Utah; Big Timber, Montana; Bryant and Sioux Falls, South Dakota; Westfield, Emmetsburg, Otto, Red Oak, and Indianola, Iowa; Chamois and St. Louis, Missouri; Pensacola and Littleton, North Carolina; Providence, Rhode Island; Weston and Wallingford, Vermont; and— fifteen days and 6,000 miles later—Vinalhaven, Maine.

These visits to various churches occurred in different regions of the country and multiple denominations, diverse cultures, urban and rural settings, new and old congregations. While most of the churches are United Church of Christ congregations, they are a diverse and comprehensive sampling of examples that any smaller church can identify with. Each has an interesting, valid, relevant story to tell. Their differences demonstrate that no single church speaks for all. Their similarities demonstrate that there is much commonality among the most dissimilar smaller churches.

This commonality reminded me of a profound "aha" experience. Twenty years ago, I was invited to give three lectures to a group of Southern Baptist denominational officials at a conference at the University of Mississippi. The lectures were about small churches, small-church ministry, and rural churches. I was quite anxious about my first foray into the South and Southern Baptist culture. I am grateful that their southern hospitality was warm and genuine, and the lectures were well received.

After the last lecture, a Southern Baptist-area minister, who worked with an association of small, remote Southern Baptist churches in rural Alabama, approached me. He thanked me and said, "The way you describe small churches is just like the churches I work with in rural Alabama." That observation was an affirming revelation to me. The churches I knew best at the time were the small, New England United Church of Christ, moderate-to-liberal churches like the one I pastored in Massachusetts. The smaller, conservative, and fundamentalist southern churches he knew were similar to the smaller churches

I knew. In fact, I believe they shared more in common than the larger and smaller churches of my own denomination and region. His comment illustrated that size has as much or more to do with determining the nature of a congregation as its denomination, theological tradition, location, ethnic identity, or anything else.

Fasten your seat belt and join me as I visit smaller churches in the West, the North, the Midwest, the South, and the East. Reflect on the differences and the common themes and realities. Compare my findings with your setting and understandings. But, first, look at the church from which I began my spiritual quest.

First Congregational Church, San Rafael, California

The trip began with the church I know best, where I've been the part-time pastor for over nine years. San Rafael (population: 55,000) is fourteen miles north of the Golden Gate Bridge and is the county seat for Marin County (population: 250,000). San Rafael and Marin County think they have it all—a beautiful natural setting; gorgeous weather; proximity to San Francisco and the rest of the Bay Area with its redwoods, dramatic Pacific coast, and wine country; and abundant cultural, educational, and employment opportunities. They also have atrocious traffic, horrendous housing prices and cost of living, an obscene gap between rich and poor, and a significant underbelly of poverty (primarily Hispanic, Asian, and African American). While Marin County gives lip service to many spiritual approaches, tilting toward New Age, in reality this church is trying to be church in a profoundly secular culture.

First Congregational moved to north San Rafael in 1960. It's a slowly growing church of about seventy-five active adult members and over twenty children. There's a pervasive family atmosphere, and the people truly enjoy one another and their church. The church has doubled its attendance, active participation, church school, and financial support since 1993. In 1970, the church built and still administers Pilgrim Park, a sixty-one-unit, affordable, housing complex on church land. In the early 1990s, Pilgrim Park was a troubled, problem-ridden apartment complex. Today, it's a model community that looks and feels like a mini-United Nations. This is a radically inclusive congregation, whose members range from very poor to wealthy and includes multiple cultures and lifestyles and is genuinely and intentionally open to all God's people.

This deeply committed church loves a challenge. When we began a building renovation in 1994, most felt our goal of $100,000 was unrealistic. In fact, we've recently finished and have almost paid for a $600,000 building renovation and expansion and the transformation of our sanctuary from drab and dreary to bright and beautiful. In 2000, the church initiated three major mission projects. First, $15,000 that had been set aside for some major, new, mission project was designated as seed money for the new Pilgrim Hill Foundation, which now spins off annual mission projects with the earnings from the Foundation. Second, the church helped start and equip the John Starkweather Computer Learning Center at Pilgrim Park. Finally, responding to the church's commitment to children and the passion of two members to feed hungry children, the church initiated the Every Dollar Feeds Kids project, through which every dollar raised goes directly to buy food for hungry children in four desperately poor schools in Mexico. In the project's first two years, $50,000 was raised, which provided over 130,000 meals. We are now seeking the participation of and partnership with other congregations, organizations, and individuals so that this program can be greatly expanded.

One-third of the church has been to a Benedictine retreat center in Cuernavaca, Mexico, on one of the annual retreat trips I lead. We house two Head Start programs, four twelve-step programs, a Korean Presbyterian church, a Fijian church, and various other organizations in our facilities. First Congregational has become unusually generous, and the members believe they can accomplish anything they attempt. This church is characterized by three qualities—vibrant worship, a deeply caring membership that gets along unusually well, and a strong sense of local-to-global mission.

Kingsbury Community Church (UCC), Vernal, Utah

After a long trek through hundreds of miles of barren openness, a night in a cheap Salt Lake City motel, and a lovely drive into the mountains, I arrived in Vernal, Utah (population: 6,600). This is Mormon country, located in the beautiful high country about three hours east of Salt Lake City. This has been a boom-and-bust community, depending on the changing fortunes of the mining, oil, and tourism industries. Greater stability is anticipated for the region with the coming of a large computer software company. I shared a brown bag lunch with full-time Pastor David Popham and four long-time members of this fifty-eight-member church. Thirty to thirty-five enjoy worshiping weekly in their round sanctuary in their round church. Kingsbury Community Church is the church in town for those who are not Mormon, Catholic, or fundamentalist. The signboard in front specifically invites those who are Methodist, Presbyterian, and Disciples of Christ.

The roots of the Kingsbury Community Church go back to 1887, to a little Sunday school that met in the Odd Fellows Hall above the Red Onion Saloon. The church was formally founded in 1903 and named after Dr. J. D. Kingsbury, home missionary superintendent for the intermountain states, from the Congregational Missionary Society. In 1904, the church received money from the Congregational Education Society in Boston and established Wilcox Academy, the first accredited school in the valley. Also in 1904, the Congregational Ladies Aid Society began serving the annual Election Day Dinner. Throughout its history, the church has prided itself on a variety of charitable mission projects.

Traditions, in addition to the Election Day Dinner, include the candlelight Christmas Eve service (that draws community people) and the Maundy Thursday service. The pastor is known for his creativity. The Pentecost bulletin features the artwork of one of the children from the church. When some have questioned the church's diminutive size, the pastor compiled a list of reasons why "I Am Not Ashamed" that includes:

- I am not ashamed that my oldest daughter gets one-on-one attention in Sunday school.
- I am not ashamed that we know each other's first names, and we don't have to wear silly name tags to remind us.
- I am not ashamed that we can take council or board meeting time to discuss issues facing individuals in the church and how we might help.

- I am not ashamed that I know by heart where each member and friend of the church lives.
- I am not ashamed that the youth call me "dude" instead of "Rev. Popham."
- I am not ashamed that when you miss a Sunday, three people will either tell me where you are, or ask about you.
- I am not shamed by the size of Kingsbury.

Soon after my visit, the Kingsbury church accepted an invitation from the Prison Ministry Fellowship (a national para-church organization) to establish an outreach ministry to about forty children of inmates in the prison system. A local Mormon group has agreed to work with the Community Church in this outreach ministry. This will be the first such program in the Utah prison system. David was pleased to share this cooperative venture with the Mormon group and commented that, if his church had been larger, they would have done this on their own. Being smaller, they needed to work ecumenically so they could reach out to all the children in their region in need of this ministry.

As in many small churches, it doesn't take much to cause major upheaval. Five families who recently moved away are sorely missed. The church's financial reserves are underwriting the church budget, and only a year's worth remains. When asked if they are pessimistic, the group I met with said quickly, "We're not pessimistic; we're concerned." Because they see themselves as an alternative to the dominant Mormon presence, this church feels that they must find a way to carry on. I'm sure they will. Like many smaller churches, the Kingsbury Community Church goes about the work of ministry and mission in relative obscurity, living up to its traditions, filling its niche in the community, and looking ahead with concern and determination.

First Congregational Church, Big Timber, Montana

The drive from Vernal, up through Wyoming, to Big Timber was spectacular. Big Timber (Population: 1,600) is a small community in southern Montana on Interstate 90. Robert Redford's movie *The Horse*

Whisperer was filmed in Big Timber. The film has contributed to the outside world's discovery of the community and region. Mining, logging, farming, and tourism provide the principal economic base.

This stop was one of the highlights of my odyssey. The hospitality of Larry and Connie Pray was a much-appreciated gift. Larry Pray, a specialist in small-town ministry, has been an answer to the church's prayer. He is well-matched with the church's people, style, and location. Essentially, Larry has two full-time jobs: pastor of the church and editor of the United Church of Christ's *Calendar of Prayer*. This church is flourishing because of the gifts and commitment of the lay people and the creative vision, spirit, and compassion of their pastor.

The church, founded in the late 1800s, has been serving the Annual Chicken Dinner to the community since 1892. Like the Vernal church, this church was preceded by a Sunday school. With 135 members, sixty to one hundred attend worship, depending on the time of year. Like every church, this one has its triumphs and struggles. When I was there, they were struggling to establish a choir and find a permanent choir director and accompanist. A thousand miles from the nearest coast, the church had turned its whole building into a beach scene in order to capture the flavor of the Vacation Bible School theme: "Beach Trek: 2001."

Larry observed that in this church, like many others, the "walls have memory," which means precedent can pave the way for contemporary action. Searching the earliest records, he discovered the story about a $690 indebtedness that remained after the church building was completed in 1903. The congregation arrived for morning worship on the day of the planned evening dedication. People got their first look at the new building and were greatly impressed. The pastor, Rev. Joseph Pope, quieted the congregation and announced that even though people were coming from around the state by train and horse, there would be no dedication that day. He announced that he would not dedicate a church that wasn't paid for. In less than fifteen minutes, the necessary pledges were garnered, and the church enjoyed a great dedication.

More recently, Larry recalled, the church talked for years about building a bell-tower entryway but never found the money or got around to it. Finally, at a church meeting, a lay leader said, "I'm sick of talking about this bell tower. Let's either build it or never mention it again." Right then, people were invited to pledge their support. Before the meeting was adjourned, enough money was pledged, the addition was built in about three months, and at midnight, December 31, 1999, the bell in the new tower tolled in the millennium.

In an enthusiastic conversation with more than a dozen church leaders, I asked what distinguished this church from others. Comments were: "it's the fun church," "we're the 'can do' church," "this church allows me to develop a personal relationship with God," and "we're child friendly." Clearly, there's a close relationship between the pastor and the church and among the people themselves. Larry uses technology to foster this. Almost weekly, he sends an e-mail message to all in the congregation who are on-line, commenting on what's happening in the parish, who's in need, and what will be happening in the upcoming worship and church life. The Big Timber church goes beyond asking people for an annual financial pledge. Each year, each member is asked to make a new covenant of faith and intention for the coming year.

When I asked what the church does particularly well, some described the annual Lenten suppers and discussions and how they seize any opportunity to feast or eat together. Others spoke out about Larry's very personal baptism services. And others commented about the recent confirmation program and noted that each confirmation class carries out a mission project.

This year, confirmation ended with a life-shaping ritual. Each of the seven young people received a letter telling them, without explanation, to come alone to a different meeting place—the bench in front of Cole Drug, the courthouse, the fire station, the lobby of the nursing home. An adult from the church picked up each youth with the terse message: "Come with me and don't say a word." The first stop was their darkened church, lit by only two candles and surrounded with recorded Russian Orthodox music, where they were each met by their mentor. The next message was: "Don't utter a word . . . listen with your heart, mind, and soul . . . listen to what God is saying: 'I set before you the ways of life and death. Choose life.'"

Each was taken by separate car and driver to a succession of locations. The first was to a manger behind the Lazy J Motel (remember, there was no room in the inn). The speaker said: "For Christians it all began here. You'll have to decide. Are you going to follow a child or a king who was drunk with power?"

They went to the river where the town doctor met them and said, "I treat people every day, but what I do is temporary. Listen to the water, the living water. The healing of the church is eternal." He spoke of the feeding of the five thousand and gave each confirmand a piece of salt cod and bread.

At the courthouse, the County Sheriff met them and led them into the courtroom, where they were instructed to sit at the defendant's table. Judge Jessie McKinney, robed, entered and commanded: "All rise." They did—quickly and somberly. She talked about the troubled, directionless people who come through her court and then, playing the role of Pilate, she said: "The mob demanded his death. What was I to do? Kids, don't ever bury your conscience. When you do, somebody gets hurt."

Then to the cemetery. A church leader, shovel in hand, approached and said: "He's not here. He's risen and alive." Asked if they would be among the living, he answered: "If your name is in the book of life." Larry then put his hand on the shoulders of each young person and said: "Enter these names: Betsy . . . James . . . Grant . . . Christine . . . Jared . . . Spencer . . . Andrew."

Then to the Lutheran Church, where their own church parish nurse and the Lutheran president of the Citizens Bank welcomed them to the church universal and washed their feet as Jesus had done.

The final stop was back to their own church where they were welcomed by their parents, the previous class of confirmands, their mentors, and other church leaders. After receiving a symbolic gift, the students were finally given permission to speak. They are still speaking about the power of the experience and its effect on their faith. This customized event illustrates how smaller churches are the right size to transform lives.

I was also impressed by the way Larry helps this small-town Montana church identify with and relate to the larger world. A few days after I was there, Larry and some church members left for a mission trip to Paraguay. A recent newsletter described how the church had donated over $4000, over and above normal giving, in one month for mission purposes. Occasionally, when something really important happens in the world, such as the bombing of the federal building in Oklahoma City and the terrorist attack on the World Trade Center, Larry provides a blank bulletin and asks his worshipers to take ten minutes out of worship to write a letter to those who are affected. This is an extraordinary church, responsive to both local and global needs.

Union Congregational, Bryant, South Dakota and the United Church of Christ, Erwin, South Dakota

A fifteen-hour drive across most of Montana and South Dakota led me to Prairie Retreat, nine miles from Union Congregational Church, in Bryant, South Dakota. Prairie Retreat is the unique ministry of Rev. Marjie Brewton and Union Church. Marjie is pastor of both the Bryant church and the UCC church in nearby Erwin. She says that she is as "at home on a tractor or in the barnyard as she is by her sewing machine, the cook stove, or in the pulpit." How she became their pastor and the nature of their shared ministry is a fascinating story. Yet, given the unorthodox way rural churches often procure their pastors, her story is not particularly unusual.

Prairie Retreat is a 160-acre farm with gardens, trees, fields, a pasture pond, and abundant wildlife in the center of thousands of acres of South Dakota prairie. Fifty years ago, when Marjie's parents, her brother, and she first moved there, it was a derelict farm. Only a fool or an optimist would have believed her father's prediction that some day this would be "the most beautiful place in the country." Marjie believes that it now is. Some years after her father's death, Marjie, her husband Ray, and her children returned to the farm to help her mother run it and survive the Midwestern farm crisis. Simultaneously, Marjie did ministry whenever and wherever she could.

Seventeen years ago, she was serving as interim pastor in nearby Chamberlain. One day, the mail carrier asked Ray if Marjie might be able to fill in on the coming Sunday in Bryant. Ray thought that she could, since Chamberlain would be interviewing a prospective pastor that day. Apparently Marjie was a hit, because a carload of deacons came to the farm the next week to ask Marjie to be their pastor. She said yes, and this farmer-preacher became pastor of what was generally considered a dying church in a dying community. As the failing farm economy forced many Midwestern farm families and those who serve, supply, or depend on them to other places and livelihoods, many churches, businesses, and even communities were wiped out. Bryant is still declining, but the church is far from dead.

Seven years ago, Marjie went out to her rock pile (the place on the farm where she often went for inspiration and renewal) and prayed, "God direct me." Later that afternoon, she returned from the rock pile with a vision of a retreat center so clear that she could draw its floor plan to scale. Marjie and Ray and the Bryant church went to work developing the center. The church loaned money for building work. The bottom level of the barn was turned into a lovely dormitory bunk house. (Wood from the old, well-worn manger was used to build one of the bunks so any retreater who wants to sleep in the manger can do so.) Ray and Marjie turned the loft of the barn into their home and the house that had been her mother's became more retreat space. The churchwomen made quilts for every bed, and they help with meals and cleaning.

Marjie bought a vacant Methodist church for $1, intending to disassemble it for the lumber. A supporter of the retreat donated $32,000 to move the whole church building sixty miles to the farm. The foundation for the church was being poured while I was there. And people have come—the first six years saw 729 overnight guests, 936 day guests, and 4,519 folks dropping in to visit. Moreover, the retreat outreach earned $1,000 for the Bryant church last year.

Union Church in Bryant, which was dying seventeen years ago, has forty-three enthusiastic members in their 110-year-old, well-maintained church building. The church, especially its women, has embraced a ministry of hospitality to one another and to their community and through the retreat. One said, "No one ever goes home without a hug and a kiss." The church and its pastor have had to learn to make do since their total budget for 2001 was $24,580. Yet even with little discretionary money, the church has a continuing commitment to support the international agricultural work of Heifer Project International.

Recently, the Erwin UCC church became part of the mix. There, twenty people (this is more than their membership) worship in their church once a month, and some travel to Bryant on other Sundays. Erwin is proud that their little, rural, Midwestern church was one of the first in the United Church of Christ to declare themselves "Open and Affirming," which means they are open to and accepting of gay and lesbian persons. They were motivated to do this as a gesture of support for the homosexual daughter of one of their members.

Ministry in locations like Bryant and Erwin is, on one hand, to help hard-pressed, rural Americans cope with the disappointments, pressures, and losses that are the stuff of life in rural America. And on the other hand, ministry helps these same folks hang on to the some-times-irrational hope that God holds before people in a remnant land. Pastors like Marjie Brewton, who've had dirt under their fingernails their whole lives, carry out ministry by living alongside their people, offering inspired worship, building a sustaining community, extending pastoral care, and organizing outreach to those who have even less. It's simply what rural pastors do in the heartland. It's their gift and their calling. Without them, rural North America would be in far greater crisis.

In 1989, Marjie wrote a little book of meditations called *Heart of the Earth*. One meditation describes the reality of a heartland neighborhood:

> Today I took a pencil and drew a picture of my neighborhood. In the twelve square miles around our farm, here is what I saw:
>
> Seven abandoned farmsteads in various stages of disrepair. Four farms occupied by widows. Two farms occupied by more than two generations of a family. There are five farms that have had farm sales within the last two years. One farmer took bankruptcy. One family moved a trailer next to the farmhouse and joined with the next generation to prevent bankruptcy. One man works away from home to make a living. One man lives 110 miles away and comes in the spring and fall to farm his land.
>
> Two men died of heart attacks. One died of cancer; another is currently fighting it. One man cannot move well because of arthritis. One man lost his memory and decision-making ability when he sprayed his fields with chemicals. One man many times moves with pain and spends

time nursing his back from doing too much heavy work. One man is hanging on—his wife just finished trade school to help support the family. . . .

There are 30 persons living on these 12 farms: Five men actively farm. Three women actively farm and take care of the home. One man works away from the farm. There is one baby. Four grade school children. Three high school students. Four retired homemakers. One retired bachelor. And two men who have been forced to retire because of their health.

PRAYER: Where is our future God? How can we hang on? How long can we survive? I am listening God . . . Are you there?

Isaiah 41:10— "Fear not, for I am with you, be not dismayed, for I am your God."[1]

Those who might like to learn more about, visit, or stay at Prairie Retreat can get more information by calling: 605-625-5085; e-mail <retreat@dailypost.com>; or through the Web site <www.prairieretreat.com>.

Sudan United Church of Christ, Sioux Falls, South Dakota

In little more than an hour, without leaving South Dakota, I traveled from the heartland world to the Sudanese refugee world. At the downtown Episcopal cathedral in Sioux Falls, the state's largest city, I met with the pastor and a lay leader of one of the five Sudanese churches located in that city. While most outsiders would assume Sioux Falls is all white and well insulated, it is home to over one thousand refugees from one of the most war-torn places on earth—Sudan. For nearly twenty years, a cruel and horrific civil war has raged between those in the predominantly Muslim northern sector of the country and the predominantly Christian and animist population in the southern sector. For two decades, Sudan has endured a latter-day slave trade, indiscriminate bombings, massive emigrations, and starvation.

Almost twenty years ago, in Marxist Ethiopia, I heard a Lutheran seminary professor say that he was frequently asked, "When they come to arrest me, imprison me, torture me, or kill me, how can I keep from denying my faith?" On this day, I met with one who has also had to wrestle with that question. Rev. Atanasio Osphaldo was born in Torip, a small town in southern Sudan. He saw bombers strafing agricultural fields at planting time, became separated from his parents and has no idea what happened to them, fled to Kenya where he received pastoral training, and took shelter with a million other refugees in a refugee camp in Uganda. He learned that Sioux Falls had become a haven for Sudanese refugees and applied for safe passage to the United States in 1995. Once here, Atanasio met a group of Sudanese who were looking for a pastor and wanted to start a church.

He had heard about the United Church of Christ, and one day he stopped by the First Congregational Church and met Rev. Arlan Fick. As they talked, the seed of an idea sprouted and took root—First Congregational would support Atanasio and his people in forming a Sudanese United Church of Christ. What was a dream in 1998 is now reality. The Sudanese church has office space and meets for Sunday school and Sunday afternoon worship at the Episcopal cathedral in downtown Sioux Falls. This new church has forty-six members. Thirty children and youth gather for Sunday school, and forty gather for worship Sunday afternoon. They worship in Arabic, but when a Caucasian is present, English translation is provided. Their worship includes spirited music and African dance. The church also comes together once a month for a prayer meeting that includes preaching, testimonies, and prayer from 10:00 p.m. to 4:00 a.m. The church meets with the other four Sudanese churches for religious support and cultural exchange. The church shares an immediate goal of having its own building.

These Sudanese people are thankful for the safety, freedom, and opportunity they have found here, but they haven't forgotten where they came from. Atanasio told me "their bodies are here, but their minds are back home." Their immediate outreach focus in Sioux Falls is to establish day care for Sudanese children, to organize training for women, and to educate Sudanese people in racial tolerance, HIV and AIDS awareness and prevention, drug and alcohol education, and crime prevention. Their hopes and plans for their homeland include training future church leadership in Sudan, providing a missionary health worker, and building one or more churches in Sudan.

There are more smaller churches in the United States than ever before. Many of these are churches like the Sudan United Church of Christ in Sioux Falls, churches of immigrant groups that are contributing to the greatly increasing diversity that is characteristic of this nation. For example, one-quarter of the churches in the regional Northern California Nevada United Church of Christ Conference are not predominantly Caucasian congregations, and all but a few of these are smaller churches.

Congregational Church, Westfield, Iowa

Dipping south from Sioux Falls, I crossed the Missouri River into Iowa, traveled a secondary state road, and came to an intersection that I knew was less than a mile from Westfield. But there was no mention of Westfield on the highway directional sign. The town is that small. In towns like Westfield (and Bryant and many other Midwestern communities), change has become synonymous with loss. Farms have been sold, schools and banks have consolidated, young people have moved away, and older folks have moved to warmer places or passed away. In many of these communities, the church is the most viable remaining organization.

Arriving in Westfield was a homecoming of sorts. From 1989–1993, I was the area minister assigned to work with this church and fifty-one others in northwest Iowa. After their part-time elderly pastor retired, I helped them search for a new pastor. From seven candidates, their search committee called a lay minister who lived an hour away. His ministry stimulated a turnaround for the church. Interest in the church renewed, and new, younger people became involved. About five years into his ministry, the church was shocked and grieved when he died suddenly of a heart attack.

They searched for someone to be their pastor, at least until their centennial. Steve Jewett, another lay pastor and the full-time owner of a glass business fifty miles away, was called on a thirty-hour-a-week basis. Steve is still there, and the church is thriving.

This is another church known for and proud of its annual fund-raising meal. In Westfield, its Harvest Supper has been held annually for well over fifty years. Events like this are not just fund-raisers. They are looked forward to as times when busy communities come, sit down with one another, share news and renew connections, and restore their sense of community and interdependence. The Westfield folks confessed without embarrassment that changing times have led them to have their Harvest Supper catered.

Steve is both loved and responded to. The Sunday school has doubled and worship attendance has increased. People say he preaches and talks to them in their own language and about things that matter. Occasionally, he preaches by dramatizing biblical characters. They particularly enjoy his children's stories when he has children bring something in a bag "that's not alive and not messy." Steve opens the bag and relates whatever is there to God and faith.

As in Big Timber, the church had been talking about building an addition for years. A member finally decreed, "Let's build it or stop talking about it!" They decided to build a dining room-meeting room, kitchen, Sunday-school rooms, and an office. Within six weeks, $50,000 was raised for an addition that would cost $93,000. It was only 105 days from groundbreaking to dedication. By dedication day their beautiful new addition was fully paid for.

Westfield and Steve Jewett disprove the notion that lay ministry, part-time ministry, and small-town ministry are merely maintenance ministries. In his part-time ministry, Steve accomplishes what needs to be done and doesn't worry about the rest. The lay people pitch in and are busy keeping the church active in his absence. This church is alive, bringing meaning to the lives of its people and making a positive difference in its community and world.

(The Former) United Church of Christ, Emmetsburg, Iowa

The next stop on my odyssey was one I looked forward to with delight and dread. I was going to Emmetsburg, Iowa, to meet with sixteen of the people who had been my parishioners from 1989 to 1993 when I was the half-time pastor of the United Church of Christ church. Emmetsburg and northwest Iowa were hurt badly by the 1980s farm crisis. During that decade, the county population decreased from 12,000 to 10,000 and Emmetsburg, the county seat, from 4,600 to 3,900. The church had withered from 398 members in 1946 to 88

total members when I was called in 1969. The church had held a
meeting to decide whether to close or to accept the state Conference
offer to create a shared position—half-time area minister and half-
time pastor for Emmetsburg. The church chose life, and I was called
as their pastor.

When I arrived, I discovered that a post had been erected in the
center of the sanctuary to prop up the roof and cables stretched across
the length and width of the sanctuary to keep the walls from collaps-
ing. In spite of the ominous symbolism, those four years were a time of
recovery, renewal, and community outreach. Some new members and
families were attracted and the church membership, attendance, Sunday school, and participation in leadership increased significantly. We
discovered, defined, and filled our niche in a heavily Catholic,
Lutheran, and Methodist community. We were known as the caring,
outreaching, hardworking, fun-loving church.

Piece by piece, we rectified the facility issues at the church building and parsonage. Two cold, decrepit rooms were transformed into a
warm and lovely Community Room. We added an accessible bathroom with changing table for the babies we hoped would come. On
"Miracle Sunday," forty-three pledgers pledged $87,000 and then
$20,000 more was pledged for the structural repair of the building and
for redecorating the sanctuary. We completed the difficult structural
work and celebrated the removal of the post and cables. Only the
sanctuary refurbishing was left.

In 1993, my wife was offered a challenging position in the software
industry in California. With mixed feelings, I began a search and was
offered the pastorate of the San Rafael church. I accepted, and we
moved in June 1993. It was very difficult to leave the wonderful people
in that active, vital, faithful church. A successor was called to serve as
area minister and pastor.

Three years later, on July 28, 1996, the Emmetsburg church closed
on the hundredth anniversary of its beautiful old building. I have never
fully understood why. After the church closed, some members trans-
ferred to other churches in the community and elsewhere. Others
remained churchless. At least one key family moved away.

I had misgivings about returning to Emmetsburg. I needed to ask
people I cared about, "What happened?" I didn't want to blame them.

I wondered if they blamed me. Seventeen of us met for breakfast at the Family Table restaurant. We reconnected, updated one another, and talked about what had happened to their church. There was no clear or single factor that would account for the church closure. But based on what was said and the conclusions I have drawn, this is what I believe happened.

I think my departure from the church took the wind out of its sails. They may not have felt ready or able to complete what we had started together. Four years of one pastor's leadership was not enough time to solidify the recovery and gains we had achieved. As my successor tackled the area minister's job, she may not have been able to dedicate the amount of time and attention that Emmetsburg needed. Key lay people were aging. Some were committed elsewhere, some may have simply been too tired to continue working at the pace we had worked, and more new people did not come. The church's vision may have left with me.

An important thing I learned from this church's closure is the importance, role, and nature of outside assistance. The state Conference was experiencing a severe financial shortfall and was forced to cut staff, including the area ministers. The Emmetsburg church was told that the state Conference could no longer pay their half of the pastor's compensation. They saw no obvious way to replace this lost revenue. The reduction of staff and the search for a new Conference minister meant that the state Conference was unable to adequately intervene to help the Emmetsburg church pursue an alternative to closing. Two volunteer consultants came from the state Conference to meet with the church. The people I met with felt that these consultants had already concluded that closure was the prudent course for the church. Apparently they did not creatively or energetically help the church explore alternatives to closing and the implications if they did close. The church was faced with serious decisions, and it appears no one could help them search for solutions that would allow them to continue choosing life.

There are two fundamental lessons for me in the closure of the Emmetsburg church. First, many, many churches, particularly in regions where population is declining, are in a fragile and precarious position. One failed pastorate, the loss of even a few key leaders and supporters, a natural disaster, escalating costs, economic decline in the community or region, a loss of vision, or a combination of two or more of these factors can be enough to lead a church to closure—unless there is wise, timely, creative, and aggressive intervention.

Second, it is easy to lose sight of the inherent value of each congregation and the cost to the membership and community in its closing. A church is family for many of its people. When a church closes, it leaves behind bereft, orphaned people. A church, even one that has dwindled or is dysfunctional, makes some kind of a contribution to its community and the community is diminished by its closing. Too many churches have been closed by those on the outside or from the inside without adequate intervention and a concerted effort to find alternative solutions.

When it comes to closing churches, I'm quite conservative. Outside observers often minimize the effects that closure may have on the members and the surrounding community. I remember the tiny church in the tiny town of Arion, Iowa. All that remained was the sewing circle of six elderly women. Yet the church was the only public institution left in the community. Schools had been consolidated and other civic institutions closed. I vowed when I worked as an area minister in northwest Iowa that I would help any church stay open that wished to continue and was able to define a mission for itself. Neither the Arion church nor any of the other churches I was responsible for closed during that time.

Emmetsburg was among the healthier and more faithful churches. Yet, today, people come from all over the region to shop at the "Heavenly Celebrations" bridal salon that occupies the building where a vital church performed vital ministry for one hundred years. It grieves me to think of all the heavenly celebrations that no longer happen there.

Oto United Church of Christ, Oto, Iowa; Rodney United Church of Christ, Rodney, Iowa; and Smithland United Methodist, Smithland, Iowa

For over a decade, Oto, Iowa, has been listed as one of the very poorest towns in the state. About ten years ago, I was notified (as area minister) that a neighboring Methodist church that had been providing pastoral leadership for the little Oto UCC church was withdrawing that leadership. The Oto church could not contribute enough money to the pastor's compensation. I went out to the tiny hill town south of Sioux City to meet with the church—which numbered about a dozen people—to discuss their future. Karen Handke, a farmer's wife in Oto, had started and was leading a successful Wednesday after school program for local children. During the meeting, I looked at Karen and suggested that one option for the church was to identify one of their own members who had gifts for ministry and call that person to be their pastor. I suggested that if such a person were available, our Conference lay ministry training program would train the person. Karen reported later that she wanted to stand on the table and say, "Pick me!" Karen wanted to try it, the church agreed, the state Conference trained her, and she's been doing a marvelous job for nine years.

Three years after Karen began in Oto (population: 100), the Methodist church in Smithland (population: 250) and the UCC church in Rodney (population: 76) were yoked with another church, but the yoke wasn't satisfactory. These neighboring churches knew of Karen and asked her to be their pastor, too. They came to an agreement, and Karen has been serving the three churches for six years. Their arrangement is called "a covenant" with the pastor, but in fact the three churches are doing much more together than merely buying part of a pastor's time. Each church determines what they can contribute to Karen's compensation, and she's free to spend her hours where she's most needed. In this arrangement, all three churches are growing larger and younger, with more families and children.

I arrived in Oto on a hot, June evening for a conversation with a dozen representatives from the three churches. Both levels of the church building were decorated with a Christmas theme for the three-church Vacation Bible School that was to begin the next day. The group was ecstatic about their pastor, their churches, and the effect their churches were having in their communities. They report that people who would never have come to church or been welcome there are now coming and are welcome. As the relationship with Karen has grown, the churches have learned to relax, trust, and follow her changes and new ways. One said, "I've learned to trust Karen and to trust Jesus Christ. Now I love to come on Sunday."

These are mission-driven churches, churches energized by the difference they're making in people's lives. A group of women make thirty to thirty-five of what they call "Ugly Quilts" that are given away each year. The Smithland church hosts a "Kids Shopping Day" each Christmas season for the children in the communities. This event is staffed by people from all the churches. All three churches donate new and like-new gifts. The purpose of the event is to enable the poor children to buy presents for their parents and siblings. Every item costs a quarter. Extra quarters are available for children who don't have any. Each year the churches prepare food boxes for poor families in the communities. People who've been helped before often now donate to help others. The after-school kids' program Karen began ten years ago is still operating. Karen has insisted, against some opposition, that the program include a nutritious meal because some of the children are very hungry.

To build interest in their churches and to minister to people's spiritual needs, the churches have revived and embellished an old-fashioned idea. They now sponsor a three-day Tent Revival at the river. The revival includes entertainment for all ages, a speaker, signing for the hearing impaired, and offerings that go to missions. To promote their revival, they adorn their cars with bumper stickers and their communities with posters. The three churches now worship together the first Sunday of each quarter and for special services. They share a common Bible-study group, mission projects, and children's programs.

It was exciting to see how Karen has grown into a gifted, committed, and mature pastor in the nine years since her tiny church that no one wanted asked one of their own to be their pastor. She is a prophet who points to God's activity in these communities. She is a pastor who people from near and far ask to do their funerals. She is a priest who leads deeply spiritual and transforming worship that's on the same level as people live and in the language they speak. She is a change agent who is instrumental in reviving three poor, rural communities. Steve Jewett and Karen Handke are living proof that ordination is not a requirement for exceptional pastoring.

First Congregational UCC, Red Oak, Iowa

After another night in a motel and an oil change for my car, I headed south to Red Oak, Iowa, a community of 6,000. Within the last ten years, this church struggled and many in the community thought it would close. At one point, the church considered shifting their worship to Thursday evening so they wouldn't have to compete with the other Sunday morning churches. I was anxious to see what had changed and why the Conference minister had recommended this as one of the smaller, healthy churches I should visit.

I arrived in time for lunch with three older women, three younger women and a baby, and the retiring seventy-seven-year-old pastor who had been with them for eight years. The tasty lunch validated the church's reputation for being "the church of the fork and spoon." There's seldom a Sunday morning when they don't linger after worship to eat together and enjoy one another.

The church's relationship with their pastor Mac McHarg explodes the myth that older pastors cannot provide dynamic, effective leadership. He exhorted them to stop living in the past, to stop just surviving. He said that if they go under, they go under, but if there's a mission they need to tackle, they should tackle it and not worry about the consequences. They listened, and it has made all the difference.

This is another mission-driven church whose practice is to identify a need and organize to meet it. Their renewal has grown out of a chain-reaction response to community needs. A retired schoolteacher started a Wednesday afternoon Celebrations program for elementary kids that offered a good meal and activities. Soon, more than twenty-five kids from the community were attending. Involvement with these kids led church members to discover shivering kids in Red Oak, kids who didn't own winter coats. This realization led churchwomen to open a clothing library specializing in children's clothing.

They soon discovered that many of their shoppers were Hispanic greenhouse workers who couldn't speak English. This discovery led to an English as Second Language (ESL) program that now has two instructors and is about to hire a third. One goal was to enable their students to be able to communicate at the store, bank, and doctor's office. A larger goal was to alleviate the divisiveness that communities experience when they have new cultures in their midst.

Red Oak's mission-responses have grown out of pressing need and the values of the membership. This is a church that prizes education and is highly committed to social justice. Their actions are congruent with their priorities. The church is populated by highly educated people who value exploring ideas and intellectual challenge. They love to go deeply into subjects and to dialogue in depth with their pastor. This is their niche, and they are beginning to attract like-minded searchers.

The church has wisely adapted to, even taken advantage of, its size. The church bylaws and organizational structure were designed for a much larger church. Under McHarg's leadership, members set the bylaws aside and adopted a governing-board structure. The governing board requires fewer people and allows people to work on what they care about rather than needing to plug everyone into one or more jobs mandated by the bylaws.

With about thirty worshipers, the church was rattling around in its large sanctuary. They moved their weekly worship into their much smaller chapel. Worshiping in the chapel helped them escape the oppressive emptiness of the sanctuary and encouraged a more intimate and participatory worship. Their small size also made it possible for them to have weekly meals during Lent, prepared by a family or several individuals.

Because Mac is retiring, the church is aggressively recruiting pastoral leadership that will understand and prize their uniqueness. They produced a compelling brochure for prospective pastors entitled "Small and Strong: A Bright Future for Us—For Everyone." They sent representatives to their Conference annual meeting with bright-yellow visors advertising: "Help Wanted—Need Minister." Without apology, they are creatively marketing themselves in a way that says who they are and invites people seeking what they have to offer. If they find a gifted pastor who is secure and intelligent enough to not get in the way of their activist laity and visionary enough to move with them into a changing future, they will be just fine.

I had one more Iowa stop scheduled. I knew of a vital and effective church that had been born out of conflict.

Crossroads UCC, Indianola, Iowa

Eight years ago, a small group of people in a Presbyterian church in Indianola, Iowa (population: 11,300, south of Des Moines), were in disagreement with others in the church over issues related to tradition and change. When attempts at mediation and reconciliation failed, the group withdrew and started meeting every other week in someone's home for worship. At each meeting, one of the members was the "preacher." The alternate weeks they visited other, more traditional churches. On these visits, they discovered they missed their more informal "house church" meetings. After several months they moved toward becoming a "church" and rented space at the public library. They also decided to affiliate with an existing denomination where they would gain a clearer identity and the status of a "new church start."

The people with whom I met fondly remember the excitement of their early days and the hard work of figuring out how to be a church and what kind of church they wanted to be. As a church born of conflict, they pledged to work hard at clear and honest communication among themselves. One impressive quality was how serious they were about being church. By choosing not to be a conventional church, these folks were choosing what Robert Frost called "the road not taken."

Despite the blank slate that starting a new church offers, they have chosen some traditional practices and structures—having a pastor, a Sunday school, and worship with hymns and a preacher. But even in this "new" church, there's been a struggle between those who want more traditional elements and practices and those who want less. For example, when I visited them, they were wrestling with whether to use the Lord's Prayer and, if so, in what form.

The Crossroads Church now rents space in the Simpson College chapel building. They have forty members and at least that many in attendance. When asked if they'd like to be much larger or have their own building, the core group I met with said no. They believe not having their own building is more of a gift than a handicap. They want to travel light, stay flexible, and remain small. They had a full-time pastor for about five years but are now looking for part-time pastoral leadership. This is a laity-centered congregation and will probably remain so, relying on a part-time pastor for coordination more than direction. Their worship is very participatory and relational. They share a strong desire for study opportunities and enjoy social activities. Mission concern is central to their identity and purpose. To be a member of this church is to be involved in Christian action. They take turns cooking meals for a homeless shelter, have sponsored two refugee families from Yugoslavia, and are extremely generous when a serious need is brought before the congregation.

I believe that freelancing, customized churches like Crossroads will be more and more common in years to come as more people in our society come to value personal involvement and community more than individualism and institutionalism. In their short history, they have worked very hard to craft and be the kind of church they feel called to be. The challenge for Crossroads will be whether they can maintain their creative intentionality and energy as they mature as a congregation with developed traditions. It was intriguing and enlightening to visit with a church that was this serious about being a faith community and that bore so much similarity to New Testament churches.

United Methodist and St. John UCC, Chamois, Missouri

I said goodbye to Iowa and drove south and east into Missouri. Throughout the trip, I had relished getting off the interstate highways and getting on to the delightfully distinctive state highways and secondary roads. South of the state capital of Jefferson, I escaped onto Route 100 and wound my way north and east through lovely rolling woods and fields to the mighty Missouri River and the riverside town of Chamois (population: 450). Chamois has six churches: two Baptist churches, a Catholic church, a Christian church, and the yoked United Methodist and St. John UCC churches. Reverend Deborah Pope, an energetic, no-nonsense, jovial woman, loves and is loved by her two churches. She's careful to treat both churches in the yoke equally. Members of both churches had been invited to meet with me. For over two hours, about a dozen of us shared snacks, hearty laughter, and poignant insights about their churches and community.

The two churches have been yoked since the mid-1960s. They are quite intentional about maintaining the separate identity of each church. The Methodists like being Methodist and don't want to give up their church. St. John UCC feels the same way. At the same time, they know they need each other to support a pastor and they enjoy the things they do together such as a community Vacation Bible

School, Children's Church once a month, a joint Bible-study group, and a Lenten series that alternates between the two churches. The Methodist church has fifty-four members with thirty attending worship. St. John has sixty-eight members with about forty in worship. The lay people recognize and appreciate that Deborah prepares a separate worship service for each church with a different sermon. They have tried proportional support of the pastor in the past, but now choose to contribute equally to her compensation.

Deborah bonded with the churches in a painful way. On her second Sunday in Chamois, she fell down the parsonage steps and broke one ankle and badly sprained the other. She crawled to a phone, called one of the churches, and exclaimed, "I need help now!" Deborah is single, and both churches rallied around to help their pastor in every way until she was back on her feet. They've been an intimate part of one another's lives since. Deborah had the wisdom and self-awareness to accept a call to a place that fits her particular style and personality. She said, "I'm bored silly by programs. It's folks I love, so I'm a lot better at a pastoral church than I would be at a program church." She said that she's not only the pastor of the church people but of their "kin folk" and community people.

Both churches actively support their denominational mission programs, give food to the area food pantry, and prepare food baskets at Christmas. But it's interpersonal, one-on-one mission at which they excel. In this kind of small community and in these kinds of churches, the pastor easily becomes a broker, matchmaker, or emissary between those in need and compassionate people who want to help. Deborah described what many rural pastors experience—the organic grapevine that gets the word out about any need to all those who want to know and stand ready to help.

I commented that each of the people attending the meeting had probably invested thousands of dollars and hours in their church and asked why they did so. One said, "I do it because it makes me feel good."

An old gentleman said, "I give because the need is there. People need help, everybody needs help, and that's why I give."

Another said, "Christ taught us to be stewards of our time and money. It's not biblical to do anything else."

Deborah said she was astounded at how hard these people work to keep their parish going.

After assisting many churches as an area minister in their search for a pastor, I have a strong conviction that a ministry won't work well or last long if there's not a close and compatible match between church and pastor. So I asked Deborah why she said yes to the invitation to come to this parish. She offered these reflections. "As soon as I drove into Chamois I had this strong feeling that I could live here. . . . They were just entertaining folks. . . . I think God matches folks up so that there will be some sort of spiritual blessing that takes place. . . . I think this is the place I was supposed to come. . . . We just all live together and try to not kill each other, but God has put us in each other's lives if for nothing else than to aggravate each other because that moves you to a new place with God."

I asked what the issues are that confront their churches. The answers were what one hears often—declining numbers, too few dollars, keeping the building maintained, finding a permanent musician, attracting the unchurched and the young. These issues are real and important and common. But what I learned in Chamois and from the other churches I visited is that when people know their church is making a genuine difference in their lives and others' lives, they find a way to resolve or compensate for the issues that challenge or unsettle them. I left Chamois thinking about the thousands of obscure, out-of-the-way churches like these two that keep on touching lives, healing communities, and contributing to the Community of God, week after week, year after year.

Epiphany UCC, St. Louis, Missouri

While most smaller churches are located in rural, small-town, and small-city settings, an increasing number are found in urban settings. Urban smaller churches include ethnic churches, new churches, intentionally small churches, and remnants of once-larger churches. Epiphany UCC, in one of the poor, transitional neighborhoods of St. Louis, is a remnant and quite extraordinary church. Aside from two, bright, hand-painted signs, Epiphany looks like a tired, run-down, inner-city church. It's the things that happen inside and because of the church that make this a story worth telling.

Eleven years ago, Epiphany was a declining, dying urban church. Members had agreed they would close the church when less than twenty people showed up four Sundays in a row or when the financial reserves dropped to less than $40,000. Attendance now ranges between forty-five and sixty, the reserves of $30,000 are $10,000 less than the agreed-on figure, and the church is vibrantly alive. The church revived, not by focusing on survival issues and institution-building strategies, but by acting faithfully, focusing on community needs, and changing the culture of the church.

The church chose to place new people in decision-making positions as soon as they were ready. It identified its mission as reaching out to the "marginal" people encountered through various neighborhood ministries. The church chose to become a "Just Peace Church" by committing to justice issues and the work of peace. It declared itself an "Open and Affirming" congregation that welcomed all persons, regardless of sexual identity. It worked successfully at becoming a multicultural congregation. Virtually everyone is involved in at least one outreach ministry.

Many churches focus on acquiring new members. Epiphany focuses on calling new "ministers" (mostly lay and volunteer) by helping young and old discern "what God is calling them to do" and providing support, nurturing, and collegiality as they fulfill their call. In this church of ninety low and middle income members, the newsletter masthead identifies two co-pastors (Michael Vosler and Tom Sawyer), a minister-in-training, a Diakonal minister, a minister of spirituality, a social advocacy minister, a musician, ten commissioned ministers, and over twenty others with formal responsibilities in the church's ministry and mission.

Michael Vosler, a fifty-something visionary, spiritual guide, and community gadfly, seems to be the one who focuses and coordinates at Epiphany. Michael describes his role as building and sustaining community and inviting people to involvement. Others said that he listens intently and is a phenomenal preacher. The church draws on the proclamation of eight "preachers" in the congregation and some complain that Michael's one or two sermons a month aren't enough.

The church is organized around thirteen ministry groups: spirituality, worship, pastoral care, personal stewardship, justice in community, educational programs, corporate accountability and responsibility, Diakonal service, outreach and evangelism, ecumenical relations, denominational support, facilities stewardship, and office tasking. Michael Vosler claims that he's not good at administration, doesn't care about it, and doesn't know what the church budget or his salary is. Yet all of these ministry groups function with considerable effectiveness.

The church building is active seven days a week with electric and eclectic activity. In addition to all the ministries of the church, they host the Joint Neighborhood Ministries (which includes a three-day-a-week food pantry, a family advocate, a family partnership, and youth and children ministries, which copastor Tom Sawyer helps staff and direct), the Grace Hill Health Clinic, the St. Louis Neighborhood Network with five staff, various other community groups, and the monthly meeting of the Benton Park Neighborhood Association. Maintaining the building is a constant challenge, yet it's the place to which people come, a symbol of hope for the community and the space necessary to make extraordinary ministry and outreach possible.

Epiphany knows the needs are too great for one, small church so the church is always looking for and working to create alliances. Through a church-based community-organizing effort, they have helped create and direct "C-4": Churches Committed to Community Concern. Church members are involved in tutoring in the public schools and are now assembling one hundred reading partners who will work with two hundred students who can't read in Garfield School, one of the lowest achieving schools in Missouri. The church's passion for community outreach has attracted activists who want to be part of a church that practices what it preaches and cares about the issues they care about.

The time the church boiler died was a defining moment. Either it had to be replaced at a cost of $25,000 or they would have to close the building. The congregation wondered if they could be the church without their building. They decided their building was critical to both their identity and their ministry in the community. The church committed to raising the money, did so, and Epiphany has even greater confidence in its ability to persevere. Now, at a cost of $100,000, they want to make their building accessible to people with disabilities.

Another defining moment was when one long-time member, Laverne, was added to the church council to literally sit in her father's seat when he was ill. At one key meeting, the council was going 'round and 'round on a tough issue. People were stuck in the position of "we don't do it that way at Epiphany." Laverne, a very quiet lady, sat and listened to the lengthy debate. Finally, she said, "Well, what we're doing isn't working." The council voted and proceeded to find a way that would work.

Another ingredient in the church's transformation has been the "boundary stretchers," those who have come into church life who didn't look like, sound like, or act like the rest of the church. These include people of different cultural and ethnic groups and life styles. Examples of this inclusivity are a phenomenal African American musician with very "rough edges," street people, and people with emotional challenges who sometimes do strange things that the congregation has learned to accept. One boundary stretcher was the man who came for the first time and said to the greeter, "I'm gay and I have AIDS. Will I be welcome here?" Gus, who had been reluctant to embrace the idea of gays in the life of the church, said, "You've come to the right church!"

How can Epiphany do so much when it's so small and so poor? One thing that makes it possible is that staff work more for love than for money. Second, people give not just generously but sacrificially. Third, people from social service agencies, seminaries, and the community see this church as the place where they want to invest themselves voluntarily. Finally, the community supports the church when the church needs supporting.

A larger question than the financial one is how does Epiphany maintain the stamina to sustain its exceptional and extensive work. Members are quite clear that, while they do substantial social ministry, they are a community of faith and not a social work agency. They take worship very seriously. They pray a lot and sing a lot. Considerable attention is given to spiritual nurture and to groups that work on discernment and support. People are encouraged and equipped to work at what they are passionate about rather than what the church wants done. There is a pervasive camaraderie that insures that people don't have to hurt alone or work alone. What keeps Vosler going is his conviction that God "lives at the margins and we have to be ever moving toward the margins to discover where the real creativity of God is going on in our time." He says that listening for God on the margins gives him energy and staying power.

I asked people at Epiphany if they were confident in the future of their church. Co-pastor Sawyer said that people there don't worry about that question. They are too active caring for and reclaiming their community to plan for the future. One said, "around here we don't worry much." My sense is that there's far too much life at Epiphany for Epiphany to die easily or soon.

We finished our pizza, and Vosler led me to the Interstate and pointed me south and east.

Laurel Branch Baptist Church, Pensacola, North Carolina

On my way to a church in eastern North Carolina, I needed to make a pilgrimage to Pensacola, North Carolina, where my father's family came from and where my great grandfather, "Little Garrett" Ray, was a Southern Baptist farmer-preacher. I followed a winding riverside road to where the paved road ends—Pensacola. The Laurel Branch Baptist Church was founded in a log cabin in the early 1800s. Today's church is a lovely, well-maintained, white clapboard building in the center of the small village. The door was unlocked (a good sign). I entered, turned on the lights, poked around, and stood in the pulpit where I pictured my ancestor in ministry standing. Looking for some-one who could tell me about the church, I went across the road to the combination general store and pool room and was directed to Ben Wilson, who lives behind the church. Eighty-four-year-old Ben was home and happy to sit me down on his cluttered front porch to tell me about his church, Pensacola, and my ancestors. He gave me a church tour and took my picture in the pulpit.

From Ben, I learned that a man who is also a drywall contractor has pastored the church for twenty-two years. It seems to be a very active, little Southern Baptist church. The building has had two additions.

Like the other churches I visited, it is generous in its mission support and quick to help those it knows who are in trouble. Even in tiny Pensacola, there's a Methodist church across the road, and one or two other churches nearby. Is that because these and many people can't get along well enough to support a larger church, or do they simply prefer a church home of intimate and manageable size? With my family roots watered and fed, I wound my way out of the mountains to the interstate and headed east.

Olive Grove Missionary Baptist Church, Littleton, North Carolina

The Olive Grove Missionary Baptist Church is an African American church affiliated with both the regional National Baptist denomination and the American Baptist Churches USA. My directions led me to a new, brick church building in a pastoral country setting, two miles from large Lake Gaston in the northeast corner of the state. This is one of the African American churches that were burned down by arsonists in 1996. The new church was across the driveway from an old, one-room schoolhouse that the church uses and will soon own. On one side of the church is the old cemetery, and on the other side is the new one.

Five lay leaders came to tell me about their church. Their pastor, Charles Walton, was meeting in Washington with leaders from the other African American churches that had also been burned. (I met with Charles a week later when we both participated in an American Baptist small church event in Providence, Rhode Island.)

The church began in the mid-1800s in a bush arbor (an opening surrounded by bushes) near where the church stands now. The land for a church building was purchased for $1.00 in 1887 from a church trustee with the provision that no more money would be expected "as long as church was held." A church building was soon built. For over a hundred years, the church carried on doing what churches traditionally do. The church only had five pastors during its first hundred years. Walton, a social worker with the county social services, was called as part-time pastor in 1991.

Everything changed for the church about 6:00 a.m., January 4, 1996. During a time when several other African American churches were burned in the South by arsonists, an Olive Grove member looked out of her window one morning and saw that her church was on fire. It quickly burned to the ground. The only thing that didn't burn was the large pulpit Bible, which is now protected in a Plexiglas case. While the fire was never officially called arson, the people believe the fire was intentionally set. At the time of the fire, Charles Walton was then serving a second church that invited Olive Grove to worship in its building.

Although Olive Grove was not an American Baptist church at the time, that denomination contacted the church and offered to help them rebuild. With $100,000 from the denomination, church savings and insurance money, and the assistance of many people who came and offered volunteer labor, the church was able to build a new building in little more than a year. When asked how the church burning changed the church, members say the experience intensified and unified relationships within the church and made the members more attentive to needs beyond themselves. Charles says it took five years and a fire for him to really become their pastor.

Olive Grove has traditional worship the first two Sundays of the month. On the third Sunday they observe "Missionary Sunday," which is a little more relaxed and often has an outside speaker. Then they don't worship again until the first Sunday of the next month. They have three major fund-raisers annually. On Men's Day, the men of the church present a program, and each is expected to make a $100 donation. On Women's Day, the women conduct the program, and they each contribute $100. These are warm-ups for Homecoming Sunday when people return, many from a great distance, for worship, catching up with one another, and eating voluminous amounts of food. There are about ten large family clans in the church and each of these customarily contributes $1000 on Homecoming Sunday. Walton says that more expression of emotion and participation in worship are the biggest differences between African American and Anglo churches.

Olive Grove is one of eight smaller churches participating in an American Baptist four-year, small church renewal program. In response to the program, each member of the Olive Grove renewal team (and some of the deacons) is starting a prayer group that they hope will involve most of their members. They want to have several groups in the church meeting for prayer, personal support, caregiving for the congregation, and outreach to new people.

As in the other churches I visited, a strength of this church is its care for the people in the church family and community. Historically in the African American community, the church has been at the center of family and community life. While this is no longer true in much of Anglo culture, the African American church is still the soul of the family and the community.

After too many miles in too few days, I was anxious to reach New England. With a tropical storm close behind, I drove quickly through Virginia, West Virginia, Pennsylvania, and New York to New England.

Weston Priory, Weston, Vermont

I've been visiting the Weston Priory, a Benedictine monastery of approximately fourteen brothers in Weston, Vermont, for over thirty years. It's been a place and community where I've found spiritual refreshment and renewal. The brothers, with their hospitable and contemplative presence on one hand and their deep commitment to peace and justice for all God's people on the other, exemplify the gospel for me. The deep community that permeates their lives, which they share with the thousands of visitors who come annually, models what a smaller congregation is the right size to be. So I called Brother Richard, the prior, and asked if I could meet with some of the brothers.

After afternoon prayers, Brothers Daniel, Robert, and Philip led me to a comfortable room where we shared a lengthy and poignant conversation. My principal question was this: As a monastic Catholic Benedictine community, what have you learned about Christian community that might be relevant to congregations of up to one hundred worshipers? To me, the terms "church" and "community" are synonymous. A church is not a church (but something else) if there is not a real sense of community. The brothers, who come out of a Catholic context in which most parishes are quite large, see congregations not as communities, but as collections of communities. This is true of some smaller churches and most larger ones. The brothers believe the strength of their community is that they are small enough to love in depth and not so small as to be weak and ineffective.

Brother Robert said he was attracted to the priory by the worship he experienced here and discovered that the worship grows out of the quality of community the brothers share. In my experience as well, quality worship grows out of genuine community, even more than it precedes it. Brother Philip commented that the work of their lives is community. Genuine community will not happen in a church unless the pastoral and lay leadership identify building community as their principal calling. I asked how their size shapes their community. They responded that their size allows them be a community instead of an institution. It enables them to communicate more deeply and honestly and to move with "one heart."

I asked how their life would be different if they had three or four times as many members. They recognize that with more members, their whole life would be different. Communication would be more difficult. They would have to spend considerably more time resolving community issues. It would be easier for brothers to hide in anonymity. Each would not be fully in relationship with each of the others. There would be more coming and going in the community and less stability. They sensed that even the language they use would change if their numbers increased.

I first encountered the priory in 1969, when the brothers left their cloister and attended an anti-Vietnam war rally in Brattleboro, Vermont. Since then, I've seen them provide sanctuary for a Guatemalan family, work in solidarity with the poor of Mexico and Central America, and be a leavening influence in the Catholic Church in the United States. Reflecting on this, I asked about their sense of their mission. It goes back to the founder of Benedictine spirituality. One of St. Benedict's sixth century "rules" for his monastic community was to treat everyone who came their way as if that person was the Christ. This Christian hospitality, radically interpreted, is the core of their mission with those who seek them out at the priory, in their collegial work with other monastic groups, and in their outreach to and advocacy for those on society's margins.

I left feeling warmly received and confirmed in the vision of community as exemplified by the brothers of the Weston Priory. Becoming an intimate and reliable community is a precious and God-given possibility for those congregations where there is not a crowd. I left even more committed to making church and community interchangeable terms.

Wilderness Friends Meeting, Wallingford, Vermont

I went to Shrewsbury, Vermont (where I used to be the only pastor in town), to attend the Sunday afternoon memorial service for a woman who had been a pillar of the community. Since I had two friends, who were members of the Quaker or Friends, meeting in nearby Wallingford, I wanted to attend their Sunday morning meeting to gain another perspective on small communities of faith. Wilderness Friends Meeting of Wallingford meets at the Paul Harris (founder of Rotary International) building on Main Street.

On this summer Sunday morning, four of us were present: the clerk of the meeting, one of my friends, an older visitor who had attended before, and me. (Usually a few more are in attendance.) There are two styles of Friends meetings. "Programmed" worship resembles other forms of Protestant worship, with listening, singing, prayers, scripture, and sermon. This meeting practiced "unprogrammed" worship. All of us arrived a few minutes early. We placed a dozen chairs in a circle and put cushions on them. At ten o'clock, we settled into silence. After about forty-five minutes, my friend reflected aloud about one of Jesus' teachings about his followers being as salt and what would happen if the salt loses its savor. There was silence then until eleven. Brief conversation was shared as we put chairs and cushions away and prepared to return to our separate worlds.

What did I take from this? The hour of silence for me was not an empty hour but a full one. There was more power and meaning in sitting in pregnant silence with three others than if I had sat alone in silence. I felt a bond among us and particularly between the two who were regulars in the meeting. I found clarity and focus in my mind and spirit. This kind of silence would not have been possible if there had been ninety or nine hundred. Even in silence, this was a communal experience, and I was glad I was present. Many smaller churches are very small. There is the very real possibility that the Spirit of

Christ will be powerfully, even especially, present when only two or three or four or a dozen gather.

Union Church, Vinalhaven, Maine

For sixteen years, my family and I have been among the "summer people" who spend as much time as they can on Vinalhaven Island, off the coast of Maine. The year-round population of twelve hundred on the island swells to over seven thousand in the summer. Currently on the island, there is a small Community of Christ (formerly Reorganized Church of Latter Day Saints) chapel, a Catholic mass at the Union Church, and the Union Church, which is the island's interdenominational church. There has also been an Episcopal prayer service and a conservative or fundamentalist study group. We frequently attend the Union Church service. Typically, there are forty to sixty in the winter and seventy to a hundred during the tourist season. The church is a member church of and receives some support from the Maine Seacoast Missionary Society, which serves the islands and remote communities of coastal Maine.

Michelle Wiley-Arey, their fifth minister in the last sixteen years, pastors the church. Michelle is in the third year of her first sole pastorate. A recent predecessor was asked to leave just a few weeks after he began. Pain over this failed ministry and unrest over having a woman pastor for the first time since 1950 left Michelle with hurdles to jump before she was unanimously voted in as permanent pastor this summer. She's an excellent pastor who is bringing vitality and purpose to her congregation. Hers is very much a pastoral ministry of presence. Her conscientious visiting of the elderly and not so elderly has been very important to stabilizing her ministry and the church.

There's been a pattern of pastors not staying very long. At the end of her first year, Michelle married a man from one of the "old families" on the island. It is my and others' hope that this connection will contribute to her having a long and effective pastorate in Vinalhaven. If that happens, the church will move from surviving to thriving. A longer tenure will contribute to the church's effort to involve some younger families.

The Union Church building is the island's primary meeting place, and its pastor is at the center of community life. Over the last two years, the church and community have rallied around to raise far more money than they thought possible—over $400,000—to fix major building structural problems and make more cosmetic renovations. One important development during Michelle's ministry has been the nurturing of a close working relationship between the Union Church and the Community of Christ. Michelle and the presiding elder attend one another's worship, sing together in a quartet, and cooperate in other ways.

There's a poignant time at the beginning of worship when people add to the printed prayer list in the bulletin and update one another about the condition of some of those on the list. This church loves music and its repertoire ranges from gospel favorites to newer sacred music and choir anthems and special music. The Union Church is quick to respond when there's any need within the island community and a deeper sense of mission is emerging.

Just as there is a gap between visitors and brothers at the Weston Priory, there is a gap between islanders and those of us who are "summer people" or people "from away." I expect the Union Church will continue evolving into the church of the whole island, where young and old, year-round and summer residents meet, worship, and serve together. I believe this church's most faithful days are just around the corner, and it will continue helping build the sense of community on this unique island.

Odyssey Findings

We've met twenty-one smaller communities of faith, bridging the spectrum of liberal to conservative, west to east and north to south, and various denominations and theological traditions. They are all healthy, faithful, and effective communities of faith, although they vary in other significant ways. Besides size and vitality, what do they share in common? As I made my coast to coast journey, I encountered several common denominators in these very dissimilar places and congregations:

1. Most, if not all, place a priority on their worship life and work to make it richer and fuller.
2. None are embarrassed by their smaller size. All of them take advantage of their size in the ways they are church together.
3. There is a genuine sense of caring and being family or community in each place.
4. They really enjoy each other and have fun together. (The tape recordings I made during the visits are full of laughter and playfulness.)
5. At most of the places I visited, there is a serious, even passionate commitment to mission and to addressing real needs and issues beyond the doors of the church.
6. These churches are not trying to be all things to all people. Rather, they have found their niche (what they do really well) and are superb at filling it.
7. Each has excellent pastoral leadership. The longer that leadership has been present, the more faithful and effective the congregation becomes. Whether the pastor is young or old, lay or ordained, part or full-time is far less important than the person's staying power, commitment, compatibility, and gifts.
8. In most, if not all the churches, there is heavy reliance on the laity and attention to equipping and supporting them and giving them opportunity to be engaged in important life-giving ministry.
9. Ministry and mission come first and by God's grace and the people's generosity there is always sufficient money and resources to meet their need.
10. In all they do, they are far more concerned with being living churches than surviving institutions.
11. Last and most importantly, in a great variety of ways, these communities are very serious about spiritual nurturing and faith development. Even the most socially active has a solid spiritual center.

These communities of faith will reappear in the pages that follow.

Questions

1. Among all the sites visited, where do you think you would feel most and least at home?
2. What differences and commonalities do you perceive in the author's visits to such a wide range of faith communities? Did you see commonalities beyond the ones the author identified?
3. If the list of the eleven common denominators of the smaller churches visited was a test of congregational faithfulness, what grade would you give your congregation? Why?
4. What ideas and practices mentioned or described would you like to see introduced to your congregation?

Suggestion

Identify one new idea, practice, or strategy from these churches and experiment with it in your church.

chapter two

A Smaller, Communal Theology

Sheila Larson is a young nurse . . . who describes her faith as
"Sheilaism." "I believe in God. I'm not a religious fanatic. I can't
remember the last time I went to church. My faith has carried me a
long way. It's Sheilaism. Just my own little voice."
                                        —Robert Bellah, *Habits of the Heart*

A small church can be defined as one in which the number of active
members and the total annual budget is inadequate relative to
organizational needs and expenses. It is a church struggling to pay its
minister, heat its building, and find enough people to assume
leadership responsibilities.
                                        —Theodore Erickson, "New Expectations"

What life have you if you have not life together?
There is no life that is not in community,
And no community not lived in praise of GOD.
                        —T. S. Eliot, "Choruses from 'The Rock'"

Christianity means community through Jesus Christ and in Jesus
Christ. —Dietrich Bonhoeffer, *Life Together*

EACH OF THESE QUOTATIONS IS FULL of theological meaning for smaller
congregations. "Sheilaism" represents an individualistic, rather shal-
low spirituality that is common in our time.[1] When over ninety percent of the population say they believe in God and less than forty
percent are active in faith communities, "Sheilaism" abounds and feels
little need for community.

To define small churches, as Theodore Erickson does in the second quote, only by what they institutionally aren't and can't do reflects a minimalist theology and an assumption that congregations are essentially only social organizations, not communities of conviction.[2]

T. S. Eliot makes a startling and intriguing statement when he asserts that people are not human and alive if they are not in community and that an association of people is not a community if it is not centered in praise of God.[3]

The final statement is by Dietrich Bonhoeffer, a product of the state church of Germany that later was complicit in the Third Reich. He envisioned a very different kind of church in his little book, *Life Together*. He felt that a Christian church that was not an intimate community is simply not the church that was founded by and lives in Jesus Christ.[4]

Many people in the pew nod off when the preacher gets too long-winded and abstract in his or her theological proclamation, just as many preachers fell asleep over obtuse theological texts during their theological education. Remembering those experiences, you the reader may be tempted to skip this chapter to get to the practical material ahead. But establishing a theological foundation is crucial. Theologian John Macquarrie stresses: "Theology is indispensable to the Church, and where theology fails, we must take this as a demand for better theology and certainly not as an excuse for turning away from it or for imagining that the Church can get along without it."[5]

An apocryphal story tells of a gathering of family members who had been on the Titanic. They met in a Liverpool hotel ballroom to learn the fate of their loved ones. All were frantically clamoring for information concerning those they cared about. Suddenly, an old, shaggy polar bear lumbered into the room. Looking sad and tearful, he asked in the suddenly hushed room, "Have you got any news of the iceberg? My family was on it. They mean the whole world to me." It hadn't occurred to the human relatives that there might have been loss of life that was other than human and that, if there was, that might be important to someone. The stunned humans were forced to rethink and expand their consciousness.

Like the humans in the ballroom, we need to rethink and expand our theological consciousness in three ways. First, our theological understandings determine the content and meaning of our lives. Second, developing and living by a theology that understands that size is theologically important is crucial for churches of all sizes. Third, living without a "smaller" theology that validates the life of smaller churches will doom them to struggle, wither, and die.

I understand theology to be one's ultimate approach to life. By this definition, every person has a theology, even those who claim no religious conviction. Out of our theology we craft our values, beliefs, and actions. A thousand years ago, Anselm gave theology its classic definition: Theology is faith seeking understanding. While probing our faith, join me in developing a different theological understanding through reading and discussing this chapter.

In the extensive literature about smaller churches, there is very little attention to biblical and theological matters. The focus is almost entirely on sociological analysis, particular areas of smaller church life, pastoral issues, and problem solving. These are important and will be considered here. But for the health and welfare of smaller churches, the first important task is to craft a theological foundation for smaller churches, one that enables them to capitalize on their strengths and keep their problems in perspective. In nautical terms, a smaller church's theology is the rudder that keeps the church stable in rough seas and charts the course toward that destination to which God is calling it.

Remember the earlier citation from Walker Percy's *The Moviegoer*. Binx Bolling believes "the search" is the answer to our being "sunk in the everydayness" of our lives, even to lifting us out of the "despair" that can lead to death. We engage in the search when we ask the ultimate theological questions, the pursuit of which season and nourish our living. What we're on to is the fruit of the truths we discover in our search. There are two primary theological questions (the search) for a smaller church: What is its essential nature? (What is it, and what is it not?) The second follows the first: What is its essential purpose? (What specifically is God, through circumstances, struggles, and opportunities, calling it to be and do?) A church that knows who and why it is can figure out how to be and what to do. In other words, any smaller church that has a solid theological foundation and adheres firmly to it can and will find a way to resolve any hardship or crisis.

Bernie Siegel, famed cancer surgeon and writer about healing and grave illness, says in Love, Medicine, and Miracles that there are three kinds of cancer patients.[6] Fifteen to twenty percent consciously or unconsciously want to die. Life is not sufficiently good and meaningful, and they really would like to get it over with. They usually die rather quickly. In Percy's terminology, these would be the people who are in despair. In the world of smaller churches, these are the churches that throw in the towel when their problems seem overwhelming.

Siegel says sixty to seventy percent are in the middle. They do what the doctor suggests. They trust in the fates and passively wait to see what will happen. Sometimes they get better; more often they linger and die. Percy would say these are the people who are sunk in the everydayness of their lives. In the smaller-church world, these are the churches that try what the denomination or pastor or respected pillar suggest and then wait to see what happens. This kind of theology puts more faith in conventional prognosis than prayer.

Then Siegel says there are fifteen to twenty percent who are "exceptional patients." These people have an undying passion to live. They use every medical, spiritual, and emotional resource available in order to live. Whether they live or die, they fill their living with purpose and passion. He says an exceptionally large percentage of these people outlive their cancer. These patients or churches have a living theology that is on to something real, powerful, and life sustaining. They live their lives in praise of God and, more often than not, are sustained, perhaps even healed, by their community of faith.

African Americans have found life and power in black theology. Poor and oppressed people, especially in Latin America, have found what they are on to in liberation theology. Many women, including those who have been victimized by others, have found new life in feminist theology. People who care about the whole of creation and witness the very real threats to it have found strength for the environmental struggle in creation theology. While these different theologies risk missing the rest of the theological forest by focusing on one kind of tree, they have often turned despair into hope and futility into faithful living for people lost in the woods. Informed by these other theologies, a smaller theology is just as crucial. This smaller theology probes the essence of what it means to be a smaller faith community, identifies the gifts of smaller churches, and nurtures exceptional patients.

Many people are in smaller churches simply because all the churches around are smaller (in rural areas), because they just happen to like that size, or because a smaller church was particularly effective in reaching out to them when they were seeking a church. A principal conviction I'm on to is that, in matters of faithfulness, size is more than a matter of preference. Whether a church can be too small or too large to be a church is less a matter of personal preference and more a matter of theological understanding.

What's the minimum size for being a faithful church? Jesus said, "For where two or three are gathered in my name, I am there among them" (Matt. 18:20). This saying occurs in the middle of the only time in the gospels that Jesus explicitly talked to his followers about church life. A question I've often pondered is whether Jesus meant that he would just be with them, or did he mean that he would especially be with them? That's a crucial question. If he meant that he would just be there, then perhaps it's enough for us to simply tolerate our little churches. On the other hand, if he meant that he would especially be there, then we should pay closer attention to our smaller churches so we can meet Jesus there and see why Jesus would find them so worthy of his presence. I believe Jesus meant he would especially be there because of the level of intimacy, compassion, and community that is potentially present. Therefore, the minimum number for a church must be two or three.

So, if two is the minimum number for a church, is there a maximum beyond which a church becomes something else, when it starts being merely a religious institution or just a crowd? Over a hundred years ago, German social scientist Georg Simmel posed the question this way: "How many people make a crowd? . . . How many grains of wheat make a heap? Since, one, two, three, or four grains do not, while a thousand certainly do, there must be a limit after which the addition of a single grain transforms the existing single grains into a 'heap.'"[7]

In *The Devils of Loudon*, a book about mass hysteria in the Ursuline convent in the town of Loudon, Aldous Huxley wrote about the difference between two or three and thousands:

"Where two or three are gathered together in my name, there I am in the midst of them." In the midst of two or three hundred, the divine presence becomes more problematical. And when the numbers run into the thousands, the likelihood of God being there, in the consciousness of each individual, declines almost to the vanishing point. For such is the nature of an excited crowd (and every crowd is automatically self-excited) that, where two or three thousand are gathered together, there is an absence not merely of deity, but even of common humanity.[8]

Is this only hyperbole or is Huxley on to something? He believes God is experienced differently and humans respond differently in a crowd, and I concur.

If you have a megachurch of, say, thirty thousand, is that still a church or has it evolved into something else? A megachurch in Korea was approaching five hundred thousand people. Is that still a church? Can it be compared to a nation that can be a nation whether it's as small as Liechtenstein or as large as China? Or is it more like a mode of transportation in which, at some point, a car turns into a minivan and then at another point the minivan becomes a bus? I believe church is not a catch-all, generic term that includes any organization that chooses to adopt the name and put a cross on the wall. A church in order to be a church must meet three criteria:

- It is and is called to be a community.
- It is built on a biblical and theological foundation.
- It acts like what it was created to be.

Church Is and Needs to Be Community

In 1995, Robert Putnam published an article in the obscure *Journal of Democracy* called "Bowling Alone."[9] The article caused a firestorm of debate. It got Putnam's picture in *People Magazine* and an invitation to Camp David. His thesis was that the social fabric of our society began rapidly unraveling in the latter third of the twentieth century. With profuse supporting data, he argued that our civil society is break-

ing down as people are socializing less and becoming more disconnected from their families, neighbors, communities, and the nation
itself. The illustration for his argument is bowling. Putnam cites statistics showing that bowling is the most popular competitive sport in
the United States. However, between 1980 and 1993, the number of
bowlers increased by ten percent while the number of people who
bowl in bowling leagues decreased by forty percent.[10] Whereas people
once bowled more in social groups, they now bowl alone.

The article received so much attention, criticism, and support that
Putnam received multimillion-dollar, foundational financial support,
hired fifty research assistants, and published the massive blockbuster,
Bowling Alone: The Collapse and Revival of American Community. He
cites mountains of data to show that fewer and fewer of us attend the
League of Women Voters election debates, give to United Way, read
the newspaper, join the Shriners and Sierra Club, participate in the
monthly bridge club, picnic with friends . . . or are active in church,
synagogue, or mosque. His term for what happens when people interact and work together is "social capital." His thesis is that with less
and less operative social capital, our society will not be able to sustain
itself.

Putnam says faith communities are the "single most important re-
pository of social capital in America."[11] They make up nearly half of all
associations between people. Half of all philanthropy and half of all
volunteering is faith-based. One-third more church members give to
charity than nonmembers. Almost twice as many church members volunteer as nonmembers. Nationwide in 1998, nearly sixty percent of all
congregations contributed to social services, community development,
or neighborhood organizing projects. Congregations are crucial to the
civic welfare. Nevertheless, there's a decline in involvement in religious communities. Churches, especially mainline ones, lament this
decline and wonder why. Putnam reports loss of membership is not
unique to congregations. People are reducing their involvement in all
areas of public life.

Why this across-the-board change? Putnam identifies the following culprits in this nation's massive disengagement: First, there has
been a generational change with younger generations choosing to be
less involved in social groupings and civic involvement. This may

account for half of the decline. The second culprit is electronic entertainment, especially television. The bumper sticker that says "Kill
Your Television" is on to something. This may account for twenty-
five percent of the disengagement. The other two major causes are
"suburbanization, commuting, and sprawl" and pressures of time and
money.[12] Some might argue with his analysis and results, but it's hard
to dispute that Robert Putnam has uncovered a trend that is alarming
and critically important.

When he writes his prescription for our national malady, Putnam
suggests that faith communities must be on the front lines of rebuilding civic responsibility and community. He specifically challenges
clergy, lay leaders, theologians, and ordinary worshipers to "spur a
new, pluralistic, socially responsible 'great awakening,' so that by 2010,
Americans will be more deeply engaged than we are today in one or
another spiritual community of meaning."[13]

Being a "spiritual community of meaning" is what our biblical and
theological tradition says we are at our core and what smaller congregations do best. When I read the creation story in Genesis, the question in my mind is: Why did God choose to create all that is? I believe
that God created because God was lonely. Light, seas, land, and plant
and animal life were not enough. So God, out of loneliness, created a
human. God's companionship was not enough for one human, so God
created another. They were content, naked, open with one another,
and were not ashamed. Where this two or three were, there was the
first community . . . until the community broke down in suspicion,
self-consciousness, and rivalry.

In 1980, Paul D. Hanson, Bussey Professor of Old Testament at
Harvard, wrote an extraordinary book, *The People Called: The Growth
of Community in the Bible*, in which he carefully proposes and documents that the primary theme of the Bible is, from beginning to end,
community. He begins with Exodus, when the Hebrew people left
servitude in a strange and foreign land and emerged as God's covenant community. Through the remaining five hundred pages, Hanson
traces the ups and downs and different manifestations and developments of God's community from the Exodus clear through to the next
to last chapter of the Bible when the prophet envisions a new community and sees that "the home of God is among mortals. He will

dwell with them as their God; they will be his peoples, and God himself will be with them; he will wipe every tear from their eyes. Death will be no more; mourning and crying and pain will be no more" (Rev. 21:3–4). Hanson asserts that true community is not of human design but God's gift:

> The entire history of the biblical notion of community points to the same transcendent referent—the God who creates out of nothing, delivers the enslaved, defends the vulnerable, nurtures the weak, and enlists in a universal purpose of shalom all those responsive to the divine call. The biblical notion of community therefore finds its final unity and focus in worship of the one true God. From that center alone, it derives its understanding of what is true, just, and good, along with the courage and power to stand on the side of truth and justice, whatever the cost. The notion of community thus arising from our biblical heritage has a potentially profound contribution to make to a threatened world groping for direction.[14]

Hanson fears that people of goodwill will settle for community as a human invention for society's health and welfare and lose sight of its divine foundation: "It is extremely important for churches and synagogues to remind their members that their communities are not a new or accidental product of recent social or historical developments. They are rather the descendants of a four-thousand-year-old history of God's seeking to form with humans an abiding and blessed relationship."[15]

Hanson is right. The beginning and end of creation is community, and this community is not just our community but also God's community and our mutual community. Jesus talked more about the Kingdom of God than anything else. Some prefer a more inclusive term like Dominion of God to convey what Jesus was envisioning. I believe it is even more true to the essence of what Jesus is foreseeing to speak of the Community of God. Kingdom speaks of patriarchy. Dominion is more inclusive but connotes that God is sovereign and we are merely God's subjects. It does not say anything about the relationship between God and creature and God and creation nor about the relationship between the creatures. We are intended for community and are most human and most in God's image when we are in community. Community is the best and last hope for the endangered creation. Therefore, the Community of God is the most authentic and promising way to speak of what God began in the biblical faith community, what Jesus was laying the groundwork for, what God is seeking to do in our own congregations, and what God in Christ is holding before us as the hope and future of the whole of creation.

This chapter began with three lines from T. S. Eliot's remarkable "Choruses from 'the Rock.'" Savor and decipher the poet's prophetic vision in a longer excerpt from the poem.

> The Church must be forever building, for it is forever decaying
>   within and attacked from without;
> For this is the law of life; and you must remember that while
>   there is time of prosperity
> The people will neglect the Temple, and in time of adversity
>   they will decry it.
>   What life have you if you have not life together?
> There is no life that is not in community,
> And no community that is not lived in praise of GOD.
> Even the anchorite who meditates alone,
> For whom the days and nights repeat the praise of GOD,
> Prays for the Church, the Body of Christ incarnate.
> And now you live dispersed on ribbon roads,
> And no man knows or cares who is his neighbour
> Unless his neighbour makes too much disturbance,
> But all dash to and fro in motor cars,
> Familiar with the roads and settled nowhere. . . .[16]

The poet merges the insight of Robert Putnam and Paul Hanson. He understands that there's a profound problem when we all "dash to and fro . . . settled nowhere." Eliot knows that this is not what the Creator intended and that society will unravel if we are neither settled nor related. He knows that since we are created for relationship, there is no life that is not in community and, since community was the fruit of God's genius, there will be no community that is not centered in the Divine, the Holy Source and Foundation of Community.

So what does Eliot's vision have to do with numbers and size? For there to be a human community, the members must know and care about one another. The smaller the community, the more intimately the members can and should know one another and the more deeply they can care about and for one another. A. Paul Hare, who has written a text book on the dynamics of size and small group research says simply, "As the size of the group decreases, the strength of the affectional ties between members increases."[17] Smaller churches are not only the right size for establishing and sustaining strong affectional ties—which is the essence of community—they are the natural size for doing this.

Before Lyle Schaller started writing about church growth strategies, he admitted, "the natural size of the worshiping congregation is that of the small church . . . the large congregation runs against the laws of nature—even in southern California and Texas."[18] In the face of enormous denominational pressure for smaller churches to "grow up" and become cost effective, Carl Dudley noted that smaller churches are "the oldest form of Christian witness, and the most numerous expression of the Christian church."[19] Later, he said that smaller churches are the "appropriate size for only one purpose: the members can know one another personally."[20]

There is a crying need for community in a society that has grown too big, too complex, too anonymous, and too disconnected. We as individuals and as the church were created for community; it is the essence of who we are. To fulfill our birthright and to manifest what our society needs from us, smaller churches that are the right size must be more intentional about being communities of meaning, mission, and hope, and larger churches should commit to creating more small communities of meaning, mission, and hope. As they do this, many of those who abandoned them or never knew them will return.

The Smaller Church's Biblical and Theological Foundation

A church is not a church if it is not a full-blooded descendent of its ancestor church—as found in scripture and history. Paul Hanson has shown that the Bible has the theme of community woven throughout it. The Bible is also a theological document that has a smaller theology running through it. Reading through the Bible's history, prophets, gospels, and epistles, the reader with an open spirit will discover that the God of scripture is clearly biased. The biblical God has empathy for and advocates on behalf of the poor, the oppressed, the refugee and dispossessed, the sick and handicapped, the young . . . and the small. Here's the evidence.

Three times in Genesis alone, God found it desirable or necessary to start over with a smaller number—with Noah and his family, when the whole society tried to settle in the large urban center of Babel, and when Jacob divided Israel into twelve smaller tribes. Israel's history is a cyclic saga of God's people growing large, then prosperous, then unfaithful, and then self-destructing, only to have a small and faithful remnant emerge, only to repeat the tragic cycle. Deuteronomy 7:7–8 records God's bias for small Israel: "It was not because you were more numerous than any other people that the Lord set his heart on you and chose you—for you were the fewest of all peoples. It was because the Lord loved you and kept the oath that he swore to your ancestors." God didn't love them merely because they were small, but their small size contributed to the qualities of dependence, humility, and loyalty that led God to love them and to covenant with them.

Among the Bible stories that illustrate God's bias is the wonderful and dramatic story of Gideon and the Midianites in Judges 6–7. It has everything Stephen Spielberg loves—intrigue, surprise, human transformation, and dramatic action. As a consequence of Israel's great sinfulness, the nation was occupied and oppressed by the Midianites. After they were "greatly impoverished," Israel cried to God for help. The angel of the Lord appeared to Joash's son, Gideon, a strange choice given his timid, even cowardly, nature. In an example of biblical satire, God's angel addressed young Gideon, who was surreptitiously threshing wheat in a wine press out of fear the Midianites might see him: "The Lord is with you, you mighty warrior." Gideon, the farthest thing from a mighty warrior, whined: "But sir, why is this happening to us?" God, who is now speaking instead of the angel, counters: "Use your might to deliver Israel from the hand of Midian." Gideon fearfully begged off with excuses: "But sir, how can I deliver Israel? My clan is the weakest in Manasseh, and I am the least in my family." Never one to entertain excuses, God cut him short: "But I will be with you."

A coward, but not stupid, Gideon proceeded to test God three times. God passed the test, so Gideon recruited an army of thirty-two thousand. Recalling Israel's past behavior, God knew that if Israel prevailed over Midian with this many soldiers, they would (as the King James Version says) "vaunt themselves" against God, saying, "My own hand has delivered me." So God winnowed the thirty-two thousand down to a piddling three hundred soldiers. This remnant army, using outrageously creative tactics, prevailed over the Midianites, who were "as thick as locusts; and their camels were without number, countless as the sand on the seashore" (Judg. 7:12).

God seems to recognize the temptation for the big to believe that they are the masters of their own destiny and that they can become their own god. The smaller, with no alternative, must rely on God's grace rather than their imposing presence and power.

The Hebrew Scriptures, particularly the prophets, repeatedly speak lovingly of and to the faithful remnant among the faithless masses. Most homes in our culture have at least one quilt made from remnants with which the quilter made something warm and beautiful out of random scraps. Some bakers keep a sourdough starter or remnant from which they can make the next zesty loaf of bread. Nothing is more satisfying to the craftsperson than to use a scrap or remnant that has been saved "just in case" and to make something useful and lovely. In the same way, these easily overlooked but plentiful biblical texts about remnant populations speak a word of hope and courage to those in our remnant congregations who are dispirited. The discerning preacher who understands and capitalizes on the power of scripture to be a transforming word can use these remnant texts to empower the powerless. Culled from the many, powerful, remnant texts are five with a note of how they might be preached or applied:

> **Genesis 45:7–8b:** Joseph said, "God sent me before you to preserve for you a remnant on earth, and to keep alive for you many survivors. So it was not you who sent me here, but God." A pastor or outside helper can say to a dwindling congregation that God has sent him or her to stabilize and rejuvenate to hearty life those who are left— God's remnant.

2 Kings 19:30–31: "The surviving remnant of the house of Judah shall again take root downward, and bear fruit upward; for from Jerusalem a remnant shall go out, and from Mount Zion a band of survivors. The zeal of the Lord of hosts will do this." The church's goal is not institutional survival. The remnant is capable of being firmly rooted in its faith and history. From the roots of that faith and history, it can bear the kind of life-giving fruit that Jesus and Paul talked about. God and God's servant leader is zealous in seeking its renewal.

Jeremiah 23:3–4: "Then I myself will gather the remnant of my flock . . . and they shall be fruitful and multiply. I will raise up shepherds over them who will shepherd them, and they shall not fear any longer, or be dismayed, nor shall any be missing, says the Lord." Again, the remnant is expected to bear fruit. The task of the shepherding pastor is to minister to its fear, despair, and feeling of insignificance so the remnant can bear fruit and multiply.

Jeremiah 31:7–8: (my favorite remnant text) "For thus says the Lord: sing aloud with gladness . . . proclaim and give praise, and say, Save, O Lord, your people, the remnant of Israel. See, I am going to bring them from the land of the north, and gather them from the farthest parts of the earth, among them the blind and the lame, those with child and those in labor, together, a great company, they shall return here." This is the message the messenger of God has sent out to the people who have been driven into exile, the people who are homeless and homesick, the people who by most accounts are of no account. The message is that it's time to come home. The prophet names the ones being called home. None of them are people one would choose to rebuild a community or nation. They are all disabled or distracted people. There's not one general, one chief executive, one movie star, one super athlete, one genius, and probably not a great leader in the mix. But from a rag-tag band of remnants, God sees a great company who will be the heart and soul of the new Community of God.

Romans 11:5–6: "So too at the present time there is a remnant, chosen by grace. But it is by grace, it is no longer on the basis of works, otherwise grace would no longer be grace." After "Amazing Grace" is sung, the preacher can remind the people that they are God's chosen and loved remnant, that they have been chosen and loved, not because they are better, but simply by the miracle of God's abundant grace. They have been called by grace in order to be angels and agents of grace for others.

Other promising remnant passages include: 2 Kings 19:3–4, 2 Chronicles 30:6b–7a, Ezra 9:8, Isaiah 10:20–22, and Amos 5:15. These remnant texts remind us that whenever there is opportunity to say any good word, people need to be affirmed for being intrepid and resolute. Most remnant people are hungry to be affirmed, respected, loved, and believed in. To criticize them for lack of faith, good stewardship, or evangelical zeal will only confirm in them their feelings of inadequacy. The remnant texts remind us that no community is too little to be loved and faithful.

Repeatedly throughout scripture, God affirms the few, the small, and the insignificant who live by grace, faithfulness, and courage. With few exceptions, biblical faithfulness does not come from or result in large numbers. God is more likely to count by ones and fives than by hundreds and thousands. God was willing to spare Sodom and Gomorrah if only ten righteous people could be found. Christ promised to be present whenever two or three come together in his name. The widow's mite was the greatest gift. The boy with only enough fish and bread for his own lunch provided food for thousands. Jesus fed thousands but only shared the Lord's Supper with the twelve who were his church. The tiny mustard seed, the pearl of great price, the leaven in the loaf, the single lamp, the lost sheep and coin, the sparrows, and the numbered hairs on a person's head are all powerful signs and symbols that small can be theologically mighty or, at least. big enough.

Let's go further with God's bias for the small and insignificant. For centuries, the Hebrew people lived with the messianic hope that God would send a royal, mighty supreme being who would liberate, judge, and rule forever. What did they get? They got Jesus, born in a borrowed stable and buried in a borrowed grave. In between, he grew up in a peasant family in a no-account backwater village. He disappeared from view from the age of twelve to his thirties. Once called, he wandered from town to town conducting an itinerant ministry and depending on the generosity of friends for food and lodging. Most of the time, his only friends and companions were a motley crew of fisher folk, tax collectors, and a few women. Up until the bitter end, Jesus avoided Jerusalem and the temple, being more at home in the countryside, with friends, and wherever the riffraff assembled. He always preferred the company of small groups to large crowds.

The revolutionary gospel Jesus preached and practiced stressed intimacy and personal relationships, discipleship, attention to individual gifts and needs, and compassion for the unloved. He did not create a mass movement or build an institution. He spent an inordinate amount of time training his dysfunctional group of twelve. His person-to-person ministry ended with his tragic, ignoble death, while his closest friends hid in the crowd. Jesus the Christ, God's messiah, came and went as a commoner. I can more easily picture him as a circuit-riding pastor than as a televangelist or a senior minister of a great church.

Even Christ's resurrection appearances were not the extravaganzas one might expect. Instead, they were encounters in a garden, on a road, behind closed doors, and on a quiet seashore. The Savior of the world was most at home in small groups, in friends' homes, on remote hillsides, by the lakeshore, and in small towns. He had a special affinity for the simple, the young, people in need, and those on the margins of the dominant culture—women, lepers, the mentally ill, prostitutes, and tax collectors. The people he selected to carry on his ministry were not the movers and shakers or the religious leadership, but the common people who readily answered his call.

We can learn much about his priorities and our discipleship by looking at those to whom he paid attention. I think particularly of the hemorrhaging woman, little Zaccheaus in the tree, the woman caught in adultery, and blind Bartimaeus, who Jesus heard above the din of the crowd. Jesus cared more about personal needs than mass markets. His paradigm for a messiah was a servant who washed feet.

The Church Acts Like What It Was Created to Be

A church to be a church, rather than something else, must be related to and bear some hereditary resemblance to its ancestor churches. The Christian church's roots are in the long line of small Hebrew faith communities, reaching back to the Exodus. The Christian church, as we know it, was born on Pentecost and initially led by those who had been mentored by Jesus. Responding to the Spirit and to Peter's extraordinary preaching, three thousand people joined that day. It could have become a megachurch. But, apparently Peter and his colleagues adopted a different church growth strategy. It seems the three thousand converts were divided into small house-churches that resembled and acted like extended family households. We read a few verses after the Pentecost story that "all the believers continued together in close fellowship and shared their belongings with one another . . . and they had their meals together in their homes" (Acts 2:44–46).

There was mentoring, caring, sharing, leadership development, evangelism, discipleship, and agape meals or communion in these small house-churches. Many, if not most, were multicultural, multiclass, multilingual, and from differing religious traditions. Women provided significant leadership in many of those churches. Apparently their evangelical zeal led the early Christians to create more churches rather than larger ones. This remained the principal church growth strategy until the latter part of the twentieth century.

What was it like in those earliest churches? 1 Corinthians 14:26–33 describes a highly participatory style of worship in that little Corinthian church. The weekly worship included a love feast or agape meal. Offerings were taken for those who were in need. There was an extensive adoption process that converts or new members experienced before they were baptized and accepted into full participation in the "church." The little, intimate churches depended on every member using his or her spiritual gifts for the welfare of all. Paul stressed that each member was an integral member of Christ's one body.

At one point, Paul criticizes the Corinthian church for losing its communal intimacy and concern for one another—which often happens when a church grows large, impersonal, and businesslike. As a result of their growth, the membership had fragmented into cliques, and each lost sight of the others' needs. The biblical model of what a church is meant to be is what a church of small numbers can naturally be—if it remembers and chooses to be.

The assumption in Paul's culture as in our culture was that bigger is better and success is the goal. Paul sought to correct this view:

> Consider your call, brothers and sisters: not many of you were wise by
> human standards, not many were powerful, not many were of noble
> birth. But God chose what is weak in the world to shame the strong;
> God chose what is low and despised in the world, things that are not,
> to reduce to nothing things that are, so that no one might boast in the
> presence of God. (1 Cor. 1:26–29)

These earliest churches were very much alternative communities
within the dominant Roman culture.

Those around us measure success by the size of the response and
equate faithfulness with success. That's not the biblical way. Faithfulness, not success, is the biblical goal. Faithfulness is more concerned
with intent, fidelity, and discipleship than with results.

The biblical expectations of a church are quite clear. The Word is
to be heard and the sacraments or ordinances are to be observed. We
are to love God, neighbor, enemy, and self and see that justice, tem-
pered with mercy, is practiced toward all. We are to incarnate the
Christ in deeds as well as words. The church is to give itself away in
redemptive action. There's nothing radically new here, although these
requirements have never been easy. While it might appear that size is
irrelevant to living up to these expectations, small size offers potentially great advantages.

Jesus had clear expectations of what should happen in faith communities. He was explicit about worship. We are to preach the gospel
to the whole creation, to pray "in this way," to celebrate the Lord's
Supper, "in remembrance of me," and to baptize in the name of the
"Father, the Son, and the Holy Spirit." In larger churches, these practices are generally carried out quite passively, as paid performers perform for the spectators.

Smaller churches can take advantage of their size and make worship
highly participatory, as it was in the earliest churches. Preaching can
directly and personally engage the lives of the people, as Jesus' preaching did, and even be dialogical. Prayer can be inclusive, personal, inter-
cessory, and can include oral prayers by several or many. The Lord's
Supper can truly be a shared family meal. Baptism can be an active
adoption into the family of faith in which the whole church partici-
pates. The word "liturgy" means "the work of the people" and our

worship should and can be much more like work than watching. Smaller church worship can look and feel very much like the worship of our earliest ancestors.

Jesus also gave his followers a mandate about education. He said, "make disciples," and, "teach them to obey everything I have commanded you." Moral instruction and institutional orientation can be given to large numbers. Perhaps we can instruct about the Bible, Christianity, church history, and right living, but Jesus commanded that we do more and do it differently. He commanded disciple-making. That is best done experientially and one-on-one. Remember how he taught: with everyday stories from the lives of the hearers, by modeling with his own life, with one-on-one Socratic dialogue, by taking two or three or the Twelve on retreat, and by sending his followers out two-by-two to practice what they had been taught. The biblical Christian-education goals are best achieved by involvement with the whole community, by providing role models and mentors, and by praxis or applying what has been taught in real life experiences. The more learners there are, the more difficult it is for each to participate in active, meaningful, memorable, and transforming ways. Large-group learning is by necessity passive learning. Large groups can divide into sub-groups, but these tend to be homogeneous collections of people of the same age, gender, or interest. This might be more pleasant and easier to administrate, but it doesn't build the community as effectively as when the community learns together in all its diversity.

A third task or mark of the church is to be a caring community. Jesus said, "Love one another." When John wrote to a little church and said, "Whoever loves a brother or sister lives in the light" (1 John 2:10), he was referring to their companions in the church. And when he said, "let us love, not in word or speech, but in truth and action" (1 John 3:18), he was talking about active caring, not happy sentiments. Tertullian, a commentator on the second-century church, said, "Look how they love one another." But you can't love someone you don't know or actively care for fifty or a hundred pews of people whom you barely recognize. It's hard for adults and kids to care for one another when the former are in the sanctuary and the latter are off in the education wing. Coffee hours are a first, but insufficient, step toward building a caring community. Smaller churches can insure that everyone knows and knows about every other person. Beyond that, utilize some of the seventy-nine caring strategies in chapter 6, "Small Enough to Care."

A final requirement of the church, the raison d'être of the Christian church, is to be a people on a mission, a people sent to save and transform the world—at least all those in its sphere of influence. Jesus said, "Love your neighbor as yourself" (Mark 12:31) (and also your enemy), and, "go into all the world" (Mark 16:15) to preach, feed, heal, clothe, visit, free the oppressed, make peace. He sent his followers out in pairs to do this and was never too busy to attend to someone in need. Larger churches do mission by sending money, by researching and developing strategies, by hiring it done, or by allowing a few like-minded enthusiasts to do it on their behalf. Smaller churches concerned more about survival than service sometimes forget that making a difference is the path from survival to life. Smaller churches can and do respond as a committee of the whole to a felt need. Often they fail to call their acts of love and mercy "mission," but that's what they are. I discovered on my cross-country odyssey that there are little churches everywhere that are making things better, helping out in real ways, loving their neighbors, making their communities more livable, and reaching around the world.

This smaller theology assumes, believes, and proposes that "church" and "community" are synonymous terms that should be spoken with the same breath. A religious group that is too large for its members to know one another (not only a few), to worship as the work of all the people, to make disciples of the whole congregation, to love and care about the whole church family, to be actively engaged in the church's mission, or to be a community of the faithful is too big to be a church. It has become something else. Or perhaps it's just a collection of little churches with a lot of people cheering (or yawning) from the sidelines. Paul says it in fewer words: "We are members of one another" (Eph. 4:25). If we've grown beyond that, we've grown too large.

Because smaller churches either haven't done their theological homework or have not believed what they have discovered, they often haven't lived up to their God-given mandate. Believing that bigger is better, they have used small size as an excuse for weak faith and meager action. They have often focused on what they think they can't do, rather than doing what they very well can do. They have often felt sorry for themselves more than empathetic for others. Some have moaned "poor us" and ignored the poor around them. Rather than relishing the camaraderie of worshiping together, they have worshiped dutifully as isolated individuals. These churches might be reassured by an observation attributed to Martin Luther: God can ride a lame horse and carve rotten wood.

Too many pastoral leaders and lay folk have not done their theological homework. They haven't noticed that God has historically chosen to do special work through small, remnant groups. They weren't paying attention when the great Jewish philosopher, Martin Buber, taught us that the "I-Thou relationships" found in intimate, caring groups are the kind of relationships prized by God. They didn't take Reinhold Niebuhr seriously in *Moral Man and Immoral Society* when he made the case that the larger the grouping, the more immoral and self-serving its attitudes and behavior.[21] They missed Paul Tillich's definition of sin as separation[22] and did not connect that with the fact that, in larger groups, relationships are more impersonal and fragmented, and it's easier to not seek reconciliation.

At their best and most faithful, what does a smaller church offer the bigger, high-tech world? Smaller churches offer high touch. They offer a place of belonging to those who feel like refugees. They offer community to those who feel isolated or estranged. They offer an opportunity to make a difference to those who feel superfluous. In a world full of sickness, they offer healing and wholeness. In a world imploding in its own complexity, they offer a simple place where people feel like they've arrived where they ought to be. They are a God-given response to this world's greatest needs.

Theologically and biblically, smaller churches are the right size to be all that God calls on a church to be and do. Building on this foundation, we will now turn our attention to the theory and practices of being faithful and effective smaller churches.

Questions

1. Reflecting on the Walker Percy quotation, are you and your church "sunk in the everydayness" or "despairing"? If not, what are you on to?

2. Do you agree that a life not lived in community is not a life and that a community not living in praise of God is not fully a community?

3. In what ways do you experience the Robert Putnam collapse of community? Where do you experience a revival of community? How could the church better be an answer to the need for community?

4. What would you question or add to the author's discussion about God's bias for that which is smaller?

Suggestion

Invite your church friends to come together for some good food, Bible study, and thoughtful conversation about their experiences, needs, and hopes for community and how that might be more fully realized in your congregation. For the Bible study, reproduce on one sheet Ephesians 2:19–22 and 4:11–16 and 25. Discuss how these verses do and do not mirror the quality of community in your church. Identify and commit to one tangible step that would deepen the level of community in your congregation.

chapter three

Theories and Tools for Understanding Smaller Churches

Saul clothed David with his armor, he put a bronze helmet on his head and clothed him with a coat of mail. David strapped Saul's sword over the armor, and he tried in vain to walk, for he was not used to them. Then David said to Saul, "I cannot walk with these; for I am not used to them." So David removed them. Then he took his staff in his hand, and chose five smooth stones . . . his sling was in his hand, and he drew near the Philistine.

—1 Samuel 17:39

In small proportions we first beauties see.

—Ben Jonson (1600s)

A big mansion is not simply a bungalow with more rooms, a big party is not simply an intimate dinner with more people, a big metropolitan hospital is not simply a clinic with more beds and more doctors, a big corporation is not simply a family firm with more employees and products, a big government is not simply a town council with more branches.

—Kirkpatrick Sale, *Human Scale*

SIZE MATTERS. SIZE DEFINES. Size determines. Size governs. Therefore, smaller churches have much in common with, and are different from, their larger cousins. Size is not all that matters, defines, determines, or governs. Each church is different. The smaller church leader who doesn't understand why and how size matters, defines, determines, and governs and how and why each church is different will encounter quicksand, landmines, and maddening futility. On the other hand, the smaller church leader who does understand how size matters, defines, determines, and governs and what is distinctive about a particular church has the insight and tools to lead that church into a more faithful and effective future.

To know a congregation, love it, care for it, and lead it, a person must understand it—who it is, where it is, how it works, and what makes it tick. Good theory makes it possible to do this. Without good theory, an observer won't have a clue. Theory may not be exciting, but it is essential. Theory is the architectural plans and tools for building or rebuilding. Theory provides the organizing principles for understanding and applying what we know. An old story reminds me of the two fundamentals that convey the essence of smaller churches:

> An old salty captain had spent forty years at the helm of an old coastal schooner transporting granite, grain, and lumber. Every morning, the old captain observed an almost sacred ritual. He dragged his old captain's chest from under his bed, fished its key from his desk drawer, opened the chest, and took out an aged scrap of paper. He read it carefully (sometimes two or three times), put it away, and spent the day following the wisdom captured on that piece of paper.
>
> One day at sea, he died of a heart attack. The first mate took command of the ship, conducted a proper sea burial, and moved into the captain's quarters. He knew of the old captain's strange morning ritual and guessed that just about all he would need to know as captain was on that paper. He found and opened the chest and took out the tattered piece of paper and read it carefully—several times. In the old captain's handwriting was a brief, cryptic message: "Port is left; starboard is right."

We will get into serious trouble sailing any sized vessel if we don't understand essentials like port and starboard and the navigational rules that are based thereon. The port reality of smaller churches is that they are the right size to be and do all that God expects of a church. The starboard reality is that they are different from other sized churches. This chapter illustrates both of these principles. The story also reminds us of the importance of theory. The old captain treasured his guiding theory, reviewed it daily, and used it to sail his ship. The theories in this chapter have been quite helpful in charting and navigating four pastorates. As you chart your own course, they may be helpful to you.

King Saul's armor was too large and unwieldy for little David to wear. But he didn't go into battle empty handed. He had his familiar sling and five smooth stones (1 Samuel 17:38–40). Your gifts, intelligence, and faith are the sling and the following theoretical understandings are stones for use in your smaller setting.

Relationships Make Them Different

There are between 350,000 and 400,000 congregations in the United States. Between 200,000 and 250,000 are smaller churches—meaning they have less than one hundred in worship or less than two hundred members. Because worship attendees are the active church, it's more precise and helpful to base church size on worship attendance. These 200,000 plus smaller churches differ from one another in geography, beliefs, denominational tradition, demographic factors, personality, and purpose. Yet, they have one crucial characteristic in common—their approximate size—that makes them more alike than they are different. I believe that their size is more important than anything else in determining how they think and act.

Size is the determining factor because relationships define and determine the church. In any organization, including churches, there are multiple levels of relationship—intimate, genuine, functional, superficial, and nonexistent. The way an organization functions is determined by the number and depth of relationships that provide the "tie that binds" when they are gathered or scattered. The following mathematical formula calculates the number of real, potential, or non-realized relationships in any group, that determine how those in the organization think and act with one another and beyond.

$$\text{Number of Relationships} = \frac{\text{Number}^2 - \text{Number}}{2}$$

Borrowing from my book *Wonderful Worship in Smaller Churches*,[1] here's what you might experience as the formula plays out in a hypothetical church. After a massive, Saturday night snowstorm in northern Minnesota, only four people managed to get to church at Maple Avenue Presbyterian Church. You were curious and wanted to know how many relationships were shared among those four people. So, using our magic formula, you multiplied or squared the number present: 4 x 4 = 16. From that answer, you subtracted the original number: 16 – 4 = 12. You divided that answer by 2 and discovered that among the four people there are six relationships. If that doesn't sound right, test it. Draw a square and number each corner: 1, 2, 3, and 4, representing our four worshipers. Draw lines between each of the four, indicating a relationship. You will see there's a relationship between 1 and 2, between 2 and 3, between 3 and 4, between 4 and 1, between 2 and 4, and between 1 and 3, for a total of six close or intimate relationships—at least if they stay together very long. This intimately shared storm experience could very well cement and color their relationships well into the future.

The next Sunday the usual twenty people show up. Do the math:

20 x 20 = 400 – 20 = 380 ÷ 2 = 190 genuine relationships

These twenty have gone through thick and thin together, like any extended family. All are in relationship with one another and most know most of the other relationships that exist between the other members. While they may have squabbled like family, they always pull together when support is needed and care deeply for one another. Generally, over eighty percent, or sixteen, are present each Sunday.

The next Sunday, the church pillar's grandchild is baptized and forty attend, including twenty guests.

40 x 40 = 1600 – 40 – 1560 ÷ 2 = 780 functional relationships

These twenty visitors are warmly welcomed. They like what they experience, keep returning, and, soon, they all, or almost all, know and enjoy working with one another. Still, over seventy-five percent or thirty attend weekly.

On Christmas Eve, all forty bring a relative or friend to experience the church they are so excited about, and eighty attend.

80 x 80 = 6400 – 80 = 6320 ÷ 2 = 3160 mostly secondary
relationships

All eighty are highly impressed and want to be part of such a success-ful church, so they start attending more or less regularly, and the forty guests join the church and get actively involved. About sixty percent of the membership, or forty-eight, are present each week. By the next Christmas, most of the eighty are involved in a congenial working relationship with one another, but most don't know too many other people very well—which begins to make a difference. While most may know most of the others, they don't know much about most of the others.

Another Christmas Eve comes around and an unusually special service using hired musicians is planned. Each of the eighty brings two guests to the service, being held in the rented high school audito-rium, while a new, larger sanctuary is being built.

$$240 \times 240 = 57,600 - 240 = 57,360 \div 2 = 28,680 \text{ mostly superficial} \\ \text{or nonexistent relationships}$$

Only about half the visitors see a reason to return, connect, and join. Growth slows significantly and levels off with about forty-five per-cent, or seventy-five to eighty, who attend on a "good" Sunday. There's now room to spare in the new sanctuary. While this is technically still a smaller church, the fact that growth has come quickly and that worship attendance is near the upper limit makes Maple Avenue now act more like a medium-sized church.

How did the numbers make a difference? The church of twenty had a special and solid intimacy. Since most members were present whenever the church gathered, any absentee was called by someone just to make sure she or he was all right. When something good hap-pened to anyone, the whole church celebrated. If someone's mother died, they all grieved. When George was out of work during his che-motherapy, the church put on an auction and raised $5,000 to help George's family. Almost everyone had some responsibility in making sure the Sunday gathering went as planned. Worship didn't begin until they were through greeting and catching up with each other. There were deacons and trustees, but most of the decisions that mattered were made during coffee hour or in the parking lot. The lay pastor, who was also a mail carrier during the week, felt like she belonged after about five years as pastor with Maple Avenue. Eight folks started and staffed an after-school homework club for the neighborhood school, and those who were working sent snacks. There was barely enough money for regular expenses and always enough for special needs.

The church of twenty felt and acted quite differently when it became a church of forty. There was a feeling of well-being and optimism as the pews and offering plates were close to full. The original twenty noticed there was a little less intimacy when the church gathered. Some felt a little less needed and slept in occasionally. Even though the church had doubled in size, it was difficult to get more than eight or ten to help with the homework club. The church was quite generous in supporting special offerings. Several people declined serving on a board or committee. The church of forty tried but couldn't quite come up with enough money to employ the pastor full-time, so they made it a four-day-a-week ministry. The pastor began to notice that the older members did not know some of the young, and the old-timers and new members didn't all know each other—at least not by more than name.

The church began to feel very different when it became a church of eighty. Some thought they should have an ordained pastor, so, with a little pressure, the pastor resigned. The church called a full-time, ordained pastor who was a little more "polished." He spent more time in his study and less time out visiting. People didn't mind, because his sermons seemed a little more sophisticated and worship a little more professional. They were also a little less participatory and personal. It was now possible to visit the Sunday service without being asked your name and invited to coffee. The new stewardship committee had to resort to an every-member canvas in order to get enough money pledged to support the $125,000 budget. The homework club closed due to lack of volunteers.

The church of 160 seemed quite different. The full-time pastor convinced the governing board that continued growth would not occur if the church didn't hire an associate pastor at least half-time. One was found, called, the growth did not continue, and the associate soon moved on. Two worship services were tried, but the results were disappointing and the "contemporary" service was canceled. The church no longer led the presbytery in per-capita giving to special offerings as it struggled to keep up with the mortgage payments on its new sanctuary. People who thought about it realized that they went home from worship feeling like they had been spectators, not participants. Old-timers complained they didn't know anyone any longer and that the new people were taking over—and they were. People only knew the people of their own generation or their interest group (choir, mission board, youth group, Bible study, etc.). A majority of members were not involved in any way beyond attending worship when they could. Maple Avenue Presbyterian had the same name, but that was about all that was the same. The little church that could had become the almost medium-sized church that might.

Why are relationships all that important? For the same reasons that families and close friends are closer and more connected and committed than mere acquaintances are. These are some of the reasons why being in relationship matters, defines, determines, and governs:

- Those who are in relationship know each other, which means they know one another's gifts, needs, nature, expectations.

- Those who are in relationship care about each other. They feel some responsibility to one another, are willing to go out of their way for one another, and will usually act in the best interest of the other.

- Those who are in relationship are committed to one other. They are committed because they have a common history and probably sense they have a common future. This means that they are invested in one another. Blood really is thicker than water. The shared atmosphere will more likely be intense and "warm."

Anthropologists believe the oldest social relationship is not the family but the tribe or small community. Even if it's not the norm today, for most of human history most people have lived and been at home in small communities.

Those who are not in relationship but are only acquaintances, or know of one another, or don't know one another at all will not be as committed to a common good or as invested in each of the others.

They will not bear any burden for the others. They will not risk vulnerability. They will not claim a common history or commit to a common destiny. The shared atmosphere will be "cool" and more superficial. But when relationships rule, those relating will bear a burden for one another, risk more vulnerability, claim a common history, and actively commit to a shared future. When relationship is compared to acquaintanceship, we see that the qualities we associate with true Christian community are the same qualities we associate with true relationships.

In 1985, the United Church of Christ published some striking research that my experience leads me to believe is comparable to other denominations and just as true today. The research looked at the correlation between size of membership and worship attendance. The research showed that churches with up to fifty members average eighty-four percent in worship every Sunday. Churches of a thousand or more members average thirty percent in worship each Sunday. When percent of membership in worship is graphed against total membership, the line goes steadily down as the total membership increases. Those who are in relationship choose to be together and feel something is missing when they're not. Those who are acquaintances, or less, have much less need or desire to be together. A community of fifty members will think and act very differently when compared to the institution of a thousand or more. Relationships make a huge difference.

How Smaller Churches Are Different from One Another and Others and What You Need to Know about Your Own Place

Understanding what makes a smaller church different can be difficult. I've surveyed a wide variety of insightful books and resources and offer some of the most helpful theories and tools for your smaller setting.

Charles Cooley and the Primary Group

One of the first building blocks in the theoretical foundation of smaller churches was laid in 1909 by Charles H. Cooley. Cooley developed the concept of the "primary group," which he defined as those groups that are:

. . . characterized by intimate face-to-face association and coopera-tion. They are primary in several senses, but chiefly in that they are fundamental in forming the social nature and ideals of the individual. The result of intimate association, psychologically, is a certain fusion of individualities in a common whole.[2]

His view was that human nature does not come at birth but through social interaction with one's primary group or community. Once hu-man nature is formed, it regresses in isolation. If Cooley is right (and I think he is), Robert Putnam's warning bells about the decline of com-munity and the increasing isolation of contemporary people are even more alarming.

Carl Dudley and the Single or Caring Cell

In the early days of the Small Church Movement, Carl Dudley built on Cooley's primary group theory and described many, if not most, smaller churches as "caring cells," or "single cells," or "culture-car-rying organisms." The smaller church is one cell, a body of the whole, connected by mutual concern, with each knowing and in relation-ship with all the others. One doesn't join the women's group or the men's fellowship but the whole church. At best, he says, relation-ships in these single cells are "warm, intimate, spontaneous, and personally satisfying." But not always. Primary group relationships can become "hot, cruel, petty, and irrational."[3] Not only do mem-bers in single cell churches all know one another, but also they are connected, if not by blood, at least by experience and concern for one another. The stuff of these connections becomes the culture that one generation carries to the next. The single cell church wants its pastor to be the "lover" who holds the cell together.

A few years ago, one of our members, a very difficult woman, died after several years in a nursing home. Two other members, Lucile and Millie, had visited her almost weekly over the entire time of nursing home confinement. When I tried to commend them for their faithful friendship, Lucile deflected my commendation by saying: "Why wouldn't we? She's a member of our church!" The difference between smaller and larger churches is determined by depth and breadth of relationships and whether they are made up of one single, large cell or multiple, smaller cells. If you map your congregation, is it made up of one cell including everyone or multiple cells divided by gender, interest, or age?

Single cell churches have several advantages. Their organizational structure is simple, rather than complex. Communication moves around the cell quickly and effectively. It's simpler to plan for one cell than for multiple cells. Generally, people know more people in a single cell church than in a multicell church. Biblically, Paul was referring to a single cell church when he described the church as many members connected with each other in one body and as "members one of another." Single cell churches are tough and strong. They can also be difficult to break into.

Robin Dunbar's Rule of 150

Malcolm Gladwell's stimulating book, *The Tipping Point: How Little Things Can Make a Big Difference*, analyzes when and why changes in our society happen. He posits that size is crucial and that when a particular size is reached, major changes occur. Gladwell was drawn to the groundbreaking work of British anthropologist Robin Dunbar who discovered by studying primates that brain size determines how many others an animal or human can effectively interact with. Dunbar developed the neocortex ratio, which is the size of the brain's neocortex relative to the size of the brain. When you plug in the neocortex ratio for humans, you get a group estimate of 147.8—or roughly 150. "The figure of 150 seems to represent the maximum number of individuals with whom we can have a genuinely social relationship," says Dunbar.[4] Beyond that size, social connections begin to break down and dysfunction becomes more likely.

Dunbar combed anthropological literature and found the number 150 popping up again and again as the demarcation line between those social organisms that were effective social units and those that weren't. This seemed to be true in groups ranging from primitive communities to military fighting units to corporate work groups. Dunbar's research led to the Hutterites, who are from the same theological tradition as the Amish and Mennonites. The Hutterites have long had a strict policy of splitting their religious colonies when they approached 150. Bill Gross, a Hutterite leader, summarized their rationale: "If you get too large, you don't have enough work in common. You don't have enough things in common, and then you start to become strangers and that close-knit fellowship starts to get lost."[5] Since congregations are more effective when they work in common, share much in common, and are a close-knit fellowship, it's difficult to argue with the Rule of 150.

Lyle Schaller and Seven Types of Churches

Over twenty years ago, Lyle Schaller made two valuable contributions to the theoretical foundation. He realized that worship attendance, rather than total membership, is the critical factor in how churches function and express themselves. He also recognized that churches of different sizes are different kinds of organizations with different characteristics and behaviors. He named seven categories of churches by size and gave each a descriptive name and metaphor. (The first two will be described in some detail after all seven are named.) The seven types of churches are:

- The fellowship or cat church has up to 35 in worship.
- The small church or collie has 35 to 100 in worship.
- The middle-sized or garden church has 100 to 175 in worship, comes in different sizes, is lots of work for the gardener, and you can never get all the weeds out.
- The awkward-sized or house church has 175 to 225 in worship, requires a variety of specialized skills, and needs constant repair.
- The large or mansion church, with 225 to 450 in worship, requires more help than it can afford and is not close knit or an efficient unit. People tend to come and go and only occupy a room in the "mansion" for the time that they're present.
- The huge or ranch church attracts 450 to 700. The senior minister is the rancher and procures hired hands to help with the ranch work.

- The mini-denomination or nation, where more than 700 worship is what we now call a megachurch and is quite self-contained and autonomous.[6]

What this book is calling smaller churches includes Schaller's "fellowship" and "small churches." One is different from the other, yet they share much similarity. Cat characteristics (up to thirty-five in worship) include: independence, self-sufficiency, willingness to be fed and cared for, not noticing the pastor's absence, able to survive abuse and neglect, no one gets on top of a cat, not wanting to be trained, instinctively knowing how to care for itself, not wanting advice or to be transformed into something else (like a dog). Collie characteristics (thirty-five to one hundred) include: coming in different sizes, enjoying being loved and returning affection, responding to sensitive handling and training, lavishly showing appreciation, warmly greeting the pastor on his or her return, but sometimes barking or even nipping at strangers.[6]

Both are more like one another than either is to any of the other types of churches. Both are alive, active, and playful. Both require care and form a relationship with their caretaker. Both are territorial.

Arlin Rothauge and Four Sizes of Churches

In the mid-1980s, Arlin Rothauge reduced Schaller's categories from seven to four and considered how size determines several other factors: the role of the pastor, what people expect, how the church engages in mission, how it incorporates new people, and what kinds of people want to participate in each size of church. Rothauge's four sizes with significant characteristics are:

- The family church has up to 50 active members. Rather than trying to be all things for all persons, this church should focus on one vocation and do that as well as it can. The pastor tends to fill the role of chaplain for the "family." It tends to attract new members through preexisting ties with family members and friends who are already part of the church. Newcomers are often attracted by the service the family church performs in the community. Often, one or more "Gatekeepers," more than the pastor, prepares the way for and lowers the bar for new people. Becoming part of the church is a gradual adoption process.

- The pastoral church has between 50 and 150 active members. This church tends to revolve around the pastor and designated leaders. It has at least two to three cells. It depends less on the matriarchs and patriarchs and more on a leadership circle. Communication is less spontaneous and needs to be more intentional. There will be more organized events and fewer happenings. New people will come through attention from the pastor. Membership is granted easily, but assimilation takes a little time. Hospitality and assimilation strategies are crucial.

- The program church has 150 to 350 active members. Democratic organization and leadership by the laity are critical for the effectiveness of this church. The pastoral leader is pastor to the leaders who are pastors for the church. Lay leaders need to be called, trained, and equipped to lead a variety of programs that are designed for differing ages and interests. The ministries, more than the minister, are the bait that attracts and the food that holds those who come to the church.

- The corporation church has over 300 active members and is complex and diverse. A charismatic, visionary leader who is able to communicate and coordinate is required. The church depends on its size to communicate success. It grows through a strong and diverse small-group ministry. It's a collection of mostly homogeneous single cells who gather weekly for a mass event—worship.[7]

Each of these church types looks, feels, and acts differently. Each requires a different kind of pastoral leader and tends to attract different types of people with different needs and expectations.

The church I served in Vermont was a family church that was becoming a pastoral church, but many of the new members were "flatlanders" (people from somewhere else) who came to Vermont from program and corporate churches. They expected their new church to function like their old churches. It didn't and couldn't.

Douglas Walrath and Social Context, Social Position, Types of Church Organization, and Cultural Appeal

Douglas Walrath, former director of the Small Church Leadership Program at Bangor Theological Seminary, was an early and pivotal contributor to the theoretical and pragmatic foundation of our understanding of smaller churches. He recognized that smaller churches are not small by accident. Generally they are the fruit of their context or situation. His chapter, "Types of Congregations and Their Implications for Planning," in *Small Churches Are Beautiful*, and his chapter, "How Change Is Challenging Small Churches," in *Developing Your Small Church's Potential*, are worth finding, studying, and applying.

Walrath says that congregations are located in three, very different, social and geographical contexts—rural country, fringe areas, and cities. He divides these three into twelve sub-settings ranging from center city to most rural: midtown, inner city, inner-urban, outer-urban, city suburb, metropolitan suburb, fringe suburb, fringe village, fringe settlement, independent city, rural village, and rural settlement.[8] Each locale has a characteristic church. What that church is like is usually determined by the locale and the types of persons in the vicinity. These sub-settings are always in flux, some growing and some declining, and the population and economy of each is always changing. Urban sprawl, in- and out-migration, and communication technologies are blurring the distinctions between these sub-settings, but they still exist. Expect that a smaller church in each of these settings will have distinctive qualities and challenges and will be called on to adapt. Smaller churches (often with limited physical and personal resources) can be very vulnerable to contextual changes around them.

A good first stop for the church leader looking at a current or prospective ministry setting would be the U. S. Census Web site <www.census.gov>. Type in your location and zip code and be prepared to learn as much or more than you want to know. Other research sites are the local library, the city hall or county courthouse, the Chamber of Commerce, the extension service, and the regional college or university. With map in hand, do your own windshield survey or ask a longtime resident or local government official to take a drive with you around your target community or county. It's hard to minister where you are if you don't understand where you uniquely are. But it's not enough to only know the social context of your congregation.

Walrath identifies churches as being in one of three social positions, which he calls the church's "posture" or position of influence in the community:

- The dominant church is the prestige church, usually larger, with old families, money, and powerful community people. Sometimes the name identifies the church—Old First or Church on the Green. It often has the tallest spire and is closest to the seat of civic power. People trying to climb the social ladder may be attracted here. They will want a pastor who fits their self-image. In different geographical regions, different denominations may automatically be found at the top rung of the social position ladder—United Church of Christ in New England, Lutheran in Minnesota, Southern Baptist in Georgia, or Presbyterian in California.

- The subordinate church or the denominational church is the other church, the one that came later, that sits in the shadow, down the block, or around the corner—the one that is more concerned with being loyal to its denominational tradition than its status in the community. It probably has more school-teachers and merchants and fewer doctors, lawyers, CEOs, and civic officials. It is likely to look for different qualities in a pastor. Since fewer people maintain their denominational loyalty, denominational churches can no longer assume those who migrate from other places will consider denomination first in selecting a church.

- The exclusive church or the distinctive church is a church for a specific group—Catholic (in a non-Catholic community), Mormon, a particular ethnic or cultural group, a church dominated by one extended family, a house church with a particular focus, or a fundamentalist church with rigid theological and social requirements. New churches determine their place on the social-position ladder by where they locate themselves, by which denomination they affiliate with, by how they market themselves, by the numerical goal they aspire to, and by who ends up populating the church.[9]

The third way Walrath classifies churches is by "church organization types." He identifies five:

- An independent church, programmatically and in terms of leadership, stands by itself. It has its own pastor and, perhaps, staff, its own building, its own program for its own people. Most churches have this as their goal.

- A yoked church has one pastor serving two or more congregations. While yoking is the most common linkage between churches, Walrath believes it may be the weakest. Churches tend to come into yokes primarily because they can no longer go it alone or can find a pastor who can afford to just serve one church. Often, the churches involved in a yoke share nothing but the pastor.

- In a team ministry, two or more pastors serve one or more congregations. If more than one church is involved, there will be a formal or informal agreement about who will do what and what will be shared. Pastors are able to share resources and talents and each is able to concentrate to some degree in her or his area of specialty or giftedness. Teams often serve a larger geographical area and pastors can cover for one another when one is off duty.

- In a cluster, two or more congregations cooperate programmatically, rather than merely sharing staff. The cluster will have some degree of formal organization and representatives will come together periodically for planning, program development, and execution. Clusters are generally more satisfying to both pastor and congregations.

- A cluster-team involves two or more pastors serving two or more churches. There is ongoing cooperation between pastors and congregations and more opportunity for sharing of leadership (pastoral and lay), programs, and resources. Experience suggests that this is the most advantageous and satisfying, as well as the most difficult to maintain.[10]

Increasingly, there is greater cooperation between denominations, particularly in small town and rural settings. In Iowa, this was called an "ecumenical shared ministry." Some denominations had worked out a process and procedure for helping churches of different denominational traditions come together to share some combination of staff, programs, and facilities. The Methodist and United Church of Christ churches in Chamois, Missouri, and the three churches in Oto, Rodney, and Smithland, Iowa, are examples of churches that continue to evolve their shared ministry. Shared ministries allow churches to maintain their historic identity when they can no longer afford to or desire to go it alone. Federating (combining everything while maintaining separate church identities), merging (combining everything into a new identity) and closing churches are recommended and utilized more today than they were ten to twenty years ago. Through merger and closure, many churches with a reason for being have been lost and many people have been left churchless.

Fourth, Walrath suggests that "cultural appeal" is another way of understanding congregations:

- Newcomer churches are found in communities where the population is increasing. New residents join a church, often one where many others have come from somewhere else. When enough newcomers become insiders, it is their church. Even in Vermont, noted for its "old Yankees," the Shrewsbury church had no one who had "always" been there. It was a newcomer church. This is true of most California and sun belt churches.

- Indigenous churches are primarily made up of people who are native to the area. These are often declining churches that find it difficult to or are unwilling to attract new people. With the United States quickly becoming a multicultural society, one of the most common types of new and smaller churches is the church made up primarily of people from a specific culture.

While the people in these churches are usually not indigenous to their locale, their churches are culturally indigenous.

- Culturally mixed churches include new and old, indigenous and immigrant, and people from diverse backgrounds. They bring differing cultural histories, economic status, values, styles, and religious histories. In these churches, it is particularly important to work at identifying those things that people have in common in an ongoing search for more commonality than differences. Heterogeneous churches such as these won't grow as easily as homogeneous churches. They often have more conflict, and they are usually more difficult to pastor. Churches like these that are able to make it work are particularly needed in our fragmented society.[11]

Walrath has been particularly helpful in his understanding that social context, social position, type of church organization, and cultural appeal are interdependent and interrelated factors in determining the health and potential of a congregation. In planning for the life and future of a church, social context, social position, cultural appeal, and type of church organization all need to be considered. For example, a small-village, dominant church that has historically been an independent church would probably be happier with its own bi-vocational pastor than yoking to share a pastor, whereas a subordinate, culturally mixed church might be quite willing to share a pastor and program with another similar church.

Tony Pappas and the Folk Society

Tony Pappas, longtime island pastor in Rhode Island, editor of *The Five Stones* journal for smaller churches, and American Baptist area minister in Massachusetts, has been instrumental in the Small Church Movement for over twenty years. In his *Entering the World of the Small Church*, Pappas constructs a helpful understanding of smaller churches based on anthropologist Robert Redfield's concept of "folk society."[12] These characteristics of folk societies are also characteristics found in most smaller churches:

- Folk societies have a small population
- Most people are connected by long-term association and know each other well
- The members have a strong sense of belonging
- The group is isolated from other groups in neighboring areas
- It has a strong identification with the area it occupies
- It often functions as if it's in "a little world off by itself"
- There is a primacy of oral over written communications
- Relationships are ends in themselves, not means for achieving some other end
- Social recognition is a greater motivator than material gain
- Valued qualities are those that contribute to long-term stability, not change
- Tradition determines actions
- Moral worth is attached to the traditional ways of doing things[13]

We should not be surprised to find that these folk or tribal characteristics also describe smaller faith communities that have descended from four-thousand-year-old biblical folk societies. The qualities on this list accurately describe most smaller churches but would be foreign to a large institution. It's clear that such a smaller society would call forth different leadership roles.

Nancy Foltz and the Characters in Smaller Churches

Nancy Foltz, professor at Pittsburgh Theological Seminary, has compiled many ways of understanding smaller churches. Particularly insightful is her list of the "characters" we are likely to find in a smaller church. How many of these can you find in the church you know best? (This is only a partial list!)

- The Matriarch and Patriarch have lived through the history of the church, are gruff on the outside and caring on the inside, and must be won over if the pastor wants to stay very long.

- The Gatekeeper (often an older man) watches the doors, enjoys greeting everyone and orienting strangers, and ushers newcomers into the family.
- The Legitimizer puts the stamp of approval on decisions, either verbally or nonverbally.
- The Cornerstone is often both a leader in church and community and the church's communicator, ambassador, and anchor.
- The Blarney Stone tells the pastor what the church won't and sometimes tells the church what the pastor can't.
- The Pebbles are the newcomers and the young, old, and sideline people.
- The Sleeper worships with eyes closed, usually without snoring.
- The Aginer or Wet Blanket may be one of the hardest workers but is against almost everything and often bickers a lot.
- The Innovator (may be the pastor) is often the first to recognize a problem or opportunity, depends on allies, and has a backup idea if the first one is rejected.
- The Border Guard knows everyone in the church family, often the honorary "aunt" or "uncle," watches newcomers, and warns pastor of brewing trouble.
- The Storyteller is the living historian who preserves the church's myth and is often a legend him or herself.
- The Early Bird and Bell Ringer arrives early and gets things organized and started on time.
- The Peacemaker works to maintain or restore harmony.
- The Spark Plug is the self-starter who sees what needs doing and does it.
- The Hugger is the friendliest of people, loves to hug and be hugged (usually appropriately).
- The Church Angel and the Holy Terror (most churches have at least one of each of these children).
- The Bird Dog points to where the pastor should direct her or his attention.

- The Captain Bluster or Steamroller makes a lot of noise and enjoys fireworks.
- The Fickle Financier uses money to register approval or disapproval and sometimes manipulates people and programs with money.
- The Busybody enjoys telling others how to do their job.
- The Sniper avoids face-to-face criticism; prefers to shoot from cover.
- The Candy, Cookie, or Gum Person understands the ministry of hospitality, is loved by the children, and usually has a pocket full of goodies.
- The Warm Shepherd is surrounded by children who feel loved by her or him.
- The Violet Lady is the flower lover who loves to decorate and make things beautiful.[14]

Most smaller churches have at least one of each and a few other characters. Most are so essential that church folks often assume the role, even when it doesn't come naturally. They make the church fun and not so fun, hot and cold, Christian and not very, real, and distinctive. Do larger churches have them? Maybe, but they're not as easily recognized, nor are they the stuff of legends.

Congregational Life Cycle Theory

Writers like Martin F. Saarinen in *The Life Cycle of a Congregation*[15] and Alice Mann in *Can Our Church Live? Redeveloping Congregations in Decline*[16] believe every congregation is somewhere in a life cycle process ranging from birth or just beginning through stages of maturation to decline and death. This theory is helpful because every congregation is in process from where it has been to where it appears to be going. The theory provides labels for the stages. Each stage has particular characteristics and requires particular leadership approaches.

Yet I have reservations about including this theory because it tempts the well-meaning helper to force-fit a congregation into an identity or stage in the cycle when it doesn't naturally fit. The labels make the stages seem more definable and predictable than they are. And they fit individuals and larger institutions better than they fit folk societies. Folk societies or smaller churches don't like to be pigeon-holed and can't be. A new pastor or family comes, and the church springs to life. A loved pastor or key family leaves, and it feels like death is just around the corner. A church is torn by conflict, and people despair. It takes on a new outreach project, and the church comes alive. A church like Epiphany United Church of Christ in St. Louis is at more than one stage at the same time. It was difficult to feel a pulse in the Oto, Iowa, church ten years ago. Today, it's as healthy and vital as any church I know.

What I find dangerous is the air of inevitability in the theory. While those who cite the life cycle theory claim the cycle can be slowed, interrupted, or even reversed, the louder message is that altering the process from birth to death is a little like stopping a runaway train. Put a fish in a bowl, give it a maintenance diet, ignore it otherwise, and it will live for a while and then die an inevitable and predictable death. But smaller churches are not fish in a bowl. Communities rise and fall. People come and go. Most importantly, people seeking to be faithful often believe the truth of Christmas new life, Easter resurrection, and Pentecost's Spirited life. The Holy Spirit is bound less by lifecycle theory than the social scientists. There are uncounted examples of people with cancer or heart disease who got treatment, changed their lifestyle and philosophy of life, and are happier than ever and healthier than in decades.

Each of the four churches I have known best were somewhere between bureaucracy or decline and death. Each of them—with good leadership, vital worship, renewed older people and new people, outreach ministries, and a vision of the future—came to vigorous life. The life cycle theory was not helpful in these situations. Others who have given more weight to this theory have found in it justification for encouraging the closure of churches when effective resuscitation could have provided a new lease on life. I would be cautious about applying the life cycle theory as a sure predictor of the future.

Robert Wilson of Duke Divinity School tells of traveling in the Southeast with a denominational administrator who we'll call Frank. Frank pointed to a little church nestled in the pines and said, "It's sad. I had the job of closing that little church about two years ago. It was no longer financially viable, a drain on the denomination. They only had fifteen or twenty members left. I led them through a process of closing the place down. Would you like to see the lovely little building?"

As they mounted the steps, Frank was alarmed to see that the front door lock was missing. Suspecting vandalism, they went inside. The church was immaculate. Fresh flowers were on the communion table. The hymn board on the front wall indicated not only the three hymns for the past Sunday but that the offering amounted to $42.25 (this was many years ago). The administrator was stupefied. Wilson said with a smile: "I'd say you did a poor job of closing this little church."[17]

Edwin Friedman and Peter Steinke and Family Systems

I find family-systems theory more helpful in understanding smaller churches. Edwin Friedman, in his classic *Generation to Generation: Family Process in Church and Synagogue*, demonstrates how churches are emotional systems, like families. They think and act like families and exhibit the same pathologies and healthfulness that one finds in families. What he says about churches in general is even truer of smaller churches that are less institutional and more familial as a result of their closer proximity and the greater intensity of their life together.

Friedman demonstrates how churches live, function, and fight like families, even to the point of inheriting patterns and personalities from their ancestors. He observes that people behave in their church family in response to the dynamics going on in their individual families. Another helpful family-system resource is Peter Steinke's *How Your Church Family Works: Understanding Congregations as Emotional Systems*.

Differences among Smaller Churches

Lyle Schaller said that smaller churches are different from other sizes of churches, but that does not mean that smaller churches are all alike. Anyone who talks of "the small church" is overlooking the wide variety among smaller churches. There is no such thing as the small church just as there is no typical human being. Each of the following, while they share many characteristics in common with other smaller churches, is distinctive, with a different history, appeal, sense of self, and view of the world:

- The always-smaller church, like the ones I served in Massachusetts and Vermont, are not troubled by that identity and will probably always be smaller unless their communities boom or they happen to get an unusually charismatic and entertaining pastor. Always-smaller churches might also be called unavoidably smaller churches, such as a Protestant church in a heavily Catholic community or one-too-many churches in an over-churched community to which no one is moving. Always-smaller churches seldom close because they are tough, resilient, and know how to be small. Even though they appear stuck in the status quo, these are often extremely faithful and effective churches. They also are more likely to resist growth for growth's sake. After all, why would a beagle want to become a St. Bernard?

- The once-large or remnant smaller church, like the Emmetsburg and San Rafael churches, is quite prevalent and often troubled. It has a sense of inferiority and—ignoring reality—wants to bring back the good old days when the pews were full and the Sunday school was overflowing. It is at greater risk of closing, because it may not have learned how to be small or is saddled with an albatross of a building it cannot support. A pastor who is quite astute, loving, and visionary is required to love the people into loving themselves, to build their self-esteem and morale by leading the people from one successful strategy to another, and to help the church discern a new, God-given identity and reason for being.

- The not-yet-large smaller church is the smaller church in the under-churched, mushrooming suburb or the new church being led by an ambitious or charismatic pastor with a good plan. This church shares a goal of not being a smaller church any longer than necessary and often has lay leaders with large-church experience and expectations. It will behave more like a larger church even while it is smaller. Sometimes, the grand vision of these churches doesn't work out, and they have to learn to be a smaller church or disband.

- An intentionally smaller church comes in various forms. There are smaller churches that stay small because the leadership jealously guards its power and excludes any who might want to share it. Then there is the highly disciplined and theologically serious church (like Church of the Savior in Washington, D.C., and its more recent incarnations) that has such demanding expectations or requirements that most prospects won't make the stiff commitment. The Indianola, Iowa, church I visited may be one of these.

- Ethnic smaller churches are the most rapidly increasing type of smaller church. Imagine, five Sudanese churches in Sioux Falls, South Dakota. Almost one-fifth of the churches in the Northern California Conference of the United Church of Christ are ethnic or non-Anglo churches. They provide an essential home away from home for their people.

- The clan smaller church is made up almost entirely of one or two large, extended families who believe blood is thicker than baptismal water. Often, the only way into one of these churches is by marriage or birth—or by being called as pastor.

- A schismatic church uses conflict to practice cell division so that it can remain small. Those who lead the dividing may be yearning to return to the size of church where they are more at home, or they may be missing the feeling of power they enjoyed when they once were large fish in a smaller church pond.

Keep these theoretical tools in your ministry toolbox, and use the ones that fit the situations you find yourself in. Each can provide insight in understanding and leading in smaller settings. But, over and above, find out what makes these churches tick, what makes them different, and what else you need to know in order to practice faithful and effective leadership in such churches.

Thirty Common Characteristics of Smaller Churches

In *Small Churches Are the Right Size*, I defined small churches by ten characteristics that generally described congregations without a lot of people. These were positive qualities around which a smaller church could develop a faithful and effective ministry. The list was often cited by others. Over the next ten years, I learned from others and my own ministry, and the list grew to twenty-six in *The Big Small Church Book*. The list was still incomplete and has now grown to thirty.

The smaller the congregation, the more true each of the following is likely to be. When these characteristics are understood and then integrated into a church's ministry and mission, they can help a church better fit the number who are present and fulfill its potential. Pretending that these are not realities will make it more difficult for a smaller church to grow. Taking the list seriously should lead to growth—if not in size, then in other measures of church health. Leaders of larger churches could use this list to help lead their churches into feeling and acting smaller, even as they accommodate more people. (This list of smaller church characteristics is in questionnaire form in the resource section.)

1. *A smaller church fulfills the common expectations of its people.*

   People join smaller churches expecting a greater level of intimacy and caring, expecting to be involved, expecting to have a say in what happens. Expecting such qualities, they participate in developing or perpetuating them. Since they are swimming in a smaller pond, they can have considerable influence in realizing their expectations. Those who don't want those qualities in their church will likely drive past a smaller church to a larger one with different qualities.

2. *Almost everyone knows almost everyone else in a smaller church.*

   This is usually the first definition of a small group. A. Paul Hare observes: "A group is usually defined as small if each member has the opportunity for face-to-face interaction with all others."[18] The smaller a church is, the more people expect not only to know one another but also to know one another's business—and they usually do. Knowledge of one another is important, because people feel and act differently with those they know. On the other hand, the belief that everyone knows everyone else is often a myth. In none of the churches where I've been pastor has everyone known everyone else. Some of the children and elders have not known each other. And, it takes a while for new folks and old-timers to get to know one another.

3. *Beyond knowing one another, the smaller church acts and feels like "family."*

This is what Tony Pappas means when he writes about the smaller church being a folk society or tribe. Others compare it to an extended family. When one celebrates, all celebrate. When one hurts, all hurt. The hatchet will be buried when one of the antagonists is in need. Feelings in the church can be as intense as feelings in the family. When a member of the family is absent, others in the family will notice and be affected by the absence. The healthy, smaller-church family meets the need we all have to be known, secure, and cared for. The place where the family gathers will be more than just God's house. It will be the home where they and God reside together.

   But beware! One doesn't just walk into a house and join the family. We enter families by birth, adoption, or marriage. This does not happen overnight. A sensitive smaller church pays attention to its adoption processes. I prefer that the worshiping congregation not grow by more than ten percent a year so that it can adopt and assimilate effectively. Also remember that families fight. Because the tie that binds them is tough and resilient, they are free to disagree and even be mad at one another. Healthy families are careful to fight cleanly, care for one another even as they fight, and then enjoy kissing and making up.

4. *Almost everyone feels and is important and needed.*

In smaller churches, a higher percentage are in worship, their people are more generous in giving, and a higher percentage serve in some leadership capacity. Larger churches hire people to do the work or they ask the most gifted. Smaller churches live by a do-it-yourself mentality. One of the most gifted lay leaders in the first church I served in Warwick, Massachusetts, recalled how it was different in the large New York parish where she came from: "I never had a chance to find out what I could do. . . . You didn't get asked to do the jobs unless you joined the groups. . . . My place was on the fringe." It is important to work to see that as many people as possible have some responsibility in the life of the church family.

Leaders need to make each person feel important and needed both for the health of the person as well as for the health of the community. I frequently quote Dietrich Bonhoeffer's counsel in *Life Together*:

In a Christian community, everything depends upon whether each individual is an indispensable link in a chain. Only when even the smallest link is securely interlocked is the chain unbreakable. A community which allows unemployed members to exist within it will perish because of them. It will be well, therefore, if every member receives a definite task to perform for the community, that he may know in hours of doubt the he, too, is not useless and unusable.[19]

5. *Organizational functioning is simple rather than complex and sometimes immediate, not delayed.*

The larger the mechanism, the harder it takes to start it, move it, and keep it moving. The more people in the organization, the more complex their interactions will be. Decisions in smaller churches can take forever to be made and then never acted on. But it doesn't have to be this way. Smaller churches will decide and act as quickly as they want. Inevitably, some things will be decided by the matriarch, patriarch, cornerstone, or pillars. The longer I'm the pastor, the more the congregation trusts me to make some procedural decisions myself. Many decisions get made before, during, or after worship simply by asking, "Who will _____?" and someone responds, "I will." Other decisions get made in the parking lot or the coffee shop. In San Rafael, when we have meetings of boards, committees, or the whole congregation, most decisions are made by consensus. This church has a firm tradition that no meeting lasts more than two hours. Decision-making is generally less complex, because fewer people are affected, the time lines are shorter, and the stakes usually aren't as high.

6. *Communication is rapid and usually effective.*

People in smaller churches want to know, expect to know, and have a right to know. Unless the church is dysfunctional, there's a grapevine that gets the word around. One of the reasons a high percentage attend worship is so that they will know who's who and what's what. As the pastor in a smaller church, I know who will be affected by a pending decision and can visit with that person. One of my roles as pastor is being the church switchboard operator or receptionist who connects those with information with those who want it. I've learned that gossip is a neutral term— sometimes constructive, sometimes destructive. So I encourage good gossip. One Saturday night before Pentecost, I wanted to encourage everyone to come to worship the next day wearing red or white. I called five people who each called five people. The next morning the sanctuary was awash in red and white.

7. *Smaller churches are known more by their distinctive personalities and less by their programs or even their names.*

Carl Dudley taught us that smaller churches find their identity in their character: "The larger congregation knows who it is because of what it does, and it must keep on doing it in order to assure its existence. The small church has identity because of the experiences that it brings from the past. . . . They find identity in their character, not in their activities."[20] Recall that Arlin Rothauge referred to the smallest churches as family churches and the larger churches as program or corporate churches. People seek out larger churches for programs that scratch where they itch. Others gravitate to smaller churches that are known not by name or their programs but as friendly churches or caring churches or Bible-believing churches or fun-loving churches or outreaching churches.

8. *A smaller church is likely to be rooted in its history and nervous about its future.*

Healthy families share a family story or history that includes legends, skeletons, heroes, humor, pathos, tragedy, and conquest. In a smaller church, many members will have personal connections with their past characters and saints. The holy moments and life-changing episodes that are remembered by those who have been around need to be taught to those who haven't. In San Rafael, when John Starkweather died, part of our job was to teach those who had come lately just why John was such a remarkable man and pillar of church and community. His legacy will help lead us into our future. Often, the church building— through windows, plaques, furnishings, pictures, and arti- facts— serves as a living museum, or as Larry Pray, pastor in Big Timber, Montana, said, "the walls have memory." One of the new pastor's first tasks is to hear the old, old stories and begin to understand how they have shaped the present church. The wise pastor finds in these stories the precedents that can guide the church into a faithful future. The pastor is no longer new when he or she becomes one of the cast of characters about whom stories are told.

Tony Pappas said that an effective, smaller-church leader must be willing to live with a sprained neck, looking both backwards and forwards. Carl Dudley noted that while a church is often afraid for its future, its history can be the solid foundation on which to build the church's future. He wrote: "To appreciate the past is not to be bound by it, but to build on it. . . . The small church will die if it loses touch with its history. . . . When the future is constructed from pride in the past, then the richest energy of the small church is released and activated."[21]

9. *A smaller church's theology is relational, horizontal, and historical.*

A church's prevailing theology is likely to grow out of its size. A larger church where people come primarily to commune with God is likely to conceive of God as transcendent, elevated, holy, mystical, other. A smaller church where people worship together as a community will likely experience God through one another as immanent, as communal, as love, as personally involved in the stuff of their lives. Since members of smaller churches are closer to their history, they are more likely to worship the God of their mothers and fathers, the God who has led them through the wilderness times toward the promised land. They are also more likely to talk about their friend Jesus than the transcendent Christ and to experience the Spirit of God as love more than mystery.

10. *Smaller churches understand and respond to mission in personal and immediate terms.*

Since smaller churches don't think in organizational or systemic concepts, it seems like just another tax when their denominations ask for undesignated mission money to support diversified, unspecified mission somewhere else. This doesn't capture their imagination. They do get excited about helping particular neighbors (even far away) and making a personal difference. When the Shrewsbury church sent twelve people to Rwanda to build a school, the church community responded generously. When the San Rafael church helped put a name and a face on poor children in Mexico, its people grew to care about these distant neighbors. The churches I visited in my cross-country odyssey actively reached out to their community. Many would rather lend a hand and be personally involved than just write a check. Smaller churches exist to care. Larger churches give to causes. Smaller churches give to people. Discerning leaders can help them do this both locally and globally.

11. *A smaller church prefers its minister be a pastor, friend, generalist, and lover; not a professional, specialist, administrator, or chief executive officer.*

A smaller church wants precisely what new pastors haven't learned to be. These churches care far less about how much the pastor knows academically and far more about how well she will get to really know and care for them. Carl Dudley says that what smaller churches want is a "lover," someone who cares effectively and personally. He wrote, "Based on the distance between pulpit and pew, three styles of pastoral relationship may be identified: specialist, generalist, and lover. . . . The small church wants a lover. . . . The pastor as lover is a source of stability, a kind of human Blarney Stone. . . . He or she is the tangible symbol of love, the lover." [22]

The professional literature talks a lot about pastoral boundaries. Certainly there are lines that should not be crossed. But, to a degree, those lines should be drawn in the sand so they can be adjusted to meet the need. If I'm not willing to change my day off in order to wait beside the deathbed or if I'm not comfortable holding a grief-stricken spouse, then I'm in the wrong line of work or at least the wrong-sized church. The tragedy of pastors leaving after two, three, or four years is that they leave just when they've gotten to know their people well enough to really do some good. I compare myself to the general practitioner in medicine and work to know as much as I can about as many aspects of ministry as possible.

12. *Smaller churches will look and feel like New Testament churches.*

Seminary students often graduate with a corporate and organizational model in mind of what a church is and does. That model comes from larger churches and doesn't fit smaller churches. Some media, journals, and books picture megachurches as the wave of the future. Whatever they are, they don't bear any resemblance to New Testament churches. The churches that the Gospels were written for and the churches we read about from Acts to Revelations were smaller churches. Get your primary understanding of what a Christian church is and does from your reading of the Gospels and epistles. When those churches messed up, learn from their mistakes. When those churches were faithful, model yourselves after them. The book of Ephesians sounds like an ideal, smaller-church mission statement.

13. *Smaller churches are people centered and oriented.*

Smaller churches aren't good at long-range planning. Encourage management by objectives and they will yawn. They don't come to worship for a private meeting with God, come to meetings solely to make decisions, or give to support an institution. They can't worship until they check in with one another. They come to worship with and work with and for people they care about. What others call gossip, they call caring. What others call mission, they call loving their neighbors—near and far. The work of faithful smaller churches is not business, budgets, and buildings; it's loving and caring in the name of God. They are the right size to be up-close and personal.

14. *Smaller churches are more likely to laugh and cry than larger ones.*

Those who are afraid of emotions will be happier somewhere else. As we know, our emotions are closer to the surface and more likely to be expressed when we're with those we know and care about. Close proximity breeds greater intensity. Expect less pretense and more honest emotion when a smaller church gathers. Don't expect worship to be as quiet as it is in larger churches. Don't expect as many stiff upper lips. Do expect that there will be a full range of emotions present, including anger and fear.

15. *Worship is their primary activity.*

Larger churches offer a full menu of activities, groups, and opportunities. Worship is the house specialty in smaller churches, the primary time it gathers, and the principal entry point into its life. Anything else (except Sunday school) is more of an appetizer or dessert. Most smaller churches worship quite well—even if the music drags or the preacher fumbles. Much that happens before, during, and after worship in smaller churches happens at other times in larger churches—like caring, education, and business.

16. *Eating together is their favorite activity.*

When someone suggested this should be added to my list of characteristics of smaller churches I felt like I'd stumbled onto the eleventh commandment. Of course it's their favorite activity! How could I have not identified that before? Some smaller churches feast, others potluck, others bring refreshments to everything, and some go *en masse* (with visitors) to a local restaurant after worship. You can be pretty sure you're in a healthy smaller church if there's usually good food present. If the people don't make time to eat together or they rush to get home to eat in private, there may well be a plague in their midst. Keep lemonade and snacks around for all meetings, and they will be better attended and more profitable.

17. *The children in smaller churches belong to the whole church.*

In larger churches, it's the parents' responsibility to control their children. In smaller churches, all the people help with the discipline and lavish affection on the church's kids. Expect to see people line up to hold a baby. Expect to see adults talking to other people's kids during coffee hour. (And make sure there's punch and cookies during coffee hour.) Every baptism of a child is a formal and poignant adoption ritual into the church family. In San Rafael, when baby Anna died, it was as though each person's own child had died. A few years later, when Jeffrey was born into the same family, it was as though each member had received a special gift from God.

18. *Smaller churches are more intergenerational and integrated than larger churches.*

Larger churches are more age-graded, with something different for each interest group. Each age group has its own space, its own leader, and its own activity. Smaller churches have the opportunity to do everything together, to have everyone learning from everyone else. In smaller churches, a sense of family is not rhetoric but reality.

19. *Smaller churches are very good at celebrating the various stages of life.*

Many birthdays and anniversaries get celebrated by the church family: Births, baptisms, confirmations, weddings, retirements, and deaths can be and often are special, acknowledged times in the collective memory of the church. The pastor who doesn't know how to do a good funeral or memorial service had better learn quickly or move on. The wedding feast we had for Steve and Fran is probably still remembered by those who were present twenty-five years ago. Big Timber, Montana, will always love Larry Pray for the way he makes baptism and confirmation unforgettable. There are many other opportunities to ritualize other life-stages and make them memorable. I offer a house blessing to those moving into a new home. A church could replace birthday celebrations with celebrations of the anniversary of people's date of baptism. Sensitive pastors could have a ritual for couples who experience a stillbirth, or when a couple divorces, or when children go off to college or the military, or when an older person moves from independent living to convalescent or nursing care. I now see one of my primary roles as ritual-maker for the people of our church. Smaller churches are small enough to remember every person from birth through life to death.

20. *Smaller churches are more story than treatise, more mythology than systematic theology.*

Tony Pappas told us that smaller churches are folk societies. Carl Dudley told us they are a culture-carrying people. Christian churches descended from Hebrew ancestors who told stories around the campfire in order to pass on from one generation to another where they came from, who they were, and what kind of God it was that had brought them that far. Jesus Christ is the country teacher/preacher/healer who used stories, sayings, and object lessons to communicate the deep truths that could not be expressed with theological argument and erudite teaching. The Bible is more an anthology of living stories and myths that tell us who we are than a systematic theology or ecclesiastical textbook that tell us what to believe and do.

Larger churches are more likely to identify themselves with interpretative brochures, mission and vision statements, financial balance sheets, statistical comparisons, and other carefully crafted documents. Smaller churches will communicate more truth and meaning by simply sharing their heartwarming, gut-wrenching, belly-laugh stories with their young and their newcomers. No opportunity should be missed to tell those stories in sermons, education with children and adults, newsletters, church history books, all-church gatherings. Someone should record them as living, oral history while the storytellers are still available. In the new sanctuary in San Rafael, we are having a special storytelling stool hand-crafted for our storytellers who tell the children's story in worship. Smaller churches are a storied people with stories to tell.

21. *Smaller churches operate on fluid "people" time.*

Starting and ending on time is not their highest priority. They watch one another more than the clock. Worship starts when people are ready to start and it's over when it's ready to be over more than when the clock strikes the hour. They wait until it feels right before making decisions. Tomorrow is far enough ahead to plan for. Two years with some pastors feels like an eternity; ten years with others flashes by in the blink of an eye. They mark time by events and memories, more than by calendar time. They trust that God's truth will be revealed in due time and that's soon enough. Garrison Keillor had it right when he said: "We Wobegonians go straight for the small potatoes. Majestic doesn't appeal to us. We like the Grand Canyon better with Clarence and Arlene parked in front of it, smiling. We feel uneasy at momentous events."[23]

22. *Most smaller church people would prefer, on the one hand, to give what is needed and when it's needed and, on the other hand, to underwrite what they value as a gesture of gratitude for God's goodness.*

It's more businesslike and less anxiety producing to have every-member canvasses and annual budgets. We like to think it's more faithful. But being businesslike is more of a value in larger organizations. Many people choose smaller churches because they prefer being less businesslike. They know they won't go broke, even if the pastor doesn't know it. I've often seen churches struggle to garner enough pledges to underwrite the budget for the next year, be drenched in red ink in July, and well in the black after Christmas. Often, smaller churches come up with unbelievable amounts of money for something the people care about or know they really need—like a new roof or money to tide a family over after their breadwinner went to jail or died. Churches don't close for lack of money.

23. *Lay people are more important than the pastor.*

Ouch! Most pastors have a little bit of a messiah complex. But it's the lay people who've carried the church through long gaps between pastors, through the lean years when the local economy crashed, when pastoral leadership was incompetent or uncaring, and when the denominational office ignored them with benign neglect. By necessity and out of faithfulness, many smaller churches have learned to be self-reliant and self-sufficient. Part of the knack of pastoring smaller churches is having the wisdom and humility to know when and how to lead and when and how to get out of the way. Especially in the early years of a pastorate, it's the lay folk who keep things going.

24. *Capable, compassionate pastoral leadership is usually required to lead a smaller church from only surviving to really thriving.*

This does not contradict the twenty-third characteristic. It is supposed that pastors have been trained to lead their people to

God's promised land. The people trust that the pastor knows God and knows God's will for God's church. The scriptures have transforming power, and the pastor ought to know how to interpret scripture to lead people to transformation. The pastor has the opportunity to lead spirited worship at least once a week, worship that addresses the people's deepest needs and fondest hopes and calls them to extraordinary faithfulness. The pastor has the opportunity to be with her or his people at the most important times of their lives and ought to be able in those times to earn their deep love, trust, and support. All but the sickest churches believe that God wants them to be more than they are and want to go there with their pastor. To take the people there, the pastor will need a durable faith, the people's confidence, leadership gifts, and staying power. Generally, the longer a pastor stays, the more effective he or she becomes. Most accomplished smaller churches have a pastoral-servant leader, leading the way by walking side by side with her or his people.

25. *Smaller churches are often hard to get into and harder to get out of.*

By getting in, I don't mean getting your name on the member-ship list. If the church acts like and is a family, a new person only becomes a family member by being adopted into the family or grafted onto the family tree. Either way, it takes time—time to learn the stories, time to learn how things are done and what's expected, time to become known and to find one's place. But once you're in and accepted, they will fight for you and to keep you. As Robert Frost said in "The Death of the Hired Man," "Home is the place where, when you have to go there, / They have to take you in."[24]

26. *Smaller churches are tough and tenacious!*

Remember the little kid in school who survived by being tough? The smaller churches that have survived have done so by being resolute and tenacious. They know how to make do. They know how to weather a storm. They know where to find water in the desert. What they may not know is that God wants more for God's people than mere survival. They may resist trusting that God is preparing a table of good things for them in the wilderness. The savvy pastor will appreciate that their toughness and tenaciousness has carried them thus far and can lead them to greater faithfulness.

27. *Smaller churches would rather do it "our way" because they're locally owned and operated.*

To survive, smaller churches have had to be independent. They've experienced more benign neglect than sensitive assistance. They believe they know what's best for them—and they may. They're not going to buy the notion of "covenant" with the wider church until they are convinced that "covenant" isn't code for giving up control of their own destiny. They are not impressed by the denomination's way, or the latest book's way, or the pastor's experience in the last church. Rather than meekly being another franchise in the "McChurch" chain of churches, they're better at being a customized, one-of-a-kind church. Each church has its own special spiritual gift, its own knack, and its own genius. The pastor won't be effective until he or she learns what that gift, knack, and genius is and that by doing it "our way," the customized way may well be God's way.

28. *Smaller churches are more effective than efficient.*

Smaller churches can be quite effective at praising God, nurturing faithful children, holding lives together, and addressing the needs of the community. The National Association of Secondary School Principals concluded in a 1996 report that creating smaller schools was an essential part of making them better. Some think it's more efficient to close the too-little church in the country in order to merge it with the bigger church in town. It might be more efficient, but it is unlikely to provide more effective and faithful ministry with those who are left in the country. Most of those little churches that outsiders think should be closed would have closed a long time ago if they weren't somehow effective. We who work with churches that are more effective than efficient need to be effective and creative ourselves in helping them find fresh ways of finding and keeping pastoral leadership, paying the bills, and doing good ministry where they are. In the end, I doubt if God awards many merit badges for efficiency.

29. *Smaller churches are better at events than programs.*

Larger churches are called "program churches." Smaller churches are better at living a seasonal rhythm and celebrating special occasions. They are going to be better at observing the church year with flair and at special worship services, fund-raising events, special trips, retreats, parties, service projects, work days, and so on, than long-term study groups, open-ended mission projects, and programs requiring long-term commitment.

30. *Smaller churches are better at meeting immediate needs than long-range planning.*

This immediacy has to do with their living on "people" time, their wariness of the future, their nuts-and-bolts way of working, and their instinctive awareness that smaller groups have less of a need for long-range plans. Don't ask a smaller church to envision how things should be in ten years. They will see that as a dumb request and a waste of time. Ask, what do you think we need to do this week, month, or year? Ask what they think Jesus would do if he were here now. Do what's in character for that particular church at that particular time. Plan one, two, or three sure-fire successes, and watch their sights expand. For them, the time that is most real is yesterday and now and, maybe, tomorrow. Perhaps they are on to what Jesus meant when he taught, "Do not worry about tomorrow, for tomorrow will bring worries of its own. Today's trouble is enough for today" (Matt. 6:34). A smaller church that is living well today will be more confident about tomorrow.

Smaller churches may be small, but they're not simple. There's more to understanding them than meets the eye. This treasure chest of theories can help those at the helm avoid the shoals, stay in the channel, follow the currents, navigate through the fog, and find the harbor. Bon voyage.

Questions

1. What theoretical assumptions now underwrite the way your church goes about being church?

2. Which Lyle Schaller-type fits your church? And, can you put a name or names beside each of Nancy Foltz's characters?

3. Which theories and approaches (from here and others) best fit and inform your situation? How and why? How can you apply them?

Suggestions

1. Gather as many people as you can and invite them to work with the number-of-relationships formula. How many relationships were present last Sunday? Provide a map of your sanctuary and ask people to write in the names of as many regulars as they can and where they sit. Draw lines between those who are related or close friends. Put squares around old-timers and circles around those who've come in the last five years. Use symbols for some of Foltz' key characters and place them by those they fit.

2. Reproduce the "Thirty Characteristics of Smaller Churches" from the resource section of this book and ask your people to fill it out, talk about it, and envision many of the ways your church might take these characteristics more seriously in their effort toward being more faithful and effective.

chapter four

Worship Is Where It All Begins and Comes Together

Our culture is a working, hurrying, and worrying culture with many opportunities except the opportunity to celebrate life.
—Henri J. M. Nouwen, *Creative Ministry*

It seems a wonder to me that in our dull little town we can gather together to sing some great hymns, reflect on our lives, hear some astonishing scriptures (and maybe a boring sermon; you take your chances) offer some prayers and receive a blessing.
—Kathleen Norris, *Dakota*

This hand to hold, this song to sing, this child to love, this voice to raise, this heart to cheer, this gift to bring, this day to give God praise!
—Daniel Damon, "This Hand to Hold, This Song to Sing"

I BELIEVE THAT WORSHIP—that time when congregations come together to celebrate life in all of its complexity and fullness—is both the most underestimated and the most important thing churches do, especially smaller churches. In fact, I believe that the hour or so, when upwards of forty percent of the people in our United States gather in their places of worship, is the most influential hour of the week in our society. For thirty years, on a weekly basis, I have had the awesome and humbling privilege of leading twenty to seventy people in worship. This is certainly the most important work I do and the most significant activity in which smaller churches and their people engage.

Worship is the most important thing smaller churches do because the worship time is the primary time when most church members gather to greet and meet, encounter God, and run the risk of being transformed. Through their meeting, they reconnect, update one another, care for each other, and do much of the work of the church—in addition to worshiping. In a society that dismisses small gatherings of faithful folk, the smaller church rediscovers in its worship that there are enough of them to love God, neighbor, and self. Worship is both the source and the foundation for everything else the church is and does. That's why it is so important for smaller churches.

In *Wonderful Worship in Smaller Churches*, I described what happens in worship and how worship has the potential to shape and transform those who have come together.

Life is hard. Whether there are two or three or one hundred present, the room is bursting with need. Some are physically ill. Others are experiencing mental or spiritual anguish. Some are angry—at family, friends, you, life, God, self. Some are in financial crisis. And others are in family crisis. Some are feeling all alone while others are desperate for some solitude. Some are working too hard and others hardly working. Others are almost paralyzed with fear. Some are feeling worthless while others are overwhelmed. Some are foundering in the face of an impending future. There may be a few who're on top of the world, whole and healthy. The worship leader who is fully cognizant of the depth of need present waiting to be addressed will exhibit great courage simply by not fleeing. The wise and sensitive pastor who's in tune with the congregation will plan and facilitate a worship experience that heals, affirms, equips, and calls the needy to new life and faithful discipleship. While we can't do that every time for every person, if we don't try we are shortchanging our calling and our people.

The primary purpose in gathering people for holy worship is not to perpetuate an institution, to merely provide one more worship service, or to flaunt a flair for impressing people. The principal purpose is to be the host who brings God and God's guests together for a celebration of life in all its fullness, so that God is worthily honored and God's guests are renewed and equipped to live again. Whether we are friend, spouse, or parent, we experience how difficult it is to address the essential need of just one other person. How then can we do that when we're faced by up to a hundred very different and very needy persons? We do it the same way we would eat an elephant—very carefully, and one bite at a time. The genius of Christian worship and the wonder of God's grace is that in the space of an hour or so, a room full of needy people can have their essential need met. How, you ask?

Knowing we have people present who are hungry for genuine community, we create opportunity for them to transcend their individualness and connect with one another. We do that by inviting people to stand up, move around, and greet one another. We do that by having multiple opportunities for corporate sharing and singing so they experience their voices blending with other voices to form one strong and beautiful voice. We do that through praising the God who is creating us for community and offering confessions that shed the pretenses that separate us. We do that by connecting with a spiritual tradition through hearing and reflecting upon God's Word and the preached word, both of which help us discover that neither in our folly nor our faithfulness are we alone. We do that by exchanging good and bad news of one another and the world and holding one another and the world in prayer. We do that by giving gifts that will sustain and expand our shared life. We do that through sacraments that welcome one another into God's baptized family and call us all to our place around God's abundant table.

We have people hungry for solitude, so we honor the need for silence and quiet reflection. Recognizing there are various forms of sickness, fear, and alienation among us, we offer carefully articulated prayers that trust God does care, answer, heal, reconcile, encourage, and equip in God's own way. Knowing we are facing many folks who feel inadequate to live up to what's expected of them, we offer a liturgy of hope, words of affirmation, sacraments of promise. Aware that life is difficult for most of our people, and that they question the adequacy of their personal resources, we use biblical resources with which they can identify and utilize religious practices that have long addressed the deepest needs of seeking people. Since it's God's job to judge and our job simply to love with wise compassion, the worship leader who uses the worship hour as a time to scold or shame is guilty of pastoral abuse. Finally, whether or not we're from an evangelical tradition that employs an altar call, we are responsible for creating a liturgy that confronts people with God's expectation, that calls them to leave different than they arrived, and that gives them the opportunity to make new promises of faithfulness.

If we don't build into worship the expectation that people will leave as healed, affirmed, equipped, and called people, they won't, and we will have squandered our call to be their pastor and priest.[1]

This is the essence and wonder of Christian worship, as experienced in all theological traditions, denominations, worship styles, and cultures. This potential of worship to connect and transform can be particularly realized when it's not a crowd but a community who have gathered. A church that worships in this manner, with such intentionality and awareness, will be full of life, hope, and faithfulness.

Many people participate in worship without a clear understanding of what worship is or what it isn't. Worship is something humans have done since they came from the cave and witnessed their first magnificent sunrise. Ever since, humans have been creating, practicing, and passing on religious rituals that give words to the unspeakable and meaning to the mystery. The Judeo-Christian community has been worshiping since God established a covenant with the earliest Hebrew people. The Christian community has been worshiping since they first learned to "pray then in this way" and to "do this in remembrance of me."

Our English word "worship" comes from the Old English word *weorthscipe*, which combines two shorter Old English words, *weorth* (worthy) and *scipe* (ship), and means to give worth or respect to someone. To worship God means to give respect to or ascribe worth to God or to give praise to the only one who is worthy of praise. To praise God embraces giving praise for all that God has done, for the whole of creation of which we are an integral part. My definition of worship is based on Jesus' Great Commandment: Worship is the ritualized response of the Christian community to God's love with the praises of their hearts, the yearnings of their souls, and the ponderings of their minds, so that the community can respond by loving each other and all of creation as they love themselves.

The word that is used to convey the practice of worship is liturgy. Liturgy means, literally, the work of the people. The reason I believe smaller churches are the right size to worship really well is that they are the right size to have all the people be workers instead of mere spectators. Danish theologian Sören Kierkegaard is noted for his observation that worship is like a stage play. The whole congregation are the actors, the worship leaders are the prompters, and God is the audience. Only in smaller churches can we actualize this understanding of worship.

Liturgy is far more than a fixed or rote form of worship. Through worship space, symbol, memory, word, and sacrament, the liturgy helps us recall what we have forgotten, gives words to feelings and substance to what is poorly articulated, and translates our joyful noises into joyful harmonies. It can begin healing a grieving heart, illuminate a muddled mind, and transform a mix of individuals into a community of believers. Without liturgy, faith would be little more than a mess of pottage. Liturgy is to faith as the constitution is to democracy.

A metaphor that expresses the nature of worship in smaller churches is the family reunion, with its fascinating rituals. Usually held annually, a family clan will rent a hall, reserve a recreation area, or return to the family homestead. The members of each generation who call those at the reunion "my family" come from near and far to renew ties and rediscover who they are and where they came from. When the clan gathers, food is put out, new additions to the family are introduced, family and personal news is updated, changes are recorded, babies are ogled and welcomed, new spouses and friends are incorporated, family stories are retold and embellished, feuds are resolved or perhaps exacerbated, and indigenous rituals are enacted. Though not much new or different may happen, the clan goes home nourished with their roots, identity, and position in the family clarified and confirmed.

Worship in smaller churches resembles a family reunion. People of various generations and stations in life behave like an extended family, no matter whether they're connected by accident, choice, or blood. They come together to praise and worship the one who gave them life and to celebrate the ties that bind them. They note who is absent and who is not. They welcome the newcomer and mourn the absent. They grieve with the grieving and celebrate with the celebrating. The old teach the young and the new the ways of the family. The young and the new give the old reason to hope. They meet, and they eat and, having practiced their power-laden rituals, having confirmed who they are, where they belong, and what they need to be doing, they are free to go . . . until it's time for another reunion. As a member of one church family told me, "If I'm not there on Sunday, the rest of the week doesn't feel quite right."

I wrote *Wonderful Worship in Smaller Churches* because there were few worship resources specifically for smaller churches. Teachers and practitioners of worship do not usually acknowledge that size is a crucial factor in the practice of worship. The unspoken assumption is that the size of the worshiping congregation is largely irrelevant in creating effective worship. This is simply not true. We plan meals for the number who will eat. We plan social gatherings for the number who will gather. We should recognize that the number present shapes the worship experience and that a worship experience planned for the number worshiping will be better targeted and more effective. Worshiping without a crowd is an opportunity that should be taken advantage of.

Wonderful Worship in Smaller Churches would be a helpful companion to this book. It's structured around twelve principles that underwrite our understanding and planning of worship with smaller churches, and fifteen practices or suggestions for creating worship based on those principles. There are abundant examples, stories, strategies, ideas, and resources. As with this book, each section ends with questions and suggestions so the book can be used as a study book and planning tool. Here are those principles and practices with brief explanatory comments. See *Wonderful Worship* for fuller descriptions, illustrations, and strategies.

Twelve Principles for Worship in Smaller Churches

Principle 1: *Worship is about the worthiness of God and ourselves.*

The purpose of worship is not to inspire or entertain. Its intent is to provide a forum through which a community of people can express their gratitude to the one who has created them as people of value, to hear God's latest word for their living, and to respond with offerings of gifts, prayers, and self.

Principle 2: *Worship is the most important thing smaller churches do.*

It's the heart and soul of smaller-church life and what gives it value, meaning, identity, and purpose. A church that worships well will feel alive, loved, capable, and ready to take on the world; a church that doesn't, won't.

Principle 3: *Smaller churches can worship very well.*

If they do it thoughtfully, they are the right size to sing beautifully, pray personally and powerfully, hear God's word as though it is just for them, give generously, baptize into God's family in that place, and commune on holy food in intimate ways that especially fit their numbers.

Principle 4: *Smaller churches are more likely to experience God as immanent rather than transcendent (and they may prefer Jesus and the Holy Spirit).*

Our theological understanding does not grow out of thin air but from our particular situation and experience. Those who worship and learn in massive cathedrals will perceive God, Jesus, and the Holy Spirit differently than those who worship in intimate communities. Our worship language and expression should grow out of our own particular experience. Most worship books and resources are written with a style and vocabulary that is rather foreign to many in smaller churches.

Principle 5: *Much more happens when they come to worship than worship.*

Smaller church worship is not a place for purists or for the faint of heart. From the time the first person arrives until the last leaves, all kinds of things will be happening among the people of God—most of it good and important. There will be community-building, care-giving, nurturing, mission, church business, and a whole lot more. Don't fight it or repress it. Seek to make the time together the most unforgettable time of the week.

Principle 6: *Their worship needs to be indigenous more than heterogeneous and not homogeneous.*

An early principle of the church-growth movement was that churches would be more successful if they were homogeneous. Smaller churches should grow out of who their people uniquely are (indigenous), and it should celebrate whatever heterogeneity is present. This is both fun and challenging and reflects the way God wills the Community of God—something like a hearty Irish stew.

Principle 7: *Most folks in smaller churches would rather folkdance than watch a ballet.*

This is not about preferences in dance entertainment. It's about smaller churches being the right size for worship that is participatory, rather than passive, and a mutual, rather than a singular, experience. During morning worship in San Rafael, there are more than twenty times in the hour when people do more than just listen. Since they have an opportunity to move, speak, sing, pray, respond, and give, every worship celebration is a liturgical dance in the broadest sense.

Principle 8: *Smaller church worship is more a public than a private experience.*

Our society is increasingly insulated, self-conscious, individualistic, and withdrawn. This is contrary to God's intention and the common good. Plan and conduct worship that is by, for, and about the whole Community of God. Our people can meditate on their own; we can help them worship communally.

Principle 9: *Worship in smaller churches is a family reunion.*

So how can we make it more of a family reunion? Include the kids as much as possible, help people share their personal and common stories, make the sacraments family rituals, and promote interaction and respect for all. The old can give the young the precious gifts of a history and tradition; the young can give the old the precious gifts of a tangible hope and future.

Principle 10: *Smaller church worship is a time for social caring and community building.*

How can worship be planned so that all the people—in the midst of worship— feel loved and cared for like a connected community? Can you see that, by the time every person leaves, each one has been smiled at, called by name, touched, listened to, and heard that God and God's church loves them?

Principle 11: *Worship in smaller churches is more emotional.*

Because more people really know more people in a smaller church, you can expect more tears shed, laughs laughed, honest anger, joyful responses, hurt feelings, and love expressed. When these emotions surface, they should not be repressed, pandered to, or exploited. The church, at its truest and best, is a safe sanctuary where people are free to fully be themselves. A remarkable thing about good religious ritual is that it simultaneously allows and tempers emotion.

Principle 12: *It's folly they resist, not change.*

None of the four smaller churches I've served were resistant to or opposed to change. They didn't want me to make them into what they were not or ram change down their collective throats. They all wanted their church experience to be richer, fuller, and more satisfying. They agreed that it was not realistic for each person to like everything that happened. So we honored those things that were considered sacred, changed one thing at a time, moved from smaller to larger changes, introduced ideas as experiments and not once-and-for-all changes, and had the ideas be their ideas as much as possible. The more they knew their pastor loved and respected them, the more open they were to changes he encouraged.

Fifteen Practices for Smaller Church Worship

Those twelve principles provide the foundation for the following fifteen building blocks or worship practices:

Practice 1: *Design every part of smaller church worship for the number expected.*

An architect designs a space for the number who will occupy it. A teacher teaches according to the number being taught—discussing with ten, lecturing two hundred. Henri Nouwen tells of celebrating the Eucharist with a group of theological students in Utrecht, Holland, in the beautiful old house where they lived. He was dismayed that the liturgy seemed to be a scaled down replica of what might be experienced in the cathedral. He doubted that a "stranger would be able to guess that these people live together, eat together, and study together. The formality of the ritual appears to create distance in word, gesture, and movement that does not exist among these men immediately before or after the liturgy."[2] If you will have twenty or eighty attending next Sunday, how can the space itself, the music, the liturgical involvement, the use of scripture, the preaching, the praying, and everything else be carried out in ways that are designed for and take advantage of the particular numbers present?

Practice 2: *The order of worship matters.*

We don't eat the dessert first or the salad last. The first act of the drama always precedes the second, which leads to the third. Why? The order matters. The traditional and correct order for worshiping is preparing to hear God's Word, hearing it, and then responding to God's Word with our lives. A bulletin that captures the attention of the worshiper, genuinely welcomes visitor and regular alike to this particular church, provides printed resources so that the people can participate together, educates, provides meditation materials for later, and orients to the full life of the congregation is worth the time and money spent. I often put as much time and thought into the liturgy as I do the sermon.

Practice 3: *Worship the God who loves the remnant, the Jesus who turns water to wine, and the Spirit who refreshes and transforms us.*

God has countless qualities that can be worshiped. Smaller churches can be strengthened with worship that focuses on the God who particularly remembered and reached out to the small and the remnant. They can be transformed by worshiping the Christ who was particularly attentive to personal need and whose ministry focused on transformation. And, they can be restored by worshiping the Holy Spirit that is a healing balm, a refreshing breeze, and life for dry bones.

Practice 4: *Design their worship as the work of the people and the fruit of their gifts.*

When my Giants, Red Sox, or 49ers play a game, each player shows up and knows that his best is needed for the team to do its best. The same is true for a symphony orchestra. Worship can be planned so that every person has a role to play and is led to play it well. With a smaller number of worshipers, I can be aware of the particular gifts of each and plan so that those gifts are incorporated—the artwork of the artist, the voices and instruments of the musicians, the ability of the speaker to speak, the generosity of the generous, the ability of the devout to pray, the flowers of the gardener, the communion bread of the baker, or the hospitality of the hospitable.

Practice 5: *Center smaller church worship on people not tasks.*

The larger the worshiping congregation, the more I have to worry about things that are not specifically about the people—time constraints, the way things look, the choreography of what we do, the performance abilities of the leaders, acoustics and sightlines, and more. With my smaller congregation, I can know at least some of the important things going on in every person's life. I can plan a worship experience that touches on the particular texture of this particular people. My goal is that our people leave knowing the worship was customized for them and none other.

Practice 6: *Make room for flexibility and spontaneity.*

Worship without form means worship without focus or coherence. Worship without some flexibility and spontaneity bores the worshiper and stifles the Spirit of God. The larger the congregation, the more structured their worship needs to be. The smaller the congregation, the more spontaneous and responsive we can afford to be. My old parishioner, Carl Nordstedt, who'd been sleeping through worship for years, said after I arrived: "At least he keeps us awake." I think it was probably the freshness of our worship and the Holy Spirit that kept his attention.

Practice 7: *Smaller churches want the song they sing to be the song of their souls.*

Who doesn't hum along, whistle while they work, sing in the shower, and have several favorite songs? How often does each person get to sing his or her favorite hymns? I keep a list of my people's favorite hymns and each favorite gets sung at least once a year. Our hymnal has a wide variety of musical styles, themes, and sentiments along with music from different cultures. When it comes to music, I care more about our people being able to sing the song of their soul than theological correctness. This contributes to why they sing so well.

Practice 8: *Smaller churches need to experience the scriptures as their own story.*

The Bible is not just hoary stories about ancient people in ancient times. Simply reading from the thick old book doesn't communicate to contemporary people. For Judeo-Christian people, the Bible is our family history and story. The scriptures can be read and discussed, read from a contemporary translation, read as dialogue, dramatized, danced, paraphrased, sung, or seen with a VCR.

Practice 9: *The smaller-church preacher is the folkdance caller.*

We said that smaller-church worship is more like a folkdance than a ballet. That makes the pastor-preacher the dance caller. It's the preacher's task to take God's dance as found in both scripture and human experience and call it in a way that his or her people can dance it accurately, powerfully, gracefully, enjoyably.

It's not the preacher's job to lecture to a passive audience. The way the preacher preaches ought to fit the number present. A preacher preaches *at* a couple of hundred and *to* a hundred or so. She can converse with fifty to seventy-five, visit with thirty or forty, and have a heart-to-heart talk with twenty or less.

Practice 10: *Worship should be seasonal, celebratory, eventful, and keyed to life's stages.*

Scripture says, "for everything there is a season." Church seasons are markers along the annual path and watering holes strategically placed throughout the year. We also have markers at crucial stages in our lives. Smaller churches are the right size to have their worship life be eventful.

Throughout the year, our colors, rhythms, symbolism, and themes change, and our lives are richer and fuller. The church's worship can mirror and amplify what is important and timely in the lives of its parishioners, community, and world.

Practice 11: *Make it a house, people, and liturgy of prayer.*

Prayer is the stream that connects those who pray to the living sea that is God. To worship is to pray, and when two or more pray, they are worshiping. Smaller church praying can be very personal and powerful. The way we pray and the content of our prayers deserve great thoughtfulness. Larger churches tend to have professional prayer-givers who pray on behalf of the people who listen. In a faithful smaller church, all the people are more likely to be active pray-ers.

Practice 12: *Customize the sacraments and make them up-close and personal.*

Sacramental occasions are times when smaller churches can really shine and get involved. Baptisms can happen in ways that make them an act of the whole church rather than a private ritual between the baptizer, the baptized, and the baptized family. Communion can be a family meal around the family table instead of a private ritual with a thimble of juice and cube of bread or wafer. Sacramental acts are precious gifts that God offers the world through the church. Smaller churches can offer these gifts in particularly poignant and powerful ways.

Practice 13: *The worship space shapes the worship and the people.*

More than we know, we are shaped, helped, or hindered by the spaces where we live and worship. Some worship spaces put up obstacles to be overcome as people attempt to worship there. Other worship spaces bring God and the people of God closer together so that the people can be touched by God and one another. In San Rafael, we transformed a sanctuary with more obstacles than we realized into a sacred space far more wonderful than we anticipated. Is it time to reconsider where your people meet God and do the work of the people?

Practice 14: *Worship so people leave feeling healed, affirmed, equipped, and called.*

What if the only question for the worship planner is: What can we do in an hour or so, so that God is worthily honored and each person leaves feeling healed, affirmed, equipped, and called? If that was the only question, how would it change what we pray, sing, speak, hear, and do? These are the key questions.

Practice 15: *Be a home of hospitality where every visitor is a guest who wants to return.*

I often quote this wisdom from Henri Nouwen:

> In our world full of strangers, estranged from their own past, culture and country, from their neighbors, friends and family, from their deepest self and their God, we witness a painful search for a hospitable place where life can be lived without fear and where community can be found. . . it is. . . obligatory for Christians to offer an open and hospitable space where strangers can cast off their strangeness and become our fellow human beings.[3]

Most smaller churches would be larger and more intimate if they were more hospitable than they are.

These principles and practices cover the worship waterfront. It would be well to give attention to each. Five subjects are so critical to the renewal of our worship that they need further exploration.

Space, Singing, Preaching, Sacraments, and Seasons

Smaller churches worship in all kinds of spaces—living rooms, storefronts, chapels, rented sanctuaries, new buildings, ancient churches, and cavernous sanctuaries that dwarf the remnant. J. A. T. Robinson wrote: "The church building is a prime aid, or a prime hindrance, to the building up of the Body of Christ. . . . And the building will always win."[4] Without doubt, the place where your church worships either aids or hinders the worship of your people.

I had the extraordinary opportunity of writing a book about worship at the time I was instrumental in helping to plan and create a space for worship for the San Rafael church. Our sanctuary had many problems. It was too large for our numbers and too long and narrow. It was filled with characterless, screwed down furniture. By its placement, the choir was the focal point of the worship space. The worship leaders were hidden behind nondescript barriers that included a pulpit and lectern and were four steps above the congregation. Tiny windows allowed little light and natural beauty in, and the artificial lighting was terrible. A rather strange lattice cross occupied the front wall.

Everything in the sanctuary was a shade of brown. Over a six-year period, we renovated the whole facility and then gutted and rebuilt the sanctuary. It took far more time, money, and effort than we anticipated—and it was worth every penny. The new sanctuary is transforming our worship and our congregation. The process we followed was a key component of the remarkable final product.

That process could be helpful for other congregations:

1. We committed ourselves to a comprehensive reworking of the facility to make it fit the needs of the congregation as it is and is becoming.

2. We hired a gifted architect who listened to the wants and don't wants of our congregation and worked closely with our pastor and committees.

3. We decided we wanted more than a pretty sanctuary; we wanted one that symbolized what we believe and facilitated the kind of worship we aspire to.

4. We studied the theology and development of liturgical space, agreed on twelve objectives we wanted to realize, and gave the architect the final word on changes. (See *Wonderful Worship in Smaller Churches* for those twelve objectives.)

5. We formed a task group to work with various artisans in the creation of two, stunning, stained-glass windows, a beautiful communion or family table, an inviting pulpit from which the Word would be heard, a baptismal fountain with bubbling water, and a distinctive cross (made by one of our men) with embracing arms. The cross was constructed so that it can be filled with flowers on Easter and other important occasions.

6. We crammed into another room for worship and then met in the midst of construction while our new sanctuary was built around us. And we did much of the work ourselves.

7. Finally, we celebrated! Now we worship in a space that is increasingly sacred for us, one that fits our growing congregation, and—most important—one that helps us do all we want to do when we worship.

Any worship space can be made more conducive to the meeting of God and God's people. From the most basic to the most adventurous, here are some steps that might be taken to make your worship space more lovely, expressive of what you believe, sacred, and complementary to your worship:

- Hold an all-church work party to clean, discard, spruce up, polish, rearrange, and replace light bulbs with more wattage.
- Repaint the sanctuary, refinish the furniture, replace the carpet.
- Improve the sound system (being able to hear in church is a right that people have).
- Do something to improve the seating and communal nature of worship—rope off or remove unused pews or rearrange the pews or chairs into a semicircle or a herringbone arrangement so people can see, hear, and be heard. (After considering chairs, we refinished and padded our pews after concluding that pews are friendlier and more communal than chairs.)
- Remove structural barriers that separate those who lead worship from those who follow the leaders and make the sanctuary more accessible for all.
- Lower the chancel platform, move the communion table closer to the people, have some new liturgical furnishings custom made for your church.

If these steps don't accomplish your goals, then be truly adventurous— renovate, rebuild, or build from scratch. Do your very best to have your worship space fit your people and your worship rather than making your people and your worship fit your worship space. The space makes all the difference.

Music and Singing

Composer Cris Williamson sang: "Love of my life, I am crying: I am not dying: I am dancing, dancing along in the madness; there is no sadness, only a Song of the Soul. And we'll sing this song; why don't you sing along?"[5] Isn't that what we all yearn to do daily and in our worship? What passes for music in many churches is dreary if not deadly. It's badly done. It's from another time and people. Many don't participate. The music used doesn't fit the season, mood, location in the service, need and desire of the people, or what the people really believe. Perhaps the singing is deadly because we don't allow the people to sing the songs of their soul.

It's getting harder for churches to find people with the skill and necessary understanding of liturgical music and worship to lead the music. It's getting harder to find people with the time and desire to be "the choir." It's getting even harder for churches to find people who are good-enough musicians to accompany congregational singing. What to do?

Do you need music in your worship? Many worship without music, but most of us would miss it and find our worship diminished without it. Do you need as much music as churches generally have (which can be as much as thirty percent of worship)? Perhaps not, but some will be disappointed. The first question is: How many people are worshiping in your faith community? The musical needs and desires of a dozen worshipers will probably be different from the church with ninety worshipers. So, pick your music according to the number of people who will be singing. You may want to have a guitar or keyboard supplement or replace your organ or piano. If you simply can't find accompaniment, perhaps you can sing *a cappella*.

Can you cast your net wider in your search for a musician? Check with your high school or nearby college for someone young and talented. Perhaps, in lieu of compensation, you can pay for music lessons for a promising student. If you changed your worship time, another church might share its musician with you. If you don't have a live musician, let technology help you. For example, Synthia, part of Suncoast Systems, Inc. (800-741-7464 or <www.suncoastsys.com/synthia.htm>), offers prerecorded music from a variety of hymnals and denominational traditions that can be connected to your keyboard, organ, or electronic piano via MIDI for between $800 and $1100. With this, you can use your computer to record and store your own music. You might go really low-budget and get a neighboring church musician to record the accompaniment for some of your favorite hymns, although the system cited above sounds more promising.

Perhaps it's your old hymnal that's giving you deadly music. A dilemma for many churches is that the people who are attending love the old hymns. Yet, the people you need and want to include can't stand them. Your traditionalists and old-timers will need to learn to tolerate (maybe even like) newer and more inclusive music, while your newer and younger folk learn to like or tolerate the old favorites. Most denominations have new hymnals that include a wider variety of music for a wider variety of tastes. For example, the United Church of Christ's *New Century Hymnal* makes it much easier to plan wonderful worship by providing both new and old music.

Consider the instrument you're using to accompany singing. The San Rafael church has an adequate organ, but the music director is a much better pianist. And, we are fortunate to have a fine, grand piano that a member gave us several years ago. Many smaller churches, including ours, find that people sing better when accompanied by a piano instead of an organ. Many churches are also enjoying adding percussion and other instruments to the instrumental mix.

A good choir contributes much to a church's worship. Unfortunately, some choirs and congregations see the choir as the performers of "good" music for the not-so-good singers to listen to and enjoy. Wonderful worship is more likely when the choir leads the congregation in singing more than when it sings on their behalf. It helps make the liturgy the work of all the people when the music comes from all the people.

Judeo-Christian people have "always" sung and made music in their worship. David, the shepherd-king, was a songwriter and musician, and we still sing his music. The first communion service ended when they "sang a hymn and went out." In the first century, Ignatius, bishop of Antioch, addressed the Ephesian church in musical metaphor: "Your accord and harmonious love is a hymn to Jesus Christ. Yes, one and all, you should form yourselves into a choir, so that, in perfect harmony and taking your pitch from God, you may sing in unison and with one voice to the Father through Jesus Christ."[6]

Some people come to worship primarily for the music and most would miss it if it weren't there. More importantly, the church sings because of what singing does and has always done for the church and its people. In its most difficult times, the church has found strength, faith, and hope in its singing, as much as in its preaching. In 1938, Dietrich Bonhoeffer, who was leading an illegal, underground seminary and worshiping community in Nazi Germany, wrote *Life Together* as a witness to how a Christian community can live faithfully in the very worst of times. He wrote these amazing words:

> The more we sing, the more joy will we derive from it, but above all, the more devotion and discipline and joy we put into our singing, the richer will be the blessing that will come to the whole life of the fellowship from singing together.
>
> It is the voice of the Church that is heard in singing together. It is not you that sings, it is the Church that is singing, and you, as a member of the Church, may share in its song. Thus all singing together that is right must serve to widen our spiritual horizon, make us see our *little company* as a member of the great Christian Church on earth, and help us willingly and gladly to join our singing, be it feeble or good, to the song of the Church [italics mine].[7]

I know from personal experience that Bonhoeffer is right. Once I had a singing range of just four notes. Now I have more notes but little control over them. Yet one reason I go to church is to sing. I love it when our little company sings as one people with one voice, and I am changed by it. I urge your smaller church to find a way to sing more, sing louder, sing better. Sing your favorites and learn some new favorites. Sing at your weddings. Sing at your funerals. Sing at your potlucks. Sing before, during, and after worship. When the song is the song of your soul, you will experience harmony and know you are alive.

Preaching

The Christian Church began with a sermon—Peter's Pentecost sermon—and there's been preaching in the church ever since. What is the essence of preaching? James F. White, who has written an important worship textbook says: "The preacher speaks for God, from the scriptures, by the authority of the church, to the people."[8] He's right and has all the components of preaching except one. The sermon is not finished until the people respond to it. In other words, the sermon at its best and fullest is a dialogue not a monologue. And smaller churches are the best size for dialogue.

The sermon should not be the main event or the climax of worship. Rather the sermon equips the people for their response through their prayers, offerings, and the words of commitment that come in response to the Word that has been heard. In the drama that is worship, the sermon is the necessary second act, the bridge that leads from the anticipation of the first act of preparation to the third act of resolution. The worship liturgy is incomplete without the Word being proclaimed and the proclaimed Word is an orphan without its relationship to the liturgy.

People are no longer interested, willing, or able to listen to speakers speak at length without interruption—except for the rare spellbinders. Mass media and frenetic living have given people a short attention span. I have adapted my preaching to this reality, my gifts, and the possibilities of our size. There is always a "sermon," but about a third of the time it's not a conventional sermon. Even the conventional sermons are getting shorter as I learn to focus better, as I know better what my people need, and as our congregation's participation in worship increases. Here are some alternatives to the traditional sermon:

- I preach a shorter, traditional sermon after the congregation engages in a brief Bible study on the text of the day.
- The sermon might be a full-blown Bible study as the whole congregation proclaims its understanding of God's Word for us.
- I sometimes invite the congregation to finish the sermon by responding to what I have said so far.
- The sermon might be a direct response to something that has happened in the parish or the world—a tragic death, a critical pending decision, a new church initiative, a major community issue, or something out of the week's news.
- A story such as "The Rabbi's Gift" (at the conclusion of this book) can be a sermon.

- One or more lay-leaders might talk about the intersection of their faith and their life or work.
- Use the works of an author or artist as the sermon. Once I read and commented on quotations of Nouwen after his death. Another time, I created a whole worship service, including a sermon, using the cartoons of Charles Schulz the week of his death.
- Sometimes I use a VCR and show a clip of a powerful film or a scene from a TV drama that speaks to issues of life and faith.
- I've costumed and dramatized a biblical or historical character.
- For a change of pace, have an "Ask the Pastor" sermon when the congregation asks or submits questions it is struggling with for the preacher to respond to.
- Occasionally, I've interviewed a noteworthy layperson as the sermon.

There are sermons waiting to be preached all around us. The Word of God can be "preached" and heard in many ways. The fundamental question is not, "Have the people heard a traditional sermon?" The real question is how can the gospel best intersect with what God is intending to do through us and in our world so that we can respond liturgically and as disciples beyond the doors of the church.

Sacraments

I grew up in the Baptist tradition in which we observed "ordinances." Ordinances emphasize remembering that Jesus instructed his followers to continue practicing baptism and communion. The United Church of Christ and Congregational tradition practices the same rituals but call them sacraments and invests them with greater significance. This tradition, along with many others, believes that through the water of baptism, God is present and acting in a real, powerful, and mysterious way to cleanse, heal, initiate, transform, and build the local and global Community of God.

While the rhetoric says that, too often too many churches have watered down baptism from the radical importance it played in the early church. Too often baptism is a warm, domesticated, photo-op for families, many of whom are never seen again. Too often the yeast has been filtered out of the wine and bread, making communion a pallid, circumspect, sanitized, individualized imitation of what it is meant to be. Too often the Lord's Supper is only a postscript tacked onto the end of an already-full worship service. Too often the traditional words are said and the people wonder what it's all about as they sip their juice and nibble their bread. We can do better.

In smaller settings, sacramental liturgies can be more communal and less individualistic, more dynamic and less passive, more personal and less generic, more imaginative and less routine. When only two or three persons are baptized a year, each baptism can be made special and memorable. For example, I prepare a special bulletin for each baptism, with the certificate photocopied on the cover and the names of the baptized, family, and godparents printed in the liturgy. I sometimes ask the congregation to bring cards, letters, prayers, and blessings for the one being baptized. We serenade the child with the following lyrics sung to the tune of "Morning Has Broken."

> [Name], we name you: And with thanksgiving,
> Offer our prayers and sing you this song.
> We are the church: your spiritual family.
> Sing we our praises to Christ our Lord.

When an infant is baptized, I carry the child around the congregation so that they can have a close look, and I say, "Look, this is your new son (or daughter). Remember what you have promised."

Powerful baptism is more than the details of the ceremony. We only baptize within the context of congregational worship because it's the church, not the pastor, who baptizes, and baptism is the doorway into both the local and universal family of God. Each church I've served had a little receptacle that was brought out for baptism and then closeted again until it was needed. For the new sanctuary in San Rafael, we commissioned a fine potter to create new communionware for us and to craft a pottery fountain with circulating water. It's a striking visual symbol and holds enough water to really get the baptized person wet. At the end of each service of baptism, I fling a handful of water over the congregation with the admonition to "Remember your own baptism!" The fountain is bubbling every Sunday so we can see and hear and be reminded weekly of our own baptism. In Big Timber, Montana, they rave about the pastor's gift for customizing every baptism with special decorations, the way Larry Pray holds the child, and the way he lovingly speaks to every child on behalf of the congregation.

Since eating together is a smaller church's favorite activity, why is communion so often a perfunctory afterthought? The most noted component of the earliest churches' worship was the agape meal that the little house churches shared every week. Smaller churches have the potential to make their communion table fellowship personal and special. The church bakers or the confirmation class can bake the bread. Others could make the wine or juice. Every church can develop its own special sacramental customs.

For many years, the San Rafael church has formed a circle around the table for communion. This is so meaningful that the church designed its new chancel to accommodate the circling of a now larger church. The beautiful communion table looks like a lovely dinner table. With one overhead light focused on the table, we light nothing else but the table for evening communion. On World Communion Sunday, people are invited to wear clothing from other cultures, and the table is decorated with an international flavor—sometimes a large inflatable globe and many different kinds of bread. Occasionally, people are invited to "bring" a special person to the table with them—such as a deceased spouse or friend, a Palestinian refugee, or a Northern Ireland Protestant and Catholic. With a little imagination, the sacraments can be memorable and awe-inspiring.

Other sacrament-like occasions, like confirmation, can be given special attention. Our confirmands write and rewrite their own Credo and then speak of their faith with the congregation. They receive gifts from the congregation. The congregation comes forward for a laying-on-of-hands ritual. The extraordinary confirmation ritual utilized by the Montana church is a wonderful model.

Weddings are sacramental occasions—especially when those being married are part of the congregation. The Warwick, Massachusetts, church removed all the pews from the sanctuary and replaced them with white-tablecloth-covered tables and conducted a church-wide wedding feast for Steve and Fran. The bride and groom read from Song of Solomon to one another, their church friends offered blessings, and we all shared a potluck and communion.

Smaller churches can be especially effective with rituals at the time of death. The whole church can be involved as some decorate the church, others greet and usher, the choir sings, individuals give witness to the significance of the person, some serve a funeral dinner, and the church family cares for family members before and after the death. When Henry died, we filled the cross with flowers. When John (a major figure in church and community) died, we put a pair of his shoes on the communion table to symbolize the shoes he left for us to fill. If you know the favorite hymns of the deceased, they can be honored by singing the hymns they loved to sing. Sacraments can and should be memorable and life-bringing occasions.

Seasonal Celebrations

Few of us eat the same dinner night after night. But in some churches, each Sunday and many of the seasons provide similar fare. However, the church year and the rhythm of community and cultural life give us wonderful opportunities for celebrating. There's Advent, Christmas, Epiphany, Lent, Holy Week and Easter, Pentecost, World Communion Sunday, All Saints' and All Souls' Days, and, in some traditions, saint's days and other occasions. Our society has other markers that the church can turn into sacred celebrations—New Year's, Martin Luther King's birthday, St. Valentine's Day, St. Patrick's Day, Mother's Day, Children's Day, Father's Day, Memorial Day, Independence Day, as well as Thanksgiving. Each community has unique occasions that the church could appropriately commemorate in some way, such as school graduations or a "blessing of the seed" service in farm country.

The church year allows us to change the colors and to redecorate the sanctuary. For the first Sunday of each season, I invite people to wear the color of that season. Communion should have a different tone in Advent and Lent than it has in the Easter and Pentecost seasons. A team of three or four could be recruited to help the pastoral leader make liturgical plans for each season. An intergenerational worship service could be created during each season in the church year. The celebration of the seasons of the church and other significant events in the lives of our people makes our worship—not what we routinely do but what we especially do. Such celebrations allow smaller churches to take a back seat to no one.

Earlier I said, "It all begins in worship." If we aren't careful, it could end there. John Westerhoff warned that if a church "loses faith in liturgy, is thoughtless in ordering of liturgy, or is careless in the conduct of liturgy, it need not look elsewhere to find vitality: It is dead at its heart."[8] In contrast, smaller congregations who enjoy taking their worship seriously, who do it in ways that are creative, spirited, and fit their size, will be faithful and effective in all they do. They will likely experience increases in attendance, membership, and giving; will have a heightened sense of mission; and will not be self-conscious about their size.

Questions

1. How do you define and understand worship?
2. Is your church's worship the work of the people? How could it be more so?
3. What is most and least effective in the worship life of your congregation?
4. Being very specific, what happens when your church gathers for worship that enables people to leave feeling healed, affirmed, equipped, and called?
5. What ideas and possibilities for worship are sparked by this chapter for your smaller church or for ones you know?

Suggestions

1. Ask your congregation to complete the worship survey that is in the resource section of this book.
2. Work with an existing group or a new task-team to discuss the principles and practices. Then begin planning and implementing strategies to strengthen what you're already doing well and to implement desired changes.

chapter five

Education

Growing Faithful Disciples

Nikos Kazantzakis tells of the wild dream told him by a monk,
Father Joachim. In this dream, Mary brings the twelve-year-old Jesus
to be cured of what obviously must be demons. Alone with the boy,
Father Joachim says to him,

"Where does it hurt my son?"

"Here, here . . ." he replied, pointing to his heart.

"And what's wrong with you?"

"I can't sleep, eat, or work, I roam the streets, wrestling."

"Who are you wrestling with?"

"With God. Who else do you expect me to be wrestling with!"

Father Joachim keeps the boy for a month, puts him in a
carpenter shop to learn the trade, speaks to him ever so gently of
God as though he were a neighbor who dropped by on an evening to
sit on the porch and chat. Father Joachim reports:

"At the end of a month's time, Jesus was completely cured. He no
longer wrestled with God; he had become a man like all other men.
He departed for Galilee, and I learned afterwards that he has become
a fine carpenter, he becomes the best in Nazareth.

—Nikos Kazantzakis, *Report to Greco*

But I contend that the church can no longer surrender to the
illusion that child nurture, in and of itself, can or will rekindle the
fire of Christian faith in persons or in the church.

—John Westerhoff III, *Will Our Children Have Faith?*

BOTH KAZANTZAKIS AND WESTERHOFF raise provocative questions
about the purpose of education for faith development. Whereas many

churches have been content to nurture nice people, something more is required if people are going to become passionate and compassionate disciples of the one for whom Christian education is named.

Westerhoff also tells the story of a crook who looted a city, and then set about trying to sell his loot, including a rare, exquisite, large rug. He cried out in the market place: "Who will give me a hundred pieces of silver for this rug?" The rug was quickly purchased. A surprised friend of the crook asked why he didn't ask more for the priceless rug. The seller, befuddled, asked: "Is there a number larger than one hundred?"[1]

With similar surprise, one might ask if there isn't more to Christian education than Sunday school, nurture of children, and programs and activities for children and youth. Will we be satisfied with only producing fine carpenters, good church members, and nice people? Does our Christian education include concern for increasing adult faithfulness? Does it include all areas of church life or only what is narrowly defined as Christian education? Is what we do by that name worth more than a mere hundred pieces of silver? Could we be giving children, youth, and adults—no matter how few—something of far greater value than we are now, especially in smaller churches? Absolutely!

Half a century ago, *Life* magazine called Sunday school the most wasted hour of the week. Since then, participation in most churches' educational programs has steadily dwindled. Of those who remain in the programs, many are unsure or reluctant to claim the name "Christian." Even fewer, by the evidence of their lives, could be convicted in any court of being disciples of Jesus Christ. For many, Sunday school, confirmation programs, and church youth groups have been rites of passage out of the church rather than avenues into church commitment and faithful living. Think about the midlife members of your congregation. How many of their adult children are not actively involved in any congregation, even though they are from wonderful families and went to Sunday school when they were young? Only a small minority of the adults of most churches participate in adult nurture in the church beyond worship. As in the story of the foolish crook, we have bartered our priceless faith too cheaply.

Actually it hasn't been cheap. Many congregations have spent all they could afford on Christian education facilities, professional and semiprofessional educators, the latest curriculum and materials, and supply closets full of equipment. Churches have tried to develop Christian education programs that resemble public school education. There is little evidence that many churches are achieving their educational objectives. Larger churches, with more resources, more sophisticated approaches, better-trained educators, and more students can't show any better results than smaller churches.

My own goal has been something like Father Joachim's. I believed genuine faithfulness would naturally result if we led our young (and old) into feeling at home and claiming a place in the Christian family. Too often, that hasn't happened. Genuine faithfulness and Christian discipleship often have not followed, even among those who are still active in our churches. It has not been enough just to hang on to our young and woo them into church involvement as young adults and adults. Congregations, including our smaller ones, need to rethink their approach to Christian education and pursue three educational goals for all of its people of all ages:

- Inclusion, or voluntary association with and involvement in the church
- Identity, or bringing people to freely confess to being Christian
- Discipleship, or helping them maturely and consciously act as disciples of Christ

Smaller churches have been fairly effective with the first goal and could be quite good at all three. Rather than trying to replicate how the church educated us or what activities might interest our young or our adults, it would be better to start by visualizing the end product. What kind of people and churches are we trying to develop?

In 1989, the Search Institute in Minneapolis surveyed 563 congregations in six denominations, ranging theologically from Southern Baptists to the United Church of Christ. These denominations asked the Search Institute to determine the nature of mature Christian faith, how people become mature in their faith, and how people can be better helped to develop mature faithfulness. The research findings are as significant and relevant now as when the results were first published. Representatives of the six denominations, reflecting a wide spectrum of Christian belief, all agreed that a person of mature faith will:

1. Trust in God's saving grace and believe firmly in the humanity and divinity of Jesus
2. Experience a sense of personal well-being, security, and peace
3. Integrate faith and life, seeing work, family, social relationships, and political choices as part of one's religious life
4. Seek spiritual growth through study, reflection, prayer, and discussion with others
5. Seek to be part of a community of believers in which people give witness to their faith and support and nourish one another
6. Hold life-affirming values, including a commitment to racial and gender equality, affirmation of cultural and religious diversity, and a personal sense of responsibility for the welfare of others
7. Advocate social and global change to bring about greater social justice
8. Serve humanity, consistently and passionately, through acts of love and justice

When the researchers applied this definition of mature faithfulness to the adults surveyed in the six denominations, only one out of three qualified as mature in their faith. The research showed that smaller churches were at least as effective as larger ones in nurturing mature faith. If these eight qualities are the desired outcome, the pursuit of them is a life-long process, beginning when the child is first brought into the church community and not ending until death.

The research went on to indicate that a church that is highly effective at developing maturity of faith in its people will have the following characteristics:

- A climate of warmth
- People feel cared for

- A climate of challenge
- Worship that touches the heart as well as the mind
- Lay and pastoral leaders who are people of mature faith
- A strong and vibrant educational ministry

Smaller churches are perfectly capable of all of these. The research went on to suggest that of these characteristics that produce mature faith, the one that matters most is effective Christian education for all ages.[2] This research clearly indicates that it takes a lot more than a functioning Sunday school, an active youth group, or even an adult Bible study to grow a church populated by mature people of faith—although each of these might be starting places.

If only one of three church people are passing the school of Christian maturity, their churches are failing for two principle reasons: First, we've assumed that by concentrating on educating children, Christian adults will result. Someone said that Jesus played with children and taught adults, while churches try to teach children and play with adults. Second, we assumed that the way you educate children (or those older) is by teaching about the Bible, about Jesus, about church history, about Christian morality, and so forth. With these assumptions, churches believed that all they needed were trained teachers, objective subject matter, attractive curriculum, up-to-date supplies and equipment, and age-graded classes in separate classrooms to get the desired results. At best, we now have church members struggling to be Christian and, at worst, poorly educated atheists. Where did we go wrong?

First, we forgot that faith cannot be taught by objective instruction. Rather, faith is caught as one experiences it in the Christian community and in the lives of faithful people from biblical times to ours. Forgetting this, we failed to intentionally and aggressively create a highly contagious atmosphere with irresistible opportunities for catching a serious case of Christianity. Secondly, we failed to observe that, for almost two thousand years, the church had been doing a pretty good job of growing faithful people. While other institutions came and went, the Christian church is still here worshiping and serving, despite its follies. There was much hoopla in 1980 over the two hundredth anniversary of Sunday schools. Most people didn't notice that if the Sunday school was only two hundred years old, then the church had effectively developed disciples and perpetuated itself for 1800 years with other approaches. The tragedy for smaller churches was that when they started trying to teach the faith the way larger schools teach chemistry, they stopped doing what they were the right size to do—providing intimate, contagious settings in which the young and not so young couldn't help but catch a serious case of faithfulness.

For over twenty-five years, Westerhoff has been shaping my understanding of Christian education and faith formation. In 1967, he published the classic *Will Our Children Have Faith?* (revised and expanded in 2000). He confessed:

> Recently, I discovered the large, important world of the small church. As a professional educator, I had often ignored these thousands of small churches and . . . I had gotten used to talking about educational plants, supplies, equipment, curriculum, teacher training, age-graded classes, and learning centers with individualized instruction. Lately, I've been confronted by churches that share a pastor and will probably never be able to afford the services of a professional church educator. At best they have a couple of small inadequate rooms attached to their church building, no audiovisual equipment, few supplies, an inadequate number of prospective teachers, and not enough students for age-graded classes . . . most small churches will never be able to mount up or support the sort of schooling and instruction upon which religious education has been founded since the turn of the century.[3]

After his mea culpa, Westerhoff recalled what the old-fashioned Sunday school, which was small and personal, was like. He cited J. A. James, who wrote in *The Sunday School Teacher's Guide* in 1816, that teaching religion is more than giving instruction and that learning facts and memorizing passages is an insignificant part of religious education. James described the Sunday schools he knew and liked with all ages preparing for and celebrating special occasions like Christmas, Easter, Thanksgiving, and Missionary Day. He described Sunday school activities that included plays and musicals, games, hikes and hunts, parties and picnics, and social service projects and community activities in which children, youth, parents, and grandparents participated together. The function of the Sunday school James described in 1816, with its activities and programs, "was to give persons an opportunity to share life with other faithful selves, to experience the faith in community, to learn the Christian story and to engage in Christian actions."[4]

Others shared James' vision and carried it forward. In 1905, John Vincent, the great Methodist leader, gave an address to the Eleventh International Sunday School Convention in Toronto entitled, "A Forward Look for the Sunday School." He predicted that, in the future, Sunday school "will be less like a school and more like a home. Its program will focus on conversation and the interaction of people rather than the academic study of the Bible or theology. The Sunday school will be a place where friends deeply concerned about Christian faith will gather to share life together."[5]

That vision captures the way it needs to be again if we want more than one-third of those in our churches to be mature in their faith. Effective, faithful Christian education has been and should be experiential and intergenerational, with people sharing deeply about faith and life. To accomplish these goals of including people in the Christian community, helping people develop Christian identity, and equipping them to be disciples of Christ, we need to provide a growing medium that will nurture such people.

The Growing Medium

Whether your green-thumb experience is a houseplant or two, a vegetable garden, or a farm of 120 acres, what kind of growing medium would you choose for developing a church of people who love their church, who confess their Christian faith, and who live as followers of Jesus? A smaller church can provide all the required resources to create a fertile growing medium with these traits.

The growing medium must be warm and hospitable. Most churches think that they're warm and hospitable and would be surprised to find that many don't experience them to be so. A mother woke her son one Sunday morning so he could get ready for church. He grumbled, complained, said that he hated going there and refused to get up. She said, "You have to get up!"

He said, "Why?"

She said, "Because you're forty years old and you're the pastor!"

In contrast, our four-year-old daughter asked when we were in our Warwick church: "Mamma, is tomorrow the day we go to church?" When the answer was yes, she exclaimed, "Oh neat!" It's a safe bet that the atmosphere in the latter church was more conducive to growing mature faithfulness.

All people of all ages yearn for places where they know they are known, where they belong, and where it is safe to be themselves. The first question for those who are planning the church's educational ministry is: How can we create a warmer atmosphere of hospitality for all ages? More specifically:

- Is the building exterior well maintained, are the entrances clearly marked, is the interior attractive and inviting?
- Are the spaces where learning is supposed to happen cluttered and drab or freshly painted and comfortably furnished?
- Are the leaders, teachers, and nurturers cold or warm persons?
- Is the content that is taught a gospel of loving good news or a religious message that is exclusive, condemning, or boring?
- Do the youngest, oldest, newest, and most vulnerable experience warm-fuzzies or cold shoulders?
- Are each of the above qualities monitored and corrected when necessary?

All that happens in the Christian education venture is a waste of time and money unless every effort is made to see that each person is treated as though he or she is an angel of God in disguise (Heb. 13:1). Directional signs, greeters, name tags, guest books, follow-up cards or calls, snacks, flowers, careful listening, affirmations, and invitations to come, stay, and come back are a few of the many ways to manifest hospitality.

The growing medium must be holistic. Christian education happens whenever and wherever the church meets, eats, worships, works, learns, plays, cares, and serves. It doesn't just happen in the designated hour when the learners are down in the basement, in the parlor, or the Sunday school room. Smaller churches, where the activities flow together, where space is used for more than one purpose, where people assume various roles, where many or most activities are intergenerational, where people know and care about one another, are particularly well suited to develop and practice a holistic understanding of Christian education. The key is understanding and remembering that every gathering and experience is a learning opportunity and that every person is a potential teacher and learner.

The fundamental question is this: How can everything we do be more inclusive, build faith identity, and nurture disciples? When the men gather for coffee, the thoughtful layman can use that opportunity for caring, nurturing, and disciple-making. When the women's group meets—whether to study the Bible, discuss an important issue, make crafts, organize a day-care program, plan a fund-raiser, or just to gossip—the opportunity is present for real Christian education and reflection on spiritual truth. When the deacons meet, they can simply rehearse how to serve communion more smoothly or they can talk theologically about why they are coming around Christ's family table and how they can insure that everyone is welcome there. Christian-education planners might study how one matures in faith rather than merely planning one more Sunday school year.

If the church teaches through everything it does and if worship is the primary time smaller churches come together, then the wise worship-planner will work long and hard to see that every minute of the worship hour is used to better encourage Christian identity and make disciples—from the first spoken word or musical note to the last. Every moment and movement in worship is an opportunity to build community, nurture spirituality, encourage honesty with one's self and compassion for others, build critical judgment and moral character, teach the fundamentals of the faith, deepen a passion for justice and peace, nurture a commitment to whole-life stewardship and evangelism, and call the worshiper to a life of discipleship. A pastor who assumes that only the sermon teaches and inspires is wasting two-thirds of the people's time.

The growing medium must be individualized. Sunday school children sing: "This little light of mine, I'm going to let it shine; let it shine, let it shine." Smaller churches are just the right size to recognize that everyone from the youngest to the oldest was born gifted and has the opportunity to release, shape, and invest that giftedness. One day Michelangelo struggled to move a large slab of marble down the street. A neighbor called out: "Michelangelo, why are you laboring so over that old rock?"

The great sculptor stopped, wiped his brow, considered the question, and said: "Because there's an angel in this rock waiting to be freed."

We formally come into the church family through the waters of baptism. At our baptism or christening, we're given our Christian name, the name bestowed on us by our parents to give us our identity. That is also when we are given the name "Christian," which is ours to own or disown. In the Christian tradition, naming is vitally important. God called Abram "Abraham" and made him father of a nation. Jesus called Simon to a life of discipleship and named him "Peter." God named Saul "Paul" and transformed him from the most vigorous persecutor of the church to its principal founder of churches. Similarly, smaller churches can be quite good at helping each person find her or his identity, place, and calling.

Those with special needs can have those needs addressed in a smaller church. I will never forget "Apple Sunday" in Shrewsbury. In a service oriented around the metaphor of apples, my sermon dramatized the Johnny Appleseed story. The service ended with the benediction, during which a helper and I moved through the congregation and presented an apple to each worshiper and pronounced the blessing from Deuteronomy 32:10: "You are the apple of God's eye." All was going well until I got to Betty. Each week, Carlene, Betty's friend and caretaker, brought Betty to worship. Betty was in a wheelchair and was blind, retarded, and had cerebral palsy. She made distracting noises during worship that annoyed some people. I took a crisp Macintosh apple from my gunny sack, placed it in Betty's hand, looked deep into her unseeing eyes, choked back the emotion that welled up in me, and pronounced: "Betty, you are the apple of God's eye!" Most of us realized in that moment that in God's eyes, Betty was an apple of the finest kind.

Throughout my ministry, it has been a privilege to watch individuals blossom through the ministry of their church. Remember the confirmation experience in Big Timber, Montana? The confirmands studied intensively, raised $748 to free slaves in Sudan as their confirmation mission-project, and sweated over the paper they each wrote on "The Truth about My Life." Imagine how "called out" they felt when their pastor placed his hand on each shoulder and said, "Your name has been entered in the book of life." Those confirmands had identified themselves as "Christian" and were well along the road of discipleship.

The growing medium must be familial. Our world divides by gender, age, size, race, religion, orientation, ability, and interest. Larger churches talk about family, but generally divide their people by some of these categories. Healthy smaller churches, either by conviction or by desire to achieve a critical mass, bring people together—as family. In four churches, we've worked at that concept. We knew it was working in Warwick when a six-year-old said to her mother, "All the people at church are part of our family, aren't they?"

To achieve what J. A. James and John Vincent were talking about two hundred and one hundred years ago, we need to bring people into intergenerational units and settings that feel like family. One way to do that is to have the education program and worship happen at separate times so people can participate together in both. Westerhoff's proposal is to have the whole church come together to prepare to worship by working with the scriptures, preparing the music, and working on the liturgy during the first hour. Then the church family incorporates its work as it worships together during the second hour. At least, have some worship services for the whole church family— perhaps one each church season. Invite a family to plan and conduct the whole worship service. Involve children and youth in planning and leading worship. A five-year-old, with a microphone, a stool to stand on, and words appropriate to her age, can lead the call to worship. Others can make music, take the offering, count the house, help with scripture, and so on. A preacher who makes the sermon graphic and well illustrated for the young may discover that the sermon is communicating better with everyone.

Who's welcome at the communion table? Just your denomination? Those who are members? Confirmed? Those who think they understand what it's all about? In Warwick, Shrewsbury, Emmetsburg, and San Rafael, everyone has been included at God's welcome table. All the children have been there. Even the Jewish member of a blended Christian-Jewish family comes to the table and partakes. Our shared vision is that the whole of creation is invited and welcomed into the Community of God.

Beyond worship, how about familial Christian education? Even if your church has classes for different ages, include as many adult and youth helpers as possible. They can teach a song, bring refreshments, tell a story, or hold a child on a lap. Organize intergenerational events, programs, and parties through the church year:

- Hold an Advent workshop
- Go caroling together and make Christmas cookies afterwards
- Throw an Epiphany party January 6
- Have a snow or beach party
- Enjoy a "Fat Tuesday" party the day before Ash Wednesday
- Plan a seder meal on Maundy Thursday
- Invite individuals and families to take turns keeping a vigil at the church from 6:00 p.m. Good Friday all the way through to 6:00 a.m. Easter Sunday
- Put on a joyous birthday of the church on Pentecost
- Go camping together or have a church family retreat
- Play kick ball together
- Take all ages to prepare and serve a meal at a soup kitchen
- Invite everyone to a church-wide Thanksgiving dinner

When our church only had one youth, we had an intergenerational confirmation group. Trying to get away from the age-graded public school model, the San Rafael church considered having a "one-room school house" Sunday school. Currently, we're envisioning regular, all-church meals and learning events. Some churches include youth and even mature children in their church committees and task groups. Think about all the things nuclear families do and adapt those experiences to your church family. Rather than dividing classes by age, divide by interest: a music group, a drama group, a mission project group.

In a smaller church that works at being familial, every child has twenty to eighty aunts, uncles, and grandparents. Every adult has many nieces, nephews, and grandchildren. In addition to the benefits to our families, on one hand, and society, on the other, when the church family acts like family, all learn more, an inclusive Christian community grows, and Christian identity is enhanced. Our young get mentors and role models and our elders rediscover their youth. Each generation is a link in a chain of faithfulness that is preserved, strengthened, and expanded.

The growing medium must be ecological. To be ecological means to care about the interrelationships of the whole environment. Whether urban or rural, we're all provincial, focusing primarily on ourselves. Yet no one and no church is an island. Christian education and being disciples should help us discover and strengthen the interrelationship of God's whole creation. What can your church do in common with other churches and faith communities in your region? What are the differences and, even more important, what are the commonalities between denominations and the world's religions? How can your church relate to other cultures and parts of the world? How can a congregation learn to conserve and replenish the precious resources of the environment? The goal is to resist isolation, to learn from and narrow the differences, and to act together on common convictions and concerns.

In the Warwick church, the church school organized an enormously successful annual community roadside clean-up. In Shrewsbury, the youth group raised hundreds of dollars by recycling beverage containers, and families experienced an Africa Day when they played, sang, crafted, and ate in African ways. In Emmetsburg, on World

Communion Sunday, we sang hymns in other languages and broke breads from around the world. In San Rafael, the church raised enough money in two years to provide 100,000 meals for hungry children in Mexico and included a Jew and a Muslim from Afghanistan in their World Communion Sunday circle on the day bombing began in Afghanistan after the World Trade Center attack in 2001. Each time we found our thread in the web that is God's ecology.

The growing medium must affirm that the biblical and historical tradition is our very own story. Many say they want the Sunday school to "teach the Bible," but it is unclear what they mean. Is the Bible to be taught as though God dictated every word, comma, and period? Should the church teach every book, chapter, verse, and word and, if not, which parts will it teach? What should be done with the contradictions and parts difficult to understand? Do we teach it as though God's revelation stopped at the end of Revelation? My approach has been to teach the Bible as the tradition out of which we have come, the story of God's relationship with our ancestors of faith, and as light and truth for our own time.

It is mind-boggling to imagine that the biblical-historical tradition began somewhere back with Sarah and Abraham and "begat" through the generations to Jesus and then through the founding of the earliest churches. That chain of revelation continued through the ages to and including the saints, church pillars, and characters in our own time and churches. When we teach the biblical tradition as our own history, then it becomes the roots for our own family tree and foundation for our own story. There is power and potential in believing that God is acting in you and me just as God acted in Jeremiah, the Marys, Peter, Paul, and Hildegard of Bingen.

Sarah, our six-year-old theologian, who understood that the church was her family, almost grasped the larger picture when she asked her mother:

Sarah: Is baby Beth God's daughter?
Mother: Yes, Sarah, she is.
Sarah: Is Joshua [her brother] God's son?

Mother: [Sensing the water is getting deeper] Yes, he is.

Sarah: And I'm God's daughter, aren't I?

Mother: Yes, Sarah you are.

Sarah: Then Daddy must be God's brother!

Sarah knew she was a direct descendant in a powerful family tree.

If the church wishes to make this biblical tradition its own, it will emphasize and celebrate the special seasons and days of its lengthy family story: the advent and birthday of Jesus, the seasons of penitence called Lent and Holy Week, Christ's breaking the bonds of death on Easter, and the birthday of the church known as Pentecost. Rather than simply teaching about the Bible and its characters, learn to identify with it and them and they will become your own.

Here are some examples of how the biblical story can be personalized:

- In the Gideon story (Judg. 6:1—7:22) have the group (intergenerational with Gideon being played by a child) read dramatically or act out the story. Ask "Gideon" what changed him from a whining wimp into a heroic leader. Ask for examples of other small groups that have surmounted great numbers or stiff odds. Discuss parallels that might be drawn between their church and the Gideon story. The resource section of *Wonderful Worship in Smaller Churches* has a condensed dramatic reading of the story.

- Ask a group to rewrite a psalm in their own words, putting their own feelings into their psalm. Then the group can chant it or sing it, just for themselves or maybe in their church's worship.

- After hearing, dramatizing, or role-playing the story of the prodigal or lost son (Luke 15:11–32), ask the group members whether they are most like the father, the younger son, or the older son? Ask: If Jesus were preaching in their church, how might he reshape this story for their time and place?

- Recall Jesus' commandment to "Go into all the world"(Mark 16:14–15). Ask the group where they think Jesus specifically wants them to go and what Jesus might want them to do. Ask how your church is doing the kinds of things he was talking about to his followers then.

- Peter and John helped start lots of churches about two thousand years ago. In the story of their encounter with the disabled man at the gate of the temple, Peter said, "I have no silver or gold, but what I have I give you . . . stand up and walk" (Acts 3:1–10). Identify and discuss the various special personal gifts and abilities that people in your group or church have besides silver and gold.

When we lay claim to the biblical tradition as our very own story, we move from a passive spectator's role to being a character in a dynamic, unfolding plot. Then, becoming a disciple is the intriguing and challenging next step.

The growing medium must be Christian. The Christian faith is an incarnational faith—the Word became flesh and lived among us. The goal of Christian education is not to entertain or even to keep our young and not-so-young in church. Rather, it is to help them become real-life disciples of Jesus Christ. The church's calling is to help people come to the place where they freely and courageously say, "Yes, I am a Christian, a follower of Jesus, and I want to live as his disciple."

There must be a substantive, serious side to our educational ventures. We need to encourage people to risk intensive and existential Bible study, to help them pursue costly outreaching ministries, to believe that God expects life-changing response from them and their little church. Any educational venture becomes substantive and serious when people wrestle with these questions: What is God calling us to be and do right here and now, and how must we respond if we really want to be disciples of Christ?

For the growing medium to be Christian, people must be treated with Christ-like care. They must be introduced to Christ-like behaviors. They must be helped to understand that there is a cost as well as a joy to discipleship. They must be given opportunities to practice Christ-like actions. And they must be invited to call themselves Christian, understanding all that that implies in their day-to-day living.

The growing medium that is all of the above must be experiential, reflective, and result in costly action. We learn best experientially. We learn a little of what we hear, a little more of what we see or read, and much more of what we experience and do. But to learn at a deep level from what we experience, we need to think about and talk to others about what we experience. What does it mean, how has it changed us, where have we encountered God in the experience? We experience, we reflect on the experience, and then we act because one can't be Christian without doing Christ-like things. James 1:22 says: "But be doers of the word and not merely hearers." The purpose of the church is not fun and games, although healthy, faithful churches have lots of fun and are full of laughter. The purpose of the church is to make a difference in the world in which it is placed. The key to transforming smaller, weaker churches into smaller, mighty churches is to help them bear fruit and make a concrete difference in their world beyond the church doors.

The Warwick church got "turned on" through its involvement in Heifer Project International. The Shrewsbury church became seriously involved with a partner church in Rwanda. The Emmetsburg church played a significant role in the redevelopment effort in its declining community. Through annual trips to a Benedictine retreat center in Mexico, the San Rafael church felt the hunger of malnourished children and committed itself to feeding hundreds, if not thousands, of them.

A church that dedicates itself to developing a fertile growing medium will achieve the educational goals of drawing people into the faith community, helping them claim a Christian identity, and leading them to live as disciples of Christ. A church that uses these eight building blocks as the foundational principles for its educational ministry can then proceed to work out the details. The following strategies can help.

Space, Methods, Leaders, Materials, Youth, Adults

When a smaller church commits itself to a faithful and effective ministry of education, it then has to wrestle with some knotty issues—such as inadequate space, uncertainty about the best educational methods, a struggle to get and keep effective leaders, what materials to use and how to pay for them, and what in the world to do with youth and adults.

Space

Smaller churches often lack adequate space, especially if they're trying to conduct several "classes" or groups simultaneously. The Emmetsburg church had one class in the cellar behind the big, old furnace and another in the balcony above the sanctuary. Virginia liked teaching her fourth and fifth graders in the furnace room, because no one cared how big a mess was made with their crafts. The balcony bunch was happy, because they could look down on whoever passed by below, and they all looked a little golden because of the beautiful light washing over them from the stained glass windows. The Warwick and Shrewsbury churches had to borrow space in nearby homes, but that was kind of fun, too. In each of these situations, what could have been a liability was seen as more of a strength.

Virtually any space can be made to work with some ingenuity, scavenging and recycling, a little paint, and some spit and polish. A group of fifth and sixth graders and I started with a bare, unused room. With the church's permission, we made it our own, arranging it and decorating it to our own tastes. In one long evening in Warwick, a group of parents transformed a drab and dreary large room by completely painting the floor, walls, ceiling, and furniture and hung a cloth divider on a wire. For about fifty dollars, we got two attractive rooms in exchange for one unattractive room.

Methods

Different methods can address a variety of needs. If you don't have enough rooms or enough kids for a class for every grade or two, try intergenerational or broadly graded groups or interest groups. Your denominational offices and educational consultants, your regional resource center, perhaps a nearby seminary, or neighboring colleagues and churches can help you with materials designed for learning centers, intergenerational approaches, or broadly graded approaches. A one-room school house is another name for a broadly graded class. Advantages to these alternatives are that dis-spirited groups of two or three will feel much better when they're part of a group of ten or twelve, teachers can work together rather than having to work alone, and the church's family spirit is enhanced.

Many smaller churches have created their own solutions. The most creative and effective educational experience in Warwick was a week-day church school that met every Wednesday after school. Our adults met for an hour of camaraderie and planning before more than thirty children tumbled down the hill from the public school. A church could do its education in family units, perhaps with a monthly church family meal and program. Or it could plan a Saturday morning monthly event for its children and their friends. Or, with some trial and error, it could combine its educational and worship efforts. There's more than one way to skin a cat and grow a mature Christian. If you're really feeling desperate, remember the church got along quite nicely without a Sunday school for eighteen hundred years.

Leaders and Teachers

What if you don't have enough or very good teachers? I don't believe in asking for volunteers or that any warm body will do. I don't solicit volunteers because our young deserve only our most loving, creative, and faithful leaders. It's better to not have Sunday school than have negative, ignorant, or bad examples as leaders. So what to do?

Make a list of every mature youth and adult in your church. With at least one trusted colleague, ask yourselves which ones of these have a love of children and young people, a living faith, and a contagious *joie de vivre* that you want your children and young people to catch. If you don't restrict yourselves to parents and to those who've been teaching for years, you will probably have a good pool of prospects. Go to the first ones on your list and say, "Out of all the people in our church, you are one of three or so people who really have what it takes to help raise our young in the faith. We really need and want you." Offer them training, whatever assistance they need, good materials, a limited time commitment (three months, nine months, etc.), and lots of warm-fuzzies. If you're going to try an alternative method, tell them they can work with one or two others. Line up others to help with refreshments, music, crafts, and substituting. Have an educator from your denomination, a really good teacher from a neighboring church, or a public school teacher spend a Saturday training them. Hold a dedication ritual for them in worship and then turn them loose to help raise your kids in the faith.

If you simply don't have the right people to lead, do something radical. Cancel Sunday school until you do. Have nothing but a child-care program (which is what we do in the summer). In the meantime, encourage all your kids to go to your denominational summer camp. Conduct two or three children's retreats during the year —you might accomplish much more than you could with forty-five minutes once a week. Thoroughly integrate your kids into the life of your church and let the whole church raise them in the faith. Or merge your Sunday school with another church's. I include this last idea only reluctantly because it communicates that you're giving up on yourselves, and it makes it harder for your children to develop identity with their own church.

Materials

Start with the basics. All you really must have is a leader with the right contagion and a Bible. Everything else is supplementary. The curriculum you choose is less important than the environment and the teachers and mentors you provide. Pick curriculum that doesn't require a large group of students for activities to be successful. Make sure the curriculum teaches what your church believes. Examine the goals of the curriculum. For example, if the emphasis is Bible knowledge and your emphasis is building the Christian community, this material will not be a good match for your congregation.

As a smaller church, you probably have limited resources and finances. A resource I recommend (especially for more evangelical churches) is *Children's Ministry Guide for Smaller Churches* (Loveland, Col.: Group Publishing, 1995) by Rick Chromey. This book advertises itself as a guide for making a "big impact on a little-bitty budget!" It's full of money-saving ideas and good program suggestions.

Some of Chromey's good ideas include: charging a nominal admission, buying curriculum that provides the original and then permits you to photocopy for each of your students, substituting for expensive materials with human talent and interesting settings, holding a "shower" and asking people to bring needed materials, posting a "wish list" of needed materials and equipment and promoting it, having your church members bring all their pennies to church and use these to buy materials (a mile of pennies is over $850), or (my favorite) asking the church to donate enough quarters to make a stack equal to the height of the pastor. (Hope that the pastor is tall.)

Youth

You want a youth group but only have one, two, or three kids. One is enough for a youth ministry. The entire time our son was in high school, he was the church's only high-schooler. Our "youth ministry" with him was to encourage his involvement in worship and church life as a lay leader, his participation in an intergenerational confirmation class, his exposure to the exceptional role models in our church, and, most important, was the serious attention our people lavished on him. I felt a mixture of sadness and delight when he said, "I'm not sure about God, but I believe in the church."

Currently, the San Rafael church has up to a dozen young people who meet every other week. Five gifted adults work with them, providing a variety of experiences: facilitating discussion meetings, involving them in church activities, promoting camp and denominational youth activities, carrying out mission projects, and enjoying fun stuff like snow trips and sleepovers.

Adults

Many churches offer little nurturing for adults besides worship. Others only offer a Bible-study group. I see adult education as the new and next frontier. As you begin to conceptualize new and more engaging adult education, build it on the eight growing medium building blocks discussed earlier in this chapter. In addition, think about and address the different stages of adult life:

- Young adult and the life-building issues that are theirs
- Midlife and the vocational and family concerns that go with this stage
- The fifties and preretirement stage, when people are asking spiritual questions like, "Is this all there is?"
- Active retirement, when people have more discretionary time and may be ready to pursue serious religious questions
- The end-of-life stage, when people are making sense of their lives and pondering what lies beyond

Each stage provides grist for the adult learning mill. The church can provide a context and forum for adults to grapple with their issues in a helpful way.

In smaller churches, I resist ongoing groups or groups for only one particular segment of the church. Interest groups open to whomever wishes to respond have more potential to build the church community and bridge the divisions between genders and generations. Use the church year as a focus for such interest groups—a Lenten study, an Advent look at cultural excess, a Good Friday day of intense Bible study, a Pentecost study of the early church, and others. Develop a church library and create a book-study group (you might start with this book). Use a retreat and "day away" format. Establish a "Sermon Wrighters" group (a "wright" is one who crafts something) to help the pastor wright or craft the next week's sermon. Plan field trips and mission-work trips. Adults will contribute lots of ideas once they believe the church cares about their issues.

Westerhoff concludes *Will Our Children Have Faith?* by answering the question his title asks: "I remain convinced that the next generation may have faith but only if the present generation in the church is faithful in living that life of faith with them."[6] If the church as a whole is intellectually and spiritually alive, serious about pursuing life's important questions, and serious about putting its faith to work, maturity of faith is a given.

Questions

1. Do you accept that the educational goals for the church are inclusion in the faith community, preparing people to claim Christian identity, and developing disciples of Christ who live as followers on a daily basis?

2. Evaluate your church's educational ministry by the eight growing medium building blocks. What's working? What's missing?

Suggestion

Ask your best cooks to come up with their best desserts. Invite everyone interested to come together for the desserts and conversation about the eight building blocks. Find out what they would suggest for Christian education in your church for every age and all ages together.

chapter six

Small Enough to Care

A Hasidic rabbi asked a disciple: "How is Moshe Yaakov doing?" The disciple didn't know. "What!" shouted the rabbi, "You don't know? You pray under the same roof with him, you study the same texts, you serve the same God, you sing the same songs, and you dare to tell me that you don't know whether Moshe Yaakov is in good health, whether he needs help, advice or comforting."

—Elie Wiesel, *Souls on Fire*

My husband said to me, "Honey, you worry too much about people!" I said, "I don't worry, I care!"

—Pearl Bailey

A Christian fellowship lives and exists by intercession of its members for one another, or it collapses.

—Dietrich Bonhoeffer, *Life Together*

THE FILM *Patch Adams* (dir. Tom Shadyac; Universal, 1998) tells the true story of a passionate medical student who desperately wants to be a doctor so he can "help people" and "improve the quality of life, not just delay death." His vision of doctoring relies less on pills and procedures and more on using holistic care to heal. In the film's prologue, Robin Williams, who plays Patch Adams, reflects on his plunge into depression and hospitalization that led to his call to enter medical school in order to become a healer.

All of life is a coming home. Salesmen, secretaries, coal miners, beekeepers, sword swallowers, all of us, all the restless hearts of the world, all trying to find a way home. . . . Your shouts disappear into the wind. How small you feel. How far away home can be.

"Home," the dictionary defines it as both a place of origin and a goal or destination. . . . As the poet Dante put it, "in the middle of the journey of my life, I found myself in a dark wood for I had lost the right path. Eventually I would find the right path but in the most unlikely place."

It's no accident that the words "hostel," "hospital," "hospice," and "hospitality" are all similar words, having the same derivation—*hospes* or "host." Patch Adams found his "home" in the mental hospital, not with the staff, but with his fellow patients. Churches—at their purest and best—more than any other organization can be home for not only one group but for all God's children. It's the communal place and people we come home to, where all are welcome, where healing often happens, where it's not genuinely home for all if it's not home for each.

We live in a hostile world full of hunger for the healing hospitality that is at the very core of the Judeo-Christian tradition. Henri Nouwen wrote, "Our society seems to be increasingly full of fearful, defensive, aggressive people anxiously clinging to their property and inclined to look at their surrounding world with suspicion, always expecting an enemy to suddenly appear, intrude, and do harm. But still—that is our vocation: to convert the hostis into a hospes, the enemy into a guest, and to create the free and fearless space where brotherhood and sisterhood can be formed and fully experienced."[1]

So how are the various Moshe Yaakovs doing at your church— each of them? What, you don't know? More than anything else, if yours is a smaller church, it's the right size for every Moshe Yaakov to know how every other Moshe Yaakov is doing. Carl Dudley agrees that such intimate knowledge is possible in a smaller church:

The single cell, a network of caring people, is the strength of the small church. . . . To the outsider the small church is a prickly ball of Christian love. But if we try to imagine the intensity of the relationship within the group, the single-cell church would "feel" like a lump of bread—textured in the middle, and solid on the crust. The inner texture and the outer toughness are universal characteristics of primary groups. But the single-cell, small church has pushed the limits of caring far beyond the capacity of most small groups to know or care about their membership.[2]

Those who are church leaders are called to push the limits to which Dudley refers. Most churches are nice to visitors. They care about those who are dear to them and for those in immediate crisis—if the crisis isn't too hidden or doesn't lead to an unending series of crises. Too often, they lack staying power and fail to push beyond the obvious need. But Christian hospitality is more than this. It plunges more deeply into people's need, it reaches more broadly to all kinds of people; it responds to every type of need; it utilizes all available spiritual and social resources in order to prevent its own depletion. A smaller church that lives up to its potential for compassion will be nothing less than a courageous cadre of caring that is radically inclusive and surprisingly effective.

Elizabeth O'Connor, the chronicler of the remarkable little Church of the Savior in Washington, D.C., writes:

> The primary purpose of the disciplines, structures of accountability, and mission of the Church is to build life together, to create liberating communities of caring. To each of us is given a gift for the building of a community of caring, a community in which we can learn to embrace our pain, and to overcome all those oppressive inner structures that would keep us in bondage and make us protective and anxious for our own futures.[3]

O'Connor is on to the truth that Christian hospitality is not just the healthy caring for the sick or the vital young supporting their ailing elders. Everyone, from youngest to oldest and healthiest to sickest, is in need of ongoing care and is capable of being a caregiver. It is in being caregivers that we fathom our own need and pain and find our own healing and hope.

There are good reasons why smaller churches are particularly the right size to be caring communities. People come to smaller churches because they want to be involved with others, rather than to worship in isolation. Since most of the people have some history with one another, they know each other well enough to tell when "I'm fine" means, "I really am fine," and when it means, "I'm afraid to let you know how I really am." Because the members are in close physical and social proximity and because they are "family" to one another, they more quickly know and take notice of one another. They notice if someone is absent or upset, and if they don't notice, they will soon find out via the grapevine. They hear about who's sick, who's recovering, and who's near death.

Smaller churches have time and can take time to care, because they don't need to be fully occupied with keeping the institution running as is true in larger organizations. If their theology is more relational, their people will be more relational. Ideally, they chose a pastor who is known more for her caring than for her spellbinding preaching and the size of her reputation. Members of smaller churches tend to not be afraid of a little emotion and are used to having it expressed. Because these churches want to hold on to their own, they won't let those who hurt flee from their pain or run away and hide. Another distinctive characteristic of smaller churches is that they express caring through everything they do—in worship, through their Sunday school, as they socialize, and in their quick response to need in their church and community.

As the people of smaller churches give and receive caring, they discover their reason for being and God's life-giving presence. Consider the biblical examples: In the marvelous story of Abraham and Sarah's hospitality (Gen. 18:1–15), God appeared to Abraham in the form of three travelers who passed by his tent in the arid desert. Abraham invited them to rest awhile in the shade of his tree, brought them water, prepared a feast for them, served them himself, and stood by while they ate. They asked about his wife, Sarah, and said that when they returned, she would have a baby son. Sarah was eavesdropping at the entrance of the tent and laughed out loud because of her and Abraham's advanced age. The idea of a child was ridiculous to her. In one translation she says: "I'm old and worn out, can I still enjoy sex?" Despite her skepticism, nine months later she gave birth to a son and named him Isaac, which means "he laughed." The message is obvious: The fruit of hospitality is life.

In Luke 24:13–35, the day after the resurrection, Jesus joins two of his followers on the road to their home in Emmaus. Failing to recognize him, they told him all that had happened in Jerusalem—none of which they understood. Upon arriving in Emmaus, the still unrecognized Jesus started to walk on but they insisted he accept their hospitality. As they shared a meal, Jesus took some bread, broke it, and gave it to them. In the sharing of bread their eyes were opened and they recognized him. Not only does life come to us as we extend hospitality, but God is present, experienced, and recognized in response to our hospitality. Remember the little churches in Oto, Rodney, and Smithland, Iowa? Churches that were dying shared hospitality with those in need and are now bursting with life and purpose. Churches that are hospitable and caring live; those who care only about themselves and their survival die.

Caring as an act of love is intrinsic to who and what churches are. Jesus made it the distinguishing characteristic of congregations: ". . . love one another. By this everyone will know that you are my disciples, if you have love for one another" (John. 13:35). Paul told the little Corinthian church that they were one body and that the eye of the body cannot say to the hand, "I don't need you." He then preached on love and stressed that love is even greater than faith and hope (1 Cor. 12, 13).

Throughout church history, the quality of caring has been its distinguishing characteristic. Tertullian, described the second-century church: "Look how they love one another." In the sixth century, Benedict of Nursia, the father of Western monasticism, required that monks graciously welcome pilgrims and the poor as though they were Christ. Benedictines are still doing this. Hospitality was a lesser but real theme for Martin Luther, John Calvin, and the sixteenth-century reformers. Hospitality was emphasized by John Wesley in the eighteenth century as he universalized benevolent hospitality, teaching that it should extend to friend and enemy, those in the community, and those outside it. Caring and hospitality are basic to the church's charter, bylaws, and mission statement—toward our own and those we barely know.

Judy and Bill Styles and their Aunt Harriet visited the Warwick church soon after moving to town. After worship, people greeted one another, and the Styles family headed home while the rest of the church headed for the coffeemaker. Carl and Rotha (two of God's finest) saw them leave, set down their coffee cups, followed them home, drove into their driveway, got out, and said: "Why didn't you stay for coffee? We wanted to get to know you!" Shocked and delighted, the Styles came back the next week and stayed for coffee. Judy was the person who taught our church to hug; Harriet was the one who wrote all the birthday cards; Bill was the woodworker who made special things for special people. Caregiving is the primary color in the fabric of that church.

Caregiving comes in all shapes and colors. I saw it in the retreat center hospitality of the little Bryant, South Dakota, church. At Epiphany Church in St. Louis, caring was evident in the greeter who reassured the visitor with AIDS that: "You've come to the right church." Caring is just as evident in their extraordinary outreach ministries. In Sioux Falls, a caring Sudanese church goes out of its way to be a home away from home for other Sudanese refugees from the holocaust in their homeland. In Red Oak, Iowa, caring took the form of churchwomen who noticed that children in their after-school program didn't have warm coats and that their parents couldn't speak English. In San Rafael, caring came in the form of over two hundred hours of labor and twelve hundred dollars in donations to build the finest ramp in the whole mobile home park for Kate, a church member who was rapidly losing the use of her legs.

Smaller churches, like a mom-and-pop grocery, can offer a little bit of everything—especially when it comes to the whole spectrum of human need. Sixty years ago, American psychologist Abraham Maslow developed what is known as "Maslow's hierarchy of needs." According to the theory, all human feelings, thoughts, and actions are directed at meeting the full range of human needs—from physical to spiritual. These needs are arranged in an ascending sequence. Lower needs must be met before one can attend to the higher ones. These needs start with our physical needs (food, shelter, clothing, physical comforts). When those are satisfied, we are better able to focus on safety and security needs; then love and belonging needs; then ego, status, and self-esteem needs; and finally what Maslow called self-actualization. We might call self-actualization self-fulfillment or living as one created in the image of God.[4]

Congregations, in their caregiving, work at each of these levels, often simultaneously. When they are really faithful and effective, they are able to help people move from the struggle to meet their most basic needs to the heights of being whom God created them to be. The little church in San Rafael and, probably, your little church is caring at each level by:

- Addressing basic needs with food and clothing for those in need
- Providing a night's lodging or creating safe and affordable housing
- Advocating for those who have been neglected and abused
- Offering a place of sanctuary and community where people experience love and belonging
- Helping people build their self-esteem
- Addressing their deepest spiritual hungers

The way churches do all this is both a mystery and a miracle.

Do we wait until a person cries out for help or are there signals or symptoms that a caregiving church can recognize and respond to? The list of warning signals are there for the observant caregiver to recognize. A church willing to care beyond pious platitudes will look for these warning signals. Is someone withdrawing from social activities or showing significant loss of interest in what was of interest before? Is a person expressing feelings of prevailing grief, depression, or loss? Is there a noticeable change of appearance, change of skin tone, or change of weight? Does a person talk of meaninglessness, hopelessness, or death? Is there something more important behind the "presenting problem" of marital stress, financial problems, etc.? Is there a change of behavior, such as becoming more aggressive or increased drinking or medicating oneself? Are a person's relationships falling apart?[5]

From time to time in every parish, these kinds of behaviors will be present and perceived. Caring and sensitive persons will not ignore them. Rather, the caregiver will listen, be compassionate, communicate concern, and offer to be an ally in seeking assistance. The caring and sensitive church will see that the hurting person is kept within the church family where the liturgical, pastoral, and social resources of the church can lead toward healing.

Churches care not just because scripture tells them to or because of historical tradition or because it comes naturally to smaller churches or because they may find their own life in the process. Churches care because it makes a difference. There's mounting documentary evidence that demonstrates that those who worship, those who are part of congregations, those who are part of caring relationships are healthier and live longer. There's solid evidence of the power of prayer to make a difference.[6] On the anecdotal level, in the four churches I've pastored, the death rate among older active participants was and is lower than one would expect for the size of church membership and the number of elderly people. I know parishioners who found a greater reason for living in the loving care of their faith community.

Seventy-Nine Caring Strategies

If a church, even the smallest church, seeks to care, it will be more effective if it does so with intentionality. Otherwise, its ministry of compassion can be superficial, haphazard, and limited to the obvious. Here is a very large sampling of caring strategies, but they are only a drop in the bucket. Use any that intrigue, fit, and have promise for your setting. Let them be triggers for your own imagination and creativity. Consider the ones you like and ignore the rest. (Some of these are for the pastor or require pastoral leadership, but many do not.) These strategies are divided into five sections: those that will build a sense of community in your congregation; those that are primarily for the pastoral leader; those that primarily engage the laity; those that relate to worship, prayer, and spiritual support; and those that reach beyond your congregation.

Community-Building

1. Develop ways to help everyone know everyone else's name and to know something about everyone else.
2. Engage a commercial company to create a photo directory of your congregation or make your own. One church created their own that included each person's name, address, phone number, birthday, and answer to interesting questions, like: "What is your message to the world?"

3. Even though you think you know each other, visitors certainly don't. Make and use permanent name tags. Have disposable name tags for visitors.

4. Have a church member take photos of every person or family. Mount them on a bulletin board with names and perhaps other information and keep the photo board up-to-date.

5. Eat together—a lot. Use any excuse for breaking bread together. Find the style of eating together that fits your church.

6. Ask each board, committee, or group in the church to plan one purely social event for the whole church in the next year.

7. Begin every group meeting at your church with meditation and community-building. Spend a few minutes around a question like: "Where did you see or sense the touch of God today?" Or, "What's different in your life since the last time we met?"

8. Have a photograph taken of the whole congregation. Make it into postcards and give them to your congregation to use. Send many from the pastor's office.

9. Print a church directory once or twice a year. Include names (including family members), addresses, phone numbers, e-mail addresses; lists of officers and committees; a birthday list; list of those who have a business or offer a service.

10. Establish a church telephone tree. One person calls five who each call five as a way of communicating important matters, news, prayer concerns, and so forth.

11. Plan church retreats, "A Day Away"—times for church folk to have a Sabbath time away from their daily lives and to be together. Although I like all-church gatherings, you could also do this with moms and kids, dads and kids, just kids, older folks, women, men, and so on.

12. Don't just call people together to meet and do business. Call them together just to play—Sunday afternoon volleyball, horseshoes, go to a good movie, eat out, go to a museum, a table game night, and other activities.

13. Once I visited every church member either at work or doing some favorite activity and took his or her picture for a slide program on the church family.

14. Create ways to get your people into each other's homes—committee meetings, progressive dinners, Bible studies, cooperative window washing or weeding parties (one hour working together at each house).

15. Decorate and furnish your church building, including the pastor's office, so people will be more likely to stop in, hang out, hang around.

16. If you don't have one, develop a church newsletter that can serve a variety of needs. It could go by e-mail to those who have that service or posted on a church Web site.

17. Do you have someone who can develop a Web site for your church? It can be a source of information for members and public relations for nonmembers.

18. Have a new, attractive outdoor sign made that lets the world know this is a caring and compassionate church.

Pastor's Caregiving

19. When it's time to seek a new pastor, hold out for one who has the gift of caring. In an interview, do you sense that she cares about you? Ask him for examples of his caring ministry. Does the candidate do all or most of the talking? A gift for listening and not just talking about oneself is almost synonymous with a gift for caring.

20. Be with parishioners the night before or morning of surgery and with the spouse or family during surgery. Don't wait until afterwards to visit in the hospital.

21. Develop your and your church's ministry at the time of death. If it's not intrusive, be with people at their time of death. Gather family and friends the night before the service to "tell stories" and share memories. Encourage memorial services and discourage funerals. Whenever possible, have the service in the church sanctuary and not the funeral home. Have a meal or social time after the service. Make a pastoral call a week and then a month after the service.

22. Invite people to work with you to plan their own memorial services. Planning ahead can help diminish fears of death,

help the person consider his or her values and priorities, and save their families anguish and sometimes conflict.

23. Establish a daily ministry in the local coffee shops. Or serve coffee or tea one morning a week at the church for whoever wants to drop in.

24. Occasionally go into your sanctuary with the church membership list. Sit where each person usually sits and pray for that person.

25. Invite or ask each person in the church (kids, too!) to meet with you individually in the sanctuary every year or so, simply to talk about "life."

26. Gather e-mail addresses of church members so you can frequently transmit group e-mails containing a prayer, a prayer request, a quotation or meditative thought, and church news.

27. Develop a card or computer file for every person or family that includes vital information and names of family members. Add information from time to time that you might otherwise forget.

28. As quickly as possible after arriving in a church, develop a "stable" of referral agencies and professionals you know and trust.

29. Whenever possible, establish partnerships with physicians and others in the helping services with whom you can collaborate, particularly when you're all working with a person who is chronically in need. (This is particularly realistic and helpful in smaller communities.)

30. Attend to your own continuing education so that your awareness and skills are continually being upgraded.

31. Study, research, and collect resources and examples of healing ministries. Then engage your leadership in developing a comprehensive healing ministry in your parish.

32. Recognize that life passages like baptisms, weddings, and deaths are primary times for offering and receiving caring. Make sure that the services you conduct for these occasions communicate the caring you intend.

33. Develop a comprehensive collection of personal rituals (house blessing, before surgery, as death approaches, divorce, engagement, holy unions) and let your congregation know that you are ready and willing to be a pastor who "has ritual, will travel."

34. Offer to conduct a ritual of forgiveness and reconciliation when two parties are seeking to repair a relationship. Conduct these rituals in the sanctuary.

35. Send postcards to homebound people while you're on vacation. It only takes a short time and people really appreciate it.

36. Remember people with cards and notes not only at times of illness or death but also on anniversaries of deaths, graduations, and times of significant achievements.

37. Make one phone call daily, not for church business, but just to say, "I was thinking of you today and wondered how you are."

38. If you're the pastor, announce (often) when and how you want to be notified of people's needs. Regularly distribute business cards that have your phone number, pager number, e-mail, and other information. People need to be trained in how to use (and not abuse) their pastor.

39. If you're the pastor, do more pastoral calling than you think you have time to do. It may be old-fashioned but it's still very effective in most churches. Call ahead for an appointment.

40. Encourage people to invite the pastor to visit them at work or for lunch on a workday so that the pastor knows something of the workday life of the laity.

Caregiving by the Laity

41. Ask an appropriate layperson to be your church's coordinator of caregiving ministries.

42. The United Church of Christ publishes *Called to Care: A Notebook for Lay Caregivers* (800.325.7061 or 800.537.3394). Use it or something similar from your denomination to train and equip a team of lay caregivers.

43. The pastor and a sensitive layperson who's been around a long time can go through the church list and do a "census" or "gift list" of who's had breast cancer, who's been divorced, who's had an addiction, who's struggled with depression or mental illness, who's been terminated from a job, who's survived the death of a spouse, and so forth; and, then, who's a counselor, who has time to be a driver, who could provide an emergency meal or emergency child care, and so on. Ask these persons if they are willing to be called on when there's a parish need for which they are suited. Encourage other parishioners to volunteer their gifts and availability.

44. Recruit articulate, courageous people to be advocates for parishioners who have to go to court, meet with the school administration, appear at the welfare office, or are having difficulty getting information from health-care professionals.

45. Ask an appropriate person to train your church leadership, including children and youth workers, in abuse-prevention in the church. The church must be a safe place for all its people!

46. Recruit and train a team of people to provide pastoral care when the pastor is away or unavailable.

47. Develop and train a church prayer chain. Where possible, use e-mail so people can easily be notified of a need for prayer.

48. Invite a homebound person to address birthday cards to each person in the congregation with a note. Then the pastor can add his or her own personal note. You could also send anniversary cards. Consider sending cards on the anniversary of a person's baptism as a substitute for birthday cards.

49. Have a nurse, doctor, or counselor (or a combination) offer a workshop on crisis intervention and hospital and nursing-home visits. Offer this to a team of church caregivers with an open invitation to anyone who might be interested.

50. Start a parish nurse program. Have a nurse in your church do health education and preventive health care with your membership and perhaps with church neighbors.

51. Ask your whole church to pray for a different church person or family each week. If you have photos of everyone on a bulletin board, you could have a special frame for the person or family who is the "Prayer Partner for the Week."

52. Find creative ways to help your church children and youth develop their caring skills. People are never too young to care. They can make and send cards, weed flowerbeds, read, and do other things.

53. Encourage each group of children and young people to carry out at least one caring project each year.

54. Find volunteers who can provide respite care for full-time caregivers in your parish, which allows them to go to the store, get a haircut, or have some time off.

55. When making pastoral calls, take one or two people with you (when you're confident there are not personal concerns that need attention). You have parishioners who would like to visit but are shy and people needing visits who would like to see others in addition to the pastor.

56. Set aside two thousand dollars from church savings for an emergency loan fund. Set a limit, request two percent interest, ask for repayment within a year.

57. Find, at least, a core of people who will do Bible study and pray faithfully, thankfully, and caringly for one another, the pastor, others in need, the whole church, and community. Where there's prayer, there's care.

Caregiving through Worship, Prayer, Spiritual Support

58. Make a video recording of your worship services (including shots of the congregation). Add recorded greetings from people. Delegate someone take it to your homebound people and watch it with them. They can then feel included in the worship and see their friends. If necessary, buy a VCR for a homebound person without one. Audio tapes are second best.

59. Establish a greeting and meeting time at the beginning of worship. We call it: "Becoming a Community."

60. Conduct your sacramental occasions in ways that facilitate caring. Make it real, personal, and communal.

61. Take communion to the homebound, those in nursing and convalescent facilities, those in the hospital, and others who wish it. Include lay members so it's the church and not just the pastor who is bringing the sacrament.

62. Preach a specifically pastoral sermon three or four times a year. Choose themes like prayer, genuine hospitality, the church as sanctuary, loving one another, loving one's enemy, or forgiveness.

63. Preach a sermon on "good" gossip and encourage it.

64. Invite a sharing of joys and concerns before the Pastoral Prayer. Remember the wider world and not just our personal joys and concerns. The San Rafael church has a Joys and Concerns Journal, in which a layperson notes every joy and concern mentioned. Those who couldn't hear or want to check a name can check the journal. The Union Church in Vinalhaven has a Prayer List in its bulletin that includes who is in what nursing home.

65. Trust, believe, and communicate that prayers for healing and help in both worship and our daily lives do heal and help.

66. Invite couples to celebrate a renewal of their vows on their tenth, twentieth, thirtieth, and other anniversaries.

67. Get a list of each person's three favorite hymns. Use them on birthdays, when someone is having a hard time, at memorial services.

68. End worship with the ancient Christian ritual of "Passing of the Peace." Encourage more than perfunctory greetings.

69. Don't just count the number attending worship. Have someone keep track of who's not there. Follow up with a note or call of concern if someone in precarious health is absent or generally after three or four absences.

Caregiving Outreach

70. Open your sanctuary daily for prayer. Have a street-side sign inviting those passing by to come in and put an ad or article in your local paper indicating your church is open for prayer and meditation.

71. Make your building available to house a twelve-step program like Alcoholics Anonymous.

72. Sponsor a blood drive.

73. Have money available to assist transients with meals, gas money, or lodging. In the interest of their dignity, I often invite them to wash some windows, do some weeding, and other chores in exchange for the gift of money.

74. Involve your church in a hands-on mission project that gives your folks an opportunity to enjoy and better know one another.

75. Hold a free ice-cream social on your church lawn for the neighborhood. Don't charge; just have a donation basket.

76. Develop a troupe of clowns, a barbershop quartet, and so on to entertain in nursing homes.

77. If you're on a busy thoroughfare, give away cold cups of water on hot days.

78. On holidays like Memorial Day, the Fourth of July, and Labor Day (when many people are killed on the highways), give away free coffee near a busy highway.

79. If you have an appropriate person to convene it, start a support group for specific groups that don't now have one— for grieving spouses, people with cancer, and others.

No church can or should attempt all of these suggestions. On the other hand, the list is not exhaustive. You and your people will have many other ideas. There are unique needs among you and in your community that these won't touch, but you can find approaches that will address those needs. A caring ministry is less a list of things we do in the church and more a style of congregational life and a way of being, as the following story illustrates.

Rachel Naomi Remen, in her best-selling book, *Kitchen Table Wisdom*, tells an Islamic Sufi story about a man who is so good that the angels ask God to give him the gift of miracles. God, wiser than the angels, suggests that they go ask the man if he even wants miraculous powers. They visited the man and asked him if he wouldn't like first the gift of healing by the touch of his hand, then the gift of conversion of souls, and finally the gift of supreme virtue. The good man refuses these gifts the angels have offered. They insist that he choose a special gift or they will choose one for him. He thinks carefully and then acquiesces: "Very well, I ask that I may do a great deal of good without ever knowing it."

The angels didn't know what to do. They thought and thought and came up with a plan. Every time the saint's shadow fell behind him, it would have the power to cure disease, soothe pain, and comfort sorrow. As he walked, behind him his shadow "made arid paths green, caused withered plants to bloom, gave clear water to dried up brooks, fresh color to pale children, and joy to unhappy men and women. The saint simply went about his daily life diffusing virtue as the stars diffuse light and the flowers scent, without being aware of it." Out of respect for his humility, the people never spoke to him of his miracles. Eventually, they forgot his name and simply referred to him as the "Holy Shadow."[7] May your church become the caring church of the "Holy Shadow."

Questions

1. How does your church now practice a ministry of caring? What's missing?

2. Who are the colleagues in your congregation who might work with you to develop or expand a caring ministry in and through your church?

Suggestion

Invite your congregation to a viewing of *Patch Adams* (have lots of popcorn and soda). Enjoy the film and one another. Discuss the film and its relevance for your congregation. Ask if your church's approach to a caring, healing ministry is more like Patch's or like the medical school's. Then ask them to come back for a second gathering to peruse this book's list of caring strategies, take a census of what you're now doing, and brainstorm what else they would like to do. All of this could provide the format for an exciting church retreat.

chapter seven

The Church Exists by Mission

Never doubt that a small group of thoughtful, committed citizens
can change the world; indeed, it's the only thing that ever has.

—Margaret Mead

But seek the welfare of the city [or the town or the country or the
earth]. . . for in its welfare you will find your welfare.

—Jeremiah 29:7

THEOLOGIAN EMIL BRUNNER MADE IT CLEAR AND SIMPLE, "The Church
exists by mission, just as a fire exists by burning. Where there is no
mission, there is no Church, and where there is neither Church nor
mission, there is no faith."[1]

Kennon Callahan said the same thing a little differently. "A congregation without a mission is a club, not a congregation."[2]

Many churches of all sizes are primarily focused on their own internal and institutional life. Feeling the press of declining membership,
rising costs, and numerical insignificance, many smaller churches re-
trench into a survival mentality and mode. Such nearsighted churches
fail to recognize that their survival, their identity as Christian churches,
and their future depend on an outer focus—mission, which I define as
all that the church does beyond its doors. Any church, no matter how
small and poor, will find a way to live if it is committed to a mission it
sees as crucial. That mission becomes its *raison d'être*—its reason for
keeping on keeping on.

Callahan described a church with which he had worked. He had suggested they turn from a survival mentality to a mission commitment.

The church was down to fourteen people. People were gradually "dying off," but they decided to "do something to be helpful" before they were all gone. They got involved with a local elementary school, helping wherever they were needed. In this involvement, they found a new lease on life. Within a year, they had about ninety people in worship.[3]

Genuine mission is less a program and more a way of life. When mission becomes a way of life, a church looks at itself as a people who can make a difference in the lives of others. Additionally, the church looks at others as persons with whom it might be in a mutual and helping relationship. Tony Pappas and Scott Planting describe a pastor's call on a man in his small village:

> I called upon a man living in our town who was dying of cancer. On the sideboard in the kitchen I noticed a bouquet of fresh wildflowers and a bowl of fruit. The man smiled and offered me an apple. He told me where the gifts came from. "Some women from the church came to visit me last night. They brought the flowers and fruit. One of them offered to wash the dishes. At first I thought they were going to try and 'save me.' I don't have much to do with their church. But they talked with me about cancer and dying. Mostly if people come they talk about the weather, or anything but the fact that I am sick. But these people really wanted to know how I was doing and if I needed anything. They didn't stay long. Before they left they said a prayer with me and they held my hand. No one had ever prayed like that with me before. Will you thank them and ask them to come again?[4]

Most likely, these churchwomen didn't visit because their church had a "program" of visiting dying people with cancer. They and their church did not leave their compassion at the church door. Instead, they felt compelled to take the love of God with them to wherever they knew there was a need for which they had the resources. Those women were there to do more than bring a little cheer, and, at the same time, they were not there to ring up one more convert. They were willing to risk addressing real need and willing to bring the resources of the church to address that need.

In 1971, the church in Warwick, Massachusetts had a total budget of $1,585 (there are no zeros missing). They doubled their budget to hire me for two days a week at thirty dollars a day. I was their first resident pastor in decades. The church had fifty dollars in its budget for "mission." But the church's crusty old treasurer refused to send the fifty dollars to the denomination, because he disapproved of how he thought they would use it. It appeared as though that church had no mission at all. But that's not accurate. Those fifteen or so people, who constituted the only active church in town, utilized a rotation of itinerant pastors and kept the doors open because they felt strongly that there had to be a Sunday school in town. They knew if they didn't do it, there wouldn't be one. The Sunday school was their "mission," even though no one ever called it that.

Mission quickly became part of the working vocabulary of that church. Some of the men started a paper-recycling project at the town dump. The church sent a letter to every home in town with an invitation to sample the new things happening at the Metcalf Memorial Chapel. A youth group was started for the youth in town. I called on anyone from the community who was hospitalized. A deacon's fund was established to assist anyone in need. In the first year, we showed a film about our denominational mission work, our children collected for UNICEF, we took our first One Great Hour of Sharing offering, and the youth group canvassed the community for the Heart Fund and put on a breakfast for Heifer Project International (HPI).

Steve, a college student and young farmer, got involved in the church and joined the youth group and choir. He heard about Heifer Project and got an idea. He wanted to spend a year as a volunteer at Heifer Project's ranch in Arkansas. He and I proposed to the church that we try to raise the annual stipend Heifer Project paid its volunteers—eighteen hundred dollars. This request created a problem, because the church had committed itself to building a new sanctuary and dining room addition on the old colonial house that was the church building. We were going to do this with one paid builder assisted by volunteer labor. Nevertheless, the church agreed to try to also raise the HPI money. Rather than the eighteen hundred dollars, they raised over three thousand dollars with various fundraisers. In the space of four years, the church was transformed from barely hanging on to literally believing that they could do anything they wanted to do. When they became a people on a mission, they became a church on fire.

Several people in the Shrewsbury, Vermont, church were involved in town government, the volunteer fire department, Amnesty International, and a range of environmental concerns. But as a church, there was little interest in mission. They needed something to identify with and commit to. The sister of our church lay leader was a Conservative Baptist missionary in Rwanda. Through her, our church established a partnership with the small Gahulire Baptist Church in a small Rwandan village. Letters, audiotapes, pictures, and small gifts were exchanged. We sent a shipment of needed Bibles. Then we learned that the school they operated for the village was termite-ridden and near collapse. It could be replaced for three thousand dollars. We accepted that challenge. In February 1988, armed with seven thousand dollars in money and needed supplies, twelve Vermonters traveled to Rwanda to meet our partner church and help with the school building. After that trip, the world was smaller and more real for those of us who traveled there and for our whole congregation.

Smart Mission at First Congregational, San Rafael

The San Rafael church illustrates how a church can discover, embrace, and find life in its mission, and it illustrates how a church can make a major difference with limited resources through what we call "smart mission." In 1993, I was called as half-time pastor of this California church. It had declined in membership from 281 members in 1957 to 50 in 1993. Due to the advocacy of Mary Moore and the existence of Pilgrim Park, there was a real, though undeveloped, mission concern. Mary, seventy years young, was what every church needs. She was the "missionary" who prodded the church to give generously to special mission offerings, recruited people to go to this important meeting and that interesting event, and stood up in worship to inform the congregation about the significant needs and issues we should be involved in.

Pilgrim Park was the sixty-one-unit, affordable, housing complex the church had built on church land in 1971. It was the first church-built housing of its kind in the San Francisco area. A property management company provided the day-to-day management, and a board of directors, composed of church members, set policies and provided the oversight management. The church had little direct involvement in Pilgrim Park.

Since mission was not on the church's front burner, there was work to be done. The church had to first address a structural issue. In response to the decrease in membership, the church had restructured into two boards—trustees, who took care of money and building, and deacons, who were responsible for everything else. The trustees seldom met and deacons' meetings were interminable.

In writing and teaching, I had started describing churches as "3-M" companies. The first M is Ministry, what a church does internally to equip itself for its mission and includes worship, education, and care of the congregation. The second M is Mission, everything the church does beyond the church doors. The third M is Maintenance, everything else (including building and money) the church does to support its Ministry and Mission. After watching the deacons struggle with an impossible workload, I suggested we experiment with three boards—a board of ministry, a board of mission, and a board of maintenance (trustees). The church agreed. It worked and still works. With a board of mission, we were no longer dependent on Mary Moore or the pastor to move us into mission. As a result, mission became the church's middle name.

Pilgrim Park was a good news-bad news story. The good news was that about 125 people had affordable housing. The bad news was that Pilgrim Park was plagued with drugs, crime, and anger at management. Disgruntled residents frequently came to my office with their grievances. Despite these problems, I had a vision of Pilgrim Park changing from an unhappy apartment complex into a healthy apartment community. The management company and the board of directors shared the vision, rolled up their sleeves, and went to work. The resident manager was replaced with one who was and is firm, fair, and compassionate. A few troublesome residents were evicted. The renovation of apartments and the relandscaping of the grounds were accelerated. Meetings were held with residents. A drug-elimination grant from HUD was used for social programs for children and young people and to make Pilgrim Park a gated community in order to control drug traffic and criminal activity. It all worked.

Today, Pilgrim Park is an award-winning, model community that looks like a little United Nations. An after-school homework club has dramatically raised the grades of the participating students. A computer learning center and the homework club were developed through grants and some money from the church. Residents are happy. The gap that existed between residents and church is steadily being narrowed. Management, residents, and the church are working closely and effectively.

People are best motivated to act when they identify with and experience people and their need. In 1995, I recruited fifteen church members (about twenty-five percent of our adults) to go with me on a ten-day retreat at a Benedictine retreat center in Cuernavaca, Mexico. The sisters lead retreats that are a rich rhythm of worship and spiritual reflection, education concerning the realities of life for the poor, Hispanic and Mexican culture, and faith in that context, and field trips to experience the culture, meet the poor, and experience projects that are helping people out of poverty. Our people were deeply sensitized and became highly motivated to reach out and address the kinds of needs we experienced. We now take retreat groups to Cuernavaca each year.

One place to start developing a mission-consciousness is with the church budget. Twenty different helping organizations receive nominal support from the board of mission budget. Having them in our budget gives them some support and keeps their work and their issues before our congregation. The following criteria help determine which groups the church supports:

- Groups need to be faith-related. (There are hundreds, even thousands, of groups we could support, so we've chosen to support faith-based groups).
- The groups we support cover the spectrum from local to global and address a broad spectrum of needs.
- We support groups in which church members participate.
- We support groups that range from those offering direct assistance (like the local food bank) to those trying to change the rules in our society (like Bread for the World).
- Finally, and most importantly, we support organizations that are cost-effective and making a genuine difference.

People won't commit their time or money until they understand the need and believe they can make a difference. Early in our consciousness-raising, the board of mission planned a yearlong, mission-education series. We had a speaker or event almost every month. These included:

- A hunger banquet in which one person got a gourmet dinner, a few got a basic meal, and most got thin soup in a can and water, followed by reflection on the experience.
- An after-worship program to honor all our members who were volunteering time and talent in various service programs was revealing and inspiring. We surveyed the whole congregation and made a construction paper balloon naming each person and the work they were doing. The balloons were exhibited on the wall in our community room. The amount of volunteer effort engaged in by this little congregation was and is amazing. Each person received a certificate and a symbolic gift.
- The main event was a mission fair. We asked every group we support in the budget to send a representative or at least a display. A panel of these representatives gave the sermon during worship. Following worship, there were games for kids, food, time to tour the displays, and opportunity to talk to the representatives. It was an exciting and educational event.

Knowing that our resources are limited and that our people are over-committed, we've tried to be "smart" in expanding the church's mission. The organization that rented the downstairs space moved to larger quarters, and the search began for a new tenant. One day, a developer knocked on my office door. He was building an office complex, and, in order to get his permits, the city was requiring him to provide a child-care center. He was having trouble fulfilling this requirement. We showed him the space. He asked if he could pay us to run a child-care program. We decided that was not our mission but agreed to help him find someone who would. The search led to Head Start, one of the best federal programs, and a deal was struck.

The result was a model of church, private sector, local government, and federal government collaboration to address a serious need. The developer was responsible for: $100,000 of renovation work to make the space suitable for young children and accessible, $100,000 in child-care scholarships, and for Head Start's rent to the church for ten years. The city changed their requirements of him to fit with what we were doing. The federal government, through Head Start, is now doing a superb job of working with twenty poor children and their families, giving them a head start in school and society. Faith-based programs using federal programs and money is not a new concept. This partnership between church and Head Start has now expanded to include another Head Start program at Pilgrim Park. Now Head Start, Pilgrim Park, and church are working closely to expand the cooperation and interdependence on what we call "Pilgrim Hill."

The people of smaller churches generally have limited time, money, and numbers of people. Yet, they are surrounded by great needs. A church practicing smart mission will seek creative methods of addressing these needs in ways that are way out of proportion to its resources.

As the San Rafael church planned the capital-funds campaign to finance its building renovation, some of our mission-minded folks asserted they didn't want to give money just for our own needs. The church quickly agreed that ten percent of what was raised would go for some new and innovative mission venture. That amount was eventually capped at sixteen thousand dollars.

That's when the excitement started. Our members were challenged to submit "grant proposals," and we offered a workshop to help them envision significant projects and write winning proposals. To be selected for funding a project had to:

- Be realistic and doable
- Address a real issue or problem in a way that could make a real difference
- Provide a fresh and creative approach
- Involve our people in a faithful and effective way

Sixteen proposals were submitted. The intention was to fund one of them, but three smart mission proposals were chosen and developed.

First, we allocated a thousand dollars to help develop the computer-learning center at Pilgrim Park. That seed money helped attract other grant funding, and the center is now equipped, staffed, and serving the children, youth, and adults of Pilgrim Park and some church and neighborhood people.

Second, a church youth proposed that fifteen thousand dollars be allocated as seed money to create the Pilgrim Hill Foundation. Rather than use all the money for one project, he thought it would be smarter to use the money to generate more money that could be used for different mission projects each year for the foreseeable future. We anticipate the foundation will attract additional donations and bequests. The money will be invested in socially responsible ways. The foundation's earnings the first year provided resources for the Pilgrim Park learning center. The second year, a thousand dollars is being used to send ten people to work on a Habitat for Humanity project.

Third, Alan and Barbara Miller, members who went on the first trip to Cuernavaca, Mexico, proposed that we do something to feed hungry children. The rationale that made this project imperative was the realization that no child should be hungry and that children cannot grow, learn, and have a decent future if they are malnourished. The initial intent was to address both local and global hunger. Investigation determined that, while there is significant poverty in our county, there are existing programs to assure that hungry children are fed here. So we chose to focus on Mexico, where we already had a reliable contact through our Cuernavaca retreat visits.

Bill and Patty Coleman had chosen to retire to Mexico to live and work with the poor. After getting to know and be trusted by many of the poor around Cuernavaca, they started an amazing program called VAMOS! VAMOS! is organized on the principle that every dollar received goes directly to serve the poor. No contributions are used for offices, promotion, or salaries for North Americans. All overhead expenses are covered by friends of VAMOS! Volunteers do most of the administrative work. Bill and Patty's income comes from royalties for Catholic curricula they've written. VAMOS! created and sustains seventy-eight programs that serve the poor, staffed with poor but well-trained Mexicans.

First Congregational partnered with VAMOS! and started Every Dollar Feeds Kids. Every Dollar pledges that every dollar received is used for nothing but buying food to feed hungry children in the schools

VAMOS! has established. In its first three years, this program raised over sixty thousand dollars, which has provided over 150,000 meals for very hungry and malnourished kids. Our church and the project's board of directors are providing whatever money is necessary to administer this grass-roots effort. We feel like we're on the front lines of ending world hunger—one child at a time. Currently, we are seeking other individuals, churches, and groups to be full partners with us in expanding our outreach to many more hungry kids. (Those interested in being involved can contact Every Dollar Feeds Kids at 415.479.2747 or <DollarsForFood@aol.com>.)

Mission is not just what the church does collectively. In fact, our church probably does more mission through what each member does once he or she leaves the building than what is done cumulatively through our various projects. As in most churches, the people sitting in our pews on Sunday morning are active in their communities, being a humanizing influence in their places of work and volunteering time and energy in a vast array of service organizations and agencies. For example, the chair of the jail ministry at the county jail sings in our choir and recruits our Sunday morning volunteers. The chair of the teen center in San Rafael teaches in our Sunday school, is a professor in the education department at the University of San Francisco, and the principal 4-H leader in Marin County. One member served in city and county government for three decades in addition to being a professor in the department of psychiatry at the University of California. His wife has been pivotal in preserving large areas of Marin County open space and other environmental causes. Through its people, this little church and most smaller churches are making a significant difference.

The Ten Commandments of Congregational Mission

God created the church for mission, to be the cadre of people commissioned to create the universal and eternal Community of God. The purpose of everything else a church does is to equip it for this awesome calling. Ten fundamental convictions can guide and strengthen the development of mission-consciousness in all types of smaller churches.

1 . *Mission is a life-and-death matter for smaller churches.*

In a "bigger is better world," smaller churches struggle to feel legitimate and needed. Many have dwindled and languished because they have lost their reason for being. Churches have closed or been closed because they (or someone else) couldn't justify their continuing existence. But smaller churches that are committed to their mission will find some way to live. To paraphrase Jesus, churches that seek merely to survive will lose their lives, but those who give themselves away in mission will find life.

On a pragmatic level, whether smaller churches live or die may depend on whether the surrounding community supports them, ignores them, or is hostile to them. God's directive to ancient Israel when it went into exile addresses the relationship between today's churches and their communities: "But seek the welfare of the city where I have sent you into exile, and pray to the Lord on its behalf, for in its welfare you will find your welfare" (Jer. 29:7). Churches that effectively reach out to serve generally attract new members and financial support. Communities that value a church will likely help it survive.

2 . *People want to make a difference.*

A woman, walking on a beach early one morning noticed an older woman picking up starfish that had washed up during the night and returning them to the sea. The younger woman asked what she was doing. The older woman explained that the starfish would die if they remained stranded. "But there are millions of starfish on the beach, how can your efforts make any difference?" countered the younger woman. After returning one more starfish to safety, the older woman said, "But at least I can save this one."

If we thought of the millions of Mexican children who are still hungry and the other hungry billions elsewhere, we might say, "Why bother?" But when we think of the several hundred children who are getting a nutritious meal and vitamin pill every school day because of our church, we know that we are making a difference, and that makes a difference to us. Other people are attracted to mission who know they can make a difference through the difference we are making.

3. *Authentic mission grows out of a church's history, unique character, and context.*

Smaller churches find meaning in their history. The symbols and stories of who they were help a church identify who they are. Carl Dudley wrote: "Memory is the strongest motive for ministry in the small cell of caring Christians."[5] A church's memory will help shape its character and help it determine what it values enough to act on. Identify the significant precedents in your history and your church can be motivated to act in similar ways.

My grandmother used to look around her big table at large family gatherings and say: "Not a shabby one in the bunch." That saying, still quoted by the Ray clan, has helped shape our character and make us a service-minded family. Your church's most authentic and sustaining mission will grow out of its character.

Context is the third ingredient in shaping a church's mission. Appropriate mission needs to fit the current situation and present needs. Red Oak organized to put coats on the children shivering their way through their Iowa winters. Then they began teaching the children's parents to speak English. Fit your mission to your situation.

4. *People have to "feel" the need.*

People in smaller churches are more likely to respond to what has touched them. Surveys, statistics, and impassioned sermons don't influence as much as direct experience. Bill Briggs, pastor of a tiny New Hampshire church in a tiny town, built that church's extraordinary mission efforts around this principle. He took people on trips, put people into particular situations, arranged for people to meet people in need. His people were then eager to act in order to alleviate the need they had felt. This approach inspired the

Shrewsbury, Vermont, mission trip to Rwanda. This is why the San Rafael church recruits people to go on retreat to Mexico and prepares a monthly meal at a neighboring homeless program.

5. *Smaller church mission needs to be hands-on, person-to-person.*

   If I carefully explain the systemic nature of injustice in the international economic alliances, people will either yawn or argue with me. If I invite them to a meeting to strategize a response to a need, they will probably be busy doing something else. But if I put a name and a face on a systemic problem, they will act. Warwick would not have raised three thousand dollars to combat world hunger, but they were happy to help when it was Steve's Heifer Project stipend they were supporting. Shrewsbury would not have raised several thousand dollars for just any school somewhere in Africa, but they did so for the school they were helping build for their partner church in Rwanda. Epiphany church in St. Louis has its people engaged in extensive, extraordinary mission because it's all hands-on, person-to-person.

6. *Smaller church mission is integral to the whole life of the church.*

   When it works as it should, smaller church mission is inspired through worship, informed through Christian education, and grows out of its care for one another. Mission is not an activity conducted by an ad hoc group of activists. Work to have mission be intrinsic to the whole life and all the people of your church. A church's mission is the fruit of all it believes.

7. *Smaller churches are better at doing mission than planning it.*

   People who like or don't mind bureaucracy will likely gravitate to a larger church. People who abhor it will enjoy a smaller one. Feasibility studies and long-range planning don't cut it for these people. If extensive research and planning needs to be done (and it often does) find a policy wonk or two to do it on behalf of the whole. Smaller churches prefer following the organizational principle of KISS (Keep It Simple, Stupid). It's the leaders' job to see a need, envision possible solutions, encourage the input of others, and then organize the church body to do what it feels called to do. Don't let your mission efforts get too complex.

8. *More gets done when you're having fun.*

The need may be serious and the work hard, but when the approach is creative and people enjoy being together, more gets done, a greater difference is made, and more people come back for the second effort. Did any group have more fun than the Shrewsbury mission committee, whose "Cow Flop Drop" raised fifteen hundred dollars for hunger programs as part of its Food Day? (Recipe for a Cow Flop Drop: A small field is divided into many squares; people purchase squares; a well-fed cow is released into the field; the person "owning" the square where the cow first flops or drops a "meadow muffin" wins first prize. The second, third, and fourth flops garner second, third, and fourth prizes.) When a leader discerns what a congregation enjoys, the germ of a mission effort can probably be discovered therein. As Jesus might have said: "Joyful are those who do good while having a little fun."

9. *Love without limits.*

More often than I want to remember, I've heard church people say they should take care of their own first. That's a natural reaction, but not a faithful one—particularly for those living in the most advantaged nation on earth. Jesus loudly and clearly said that all people everywhere are our neighbors. To think globally and act locally can be effective, but it's even more faithful to think globally and act globally as well as locally. Churches should be encouraged to balance their local and global mission commitments.

10. *Smart mission is both smart and faithful.*

Out of the thousands of well-meaning things a church can commit to, what is the smart and faithful mission? Heifer Project International has built its outstanding self-help program around the folk adage "give a person a fish and you feed him for a day, teach him to fish and you feed him for a lifetime." Habitat for Humanity doesn't just give people a voucher for a night's lodging. It involves them in building their own permanent home. That's smart mission.

A magazine ad asks me to "adopt" a beautiful big-eyed child somewhere in the world by sending a certain amount of money every month. It doesn't tell me what really happens to the money I send or how much is siphoned off to pay for the ad and salaries for the organization's staff. That kind of support may be considered mission, but I wouldn't call it smart mission. But what if every single dollar I give buys nothing but nutritious food for a hungry child in a school where the child is learning to read and write so that she or he can be self-supporting someday? What if a little church persuades friends and neighbors and strangers to also contribute generously to feeding truly hungry school children? That's smart mission.

Smaller churches have too few resources to squander them on appeals to the heart that are not also "smart." Pick your projects thoughtfully and design them strategically so that you get maximum benefit from your investment of time and money and accomplish the greatest good.

Deciding What to Do and Gearing Up to Do It

A smaller church can do more than most would imagine. For many examples of the mission that other congregations have engaged in and for suggestions for organizing for your own mission, get the book *Acting on Your Faith: Congregations Making a Difference* by Victor N. Claman and David E. Butler. It has seventy stories of what other churches have done (with photos), along with suggestions for identifying and developing your own mission venture. Here's a sampling of what other, smaller churches have done:

- Seventh Day Adventist Church, Barberton, Ohio, 130 members, started the New Start Bakery as part of their community center. Some bread is sold to help support the center, some is used for school lunches, and some is given away.

- Case Community United Methodist Church, Detroit, Michigan, 140 members, is focused on the inner-city poor and homeless, serving three thousand meals a week, offering a free medical clinic, operating a drop-in center for homeless people and another for developmentally disabled, and so on.
- Bethany Presbyterian Church, Cleveland, Ohio, seventy-five members, operates a half-day, three-day-a-week preschool for thirty-five families and charges each one two dollars a day.
- Our Redeemer Lutheran Church, Livingston, California, eighty-five members, acquired seven acres to be farmed on a cooperative basis by migrant farmers.
- Santa Fe Episcopal Church, San Antonio, Texas, a seventy-five-family Anglican church in a Mexican-American neighborhood, was on the verge of closing. It called a Hispanic priest and began a variety of social programs that have, as a result, revived the church.
- Community Church, Franconia, New Hampshire, one hundred members, formed a partnership with a village in Honduras and has been sending mission teams to do development work since 1985. These teams work in the medical clinic started by the church, have developed a water system, and are working on agricultural programs. This is only one of several of their outreach efforts.[6]

As you think about getting started or adding to your mission commitment, you have some choices to make.

- What will fit the history, character, and context of your church? What kinds of projects fit the priorities and experience of your people? (The San Rafael church had a real concern for children and an interest in Mexico, so that's the direction they went in.)
- Is your church oriented toward social justice issues, is it likely to respond to an educational or development concern, or does it have an evangelistic concern?

- Do you want to work at the charitable level, the development level, or the social-change level?
- Or perhaps there's a pressing need staring your people in the face that they must respond to?

Rather than trying to start several projects, pick one to rally around. Focus on it and expect that it will evolve into other involvements.

Smaller churches do best with the KISS (simplicity) approach, yet being faithful and effective in mission requires creative imagination, discernment, and appropriate planning. After looking at a wide variety of planning tools, I recommend the two that follow. Decide which best fits you or mix and match. Both will fit the uniqueness of a smaller church and should lead it to a new and wonderful vision for mission.

Twelve-Step Planning Process

This process takes seriously a church's uniqueness and how it understands "mission." It uses the gifts that are already present in a church and targets specific needs and opportunities. It can be used by the whole church (sometimes working in smaller groups, perhaps at a retreat), a mission committee, the church's official board, a task force, or an ad hoc group. Use the process over a couple of intensive evenings, a day, or a weekend. Have someone experienced in group-process guide your group. Use lots of newsprint so that you can keep track of your work. Supply lots of good food to keep people well fueled for the task.

1. Begin with some community-building around the question: What are your hopes and fears for our church and community? Or, if Jesus were to visit our community, what local or global situations or conditions would alarm or intrigue him, and what would he want to do in response?

2. Lead the group in a communal Bible study on one or two of the following texts. Choose the one(s) that you find most provocative and pertinent: Amos 5:21–24; Matthew 5:43–47; Luke 4:16–21; Luke 10:25–37; Ephesians 2:13–15.

Discuss these questions in response to the text:

- In general, what might God be saying through this passage?
- Through this passage, what might God be saying to us in this particular time and place?
- If our church was to stake its life on this passage, what would we do and how would we do it?

(Without getting bogged down or hurrying, work your way through the following steps and questions, being honest and creative.)

3. What is your church's present understanding of mission? How would you or they define it? Does this understanding of mission fit the scripture you studied?

4. What does your church see as the key reasons for its existence? Or, what is its mission or calling as a church? Or, what does it believe and how does it act on its beliefs? Consider both your history and your present convictions.

5. Make a list of the ways that your church is now engaged in mission? Is there rhyme or reason to it? Is it balanced? All local? All global? Does it involve more than giving money?

6. What is unique about your church—its history, personality, style, context, and resources?

7. Answer and discuss the following four questions:

- What does your church do really well?
- What special talents and resources are present in your midst?
- What issues, needs, persons do your people already care deeply about?
- What issues and needs do your people have personal experience with?

8. *(Do the following in groups of no more than ten people. Respond in brainstorming fashion—without stopping to evaluate.)* List on newsprint up to fifteen or even twenty specific needs and opportunities that surround your church. *(Decide how large a*

geographic area you want to consider.) Putting numbers in the margin, arrange them in order from the most to the least important. *(Combine those that are naturally related.)* If you've been in more than one group, report back to the whole group.

9. As you begin to consider how you might reach out in mission, list the limiting factors or handicaps you'll need to keep in mind?

10. What resources—both physical and human, both in and outside the church—are available to you that might be used as you reach out in mission?

11. Learning from all that you've identified and decided:

   - What specific action are you most excited about and feel called to do?
   - How will you enlist others (your whole church?) to work with you?
   - Specifically how will you do it? What steps will you take?
   - What will it cost? Where will those resources come from?
   - Who will do it?
   - What help do you need (from other faith communities, the community, social services, your denomination)?
   - How soon can you start? What happens then and after that?
   - Who will call you together and keep you on track as you proceed and when will you meet next?

12. With all the gusto you have left, hold hands, sing the doxology or some exuberant song, pray, eat the rest of the food, and go home with God's blessing.

Bill Briggs's Four-Stage Process

Here is a second, effective method of moving a smaller church into mission. Bill Briggs, battered and bruised after difficult ministries in difficult times in Chicago and Buffalo, retreated in 1972 to the tiny

Franconia Community Church (twelve active members) in Franconia, New Hampshire (population 800). It was a church of older members who were despairing about their future. Using the following simple process, the church came alive through its extraordinary mission ventures. Bill tells the story in a little, exciting book (out of print), *Faith through Works*. Here is their simple and effective four-stage process:

Core Group ➤ Experiencing ➤ Reflecting ➤ Responding

First, out of the church, develop a core group of people who really care about one another. The core group gets to know and love one another as they engage in disciplined prayer and mission-oriented Bible study. When they are a cohesive and caring group, it's time for experiencing.

The second stage is for the core group to experience a need in this world. One core group of four people helped deliver a bus to a Catholic mission in Guatemala. Another visited a faith community in Washington, D.C., that was engaged in social ministries. A third visited a self-help, poor-people's project in Maine. It's important that the core group personally experience real need so that their subsequent action is a passionate and compassionate response and not a vague and half-hearted action.

The third stage is to come back and come together for "real thinking" and "real praying," for reflecting on what they've experienced and what a faithful and effective response could be. Real thinking looks back to the source of the need or problem and ahead to the nature and consequences of possible action. During this stage, the core group meets for a stream-of-consciousness kind of brainstorming in which every person suggests every action that comes to mind, often in response to what others have brainstormed. Real praying opens the group to God's revealing and seeks the courage to respond to God's leading.

The fourth stage is responding with appropriate and faithful action. The core group uses three criteria for discerning the right action:

- Is it appropriate to the scriptures?
- Is it appropriate for the receiver of the action?
- Is it appropriate for the core group and church?

When they're sure the criteria have been met, they're ready to come to the church members, seeking not its permission or money but its blessing. With the congregation's blessing and the participation of many, the mission is carried out. As a result, out of completed missions, new core groups were born and new mission ventures evolved.[7]

Using the simple process, a number of creative projects emerged. The Noah's Ark Craft Cooperative provided a needed outlet for area craftspeople and raised money for other mission efforts. The four retired women who had gone to Guatemala returned and told their story. A 6.2-mile road-race (that became an annual event) was organized to raise money to support a land reform program in Guatemala, which led to purchasing and delivering a van to the mission in Guatemala. A wood co-op was established to help poor people procure their winter firewood. A nursing home ministry was established at the Willows Nursing Home. One person was so passionately concerned about the tragic plight of Southeast Asian boat people after the Vietnam War that a refugee task force was established, ultimately resulting in bringing many refugees to a new life in New Hampshire. Like an unstoppable chain reaction, one mission project after another happened and met a variety of needs. And a dying, despairing rural church found its avenue to new life through dynamic mission.

An alternative to these thoughtful processes is the way it worked at Church of the Savior in Washington, D.C. During the sharing time in their worship, it was the custom that, if a person felt a strong call to a new mission venture, that person would stand and articulate the call. If one or two or more responded positively to the call and offered to help, the church blessed them and encouraged them to develop the new mission. If no one responded, it was assumed that the time wasn't right and the call was moved to the back burner to simmer for a while longer.

Twice I've been blessed with churches that came to the realistic assessment that they could do just about anything they felt called to do. I pray your church will come to the same amazing conviction. Once it believes that, it will act accordingly and change its world. An anonymous axiom says:

A vision without a task is a dream;
A task without a vision is drudgery;
A vision and a task is the hope of the world.
A church with a vision and a task will never die.

Questions

1. What is your church's history and understanding of mission?
2. What does your church do beyond the doors of your building on behalf of God's universal community?
3. Can you identify a nagging or pressing mission need you would like to act on?

Suggestion

Implement one of the processes described here and see where it leads.

chapter eight

Raising Morale, Elevating the Spirit

All of us at Christ Church, Island Pond, are conscious of belonging to a small parish on the virtual edge of nowhere. Half of us are a good deal past what is commonly, if erroneously, referred to as "the prime of life." The resulting self-image is not enhanced by the memory that we were a thriving and "important" parish only a generation ago.

—Garret Keizer, A *Dresser of Sycamore Trees*

As the internal-combustion engine runs on gasoline, so the person runs on self-esteem: if he is full of it, he is good for a long run; if he is partly filled, he will soon need to be refueled; and if he is empty, he will come to a stop.

—Unknown

CHRIST CHURCH IN ISLAND POND, in rural northeast Vermont is not unusual. It's not big or splashy. By the world's standard, momentous things don't happen there. It would be reasonable and expected that this church feels insignificant, perhaps inadequate. However, when a church's self-esteem and morale are run down or fully depleted, it should and can do the things that will fill its tank.

The largest problem facing smaller churches is not a shortage of people or money. Instead, their most dominating and debilitating problem is more often low morale, resulting in negative self-esteem. This has become patently clear to me as I've been with smaller churches and their leaders from coast to coast for three decades. This sense of inferiority is often revealed in how they describe themselves:

- We're *just* a little church.
- I'm *just* a small church pastor.
- We *only* have thirty in worship and twenty in Sunday school.
- We're small now, *but* our pews used to be full.
- We *can't* afford a full-time pastor.

Words like "just," "only," "but," and "can't" communicate feelings of inadequacy. This sense of inadequacy is a cancer that often erodes how smaller churches see their place in the world and how they think and act, worship and work. Such churches think they're too insignificant to do the things "real" churches do: to attract others, to play a positive role in their communities and world, or to have a promising future. Feelings of inadequacy, insignificance, and insufficiency lead them to substitute institutional survival for faithful ministry and mission. They cease being generous with time and money. They resort to blaming and bickering. Despair replaces hope. Good enough replaces a pursuit of excellence.

This shouldn't be and doesn't have to be the way it is in smaller churches. The Bible gives no merit to size alone. Faith communities in the Bible and throughout history have been mostly small. Yet, historically, they have been plenty big enough to be spirited, thriving communities of faith and action. If a church feels worthy, legitimate, confident, and able, it is likely to be a delightful community in which to be. It will probably be attractive to others and be able to do just about anything it sets its mind to.

Self-image is absolutely critical because it determines everything else. This is why building self-esteem and morale has been central to everything I say and do in ministry. It makes all the difference and should be central to the ministry of every leader in smaller churches.

A church's sense of self-worth and morale determine:

- How much the members invest of themselves
- How generous they are with their resources
- How open they are to outsiders

- How embracing they are of change
- How committed they are to their mission in God's world
- How much fun they have
- How easily and quickly they resolve their conflicts
- How resolute they are in finding solutions to any problem
- How hopeful they are about the future

What the psalmist prayed, in regard to humans, might also be prayed in regard to churches: "What are human beings [churches] that you are mindful of them . . . ? Yet you have made them a little lower than God, and crowned them with glory and honor. You have given them dominion over the works of your hands" (Ps. 8:4–6). A smaller church that believes it is a recipient of God's glory and honor can live fully as a community of God with all that that encompasses and implies.

Smaller churches feel illegitimate and inadequate for several reasons. First and most important is the power of sizeism (see the Introduction). Kirkpatrick Sale graphically makes the point:

> It has become part of the American character not only to accept bigness but actually to admire, respect, love at times even worship bigness. Size is the measure of excellence: in cars, tomatoes, cigarettes, houses, breasts, audiences, salaries, freeways, skyscrapers, muscles, children, penises, and fish. . . . Or as one nineteenth-century German journalist summed it up: "To say that something is large, massive, gigantic, is in America not a mere statement of fact but the highest commendation."[1]

Ample-to-massive size is admired, respected, even loved in the church as well as the world. Not to be large in our society is a sign of inadequacy; not to lust after growth is a sign of folly or futility.

Secondly, smaller churches despair over failure. For example, if they lose their present pastor or a prospective pastor to a church that can pay a higher salary, or if they remember when their sparsely filled pews and the Sunday-school rooms were once full, or if they can't meet their denomination's financial goals, or if a young family leaves to join the full-service church up the street, they will begin to obsess about whether it was their fault. Despair over past and present failure leads to expectations of continuing failure, which leads to an ongoing sense of failure, which too often leads to closure. Church meetings and after church conversation are confined to wrestling with real and perceived problems, rather than plotting greater faithfulness.

Other factors that diminish or deplete a smaller church's self-esteem and morale are: loss of or lack of capable and caring leaders, frequent pastoral changes or loss of a beloved pastor with questionable prospects for a suitable replacement, spiritless worship, a few negative or hostile members or a divided membership, financial crisis, failure to have some good-time events, barely enough money for basic needs with no money for things that would enhance their life.

Sometimes, it's not what's happening in church but what's going on outside of church that erodes a church's self-esteem and morale. Crisis or despair within people's personal lives or the life of the surrounding community or region can draw down the sense of worth and energy within a church. The exodus of young people and young adults for greener pastures, the closing of a local company or industry, or even the loss of the local high school to consolidation can breed despair in a church.

Finally, the experience of not measuring up depletes a congregation's energy and diminishes its experience of community. Members forget they are part of a gifted church, that they enjoy (or used to enjoy) one another, and that their church gives meaning to their lives. Most importantly, they forget that they are called to make and are capable of making a lifesaving difference right where they are. When they lose the joy of the ministry that happens among them and lose their sense of mission or belief that they can change the world, they become a hollow shell of what they once were and have no vision of what they might be.

The bad news is that poor self-esteem and low morale are endemic in smaller churches. The good news is that, no matter how poor and low they are, self-esteem and morale can be elevated and can often be raised significantly. The required ingredients for building a smaller church's self-worth and self-confidence are these:

- At least one caring and capable leader (lay or pastoral)
- Openness to thinking and acting a little differently
- Awareness of which areas of church life need bolstering or enhancing
- Some strategies for changing the way folks feel about their church

"If it ain't broke, don't fix it." This common and catchy phrase is of limited value. If something is not broken, why not build on it? Sometimes it's not easy to tell if something is broken or not. If it is broken, it may not be fixable. If it is broken, some parts and tools are probably required to fix it. And, if it's broken, how can you fix it so that it isn't likely to break again? The Church Morale Inventory (see Resources, page 272) is a diagnostic tool for determining what in your church might be broken and what's perfectly fine. I know from experience that each area of church life is either improvable or fixable. I also know that the things that "ain't broke" should be celebrated and enhanced.

I first published the Church Morale Inventory two decades ago and have used it in many consultations and workshops. Others have used it with minor modifications. The updated inventory could be used by any church but is particularly useful with smaller churches. It could be used by a church's leadership, but, the more people who fill it out, talk about it, and use it as a springboard, the better.

It would be a helpful resource for a one-day or overnight retreat. Try to have an outside leader who understands churches and group process administer the inventory and lead the analysis and planning that should follow it. Try to have those present to whom the church defers before ideas are tried or actions taken. Use it in a warm and friendly setting where there will not be frequent interruptions. Provide an inventory sheet and pencil for each person and some newsprint and markers for the discussion that should follow. Allow at least two hours for completing the inventory, for discussing it, and for strategizing. Completion of the inventory by a good cross-section of the church will identify particular areas of church life needing attention. Discussion will help people see that others may perceive their church differently than they do.

The following worship or meditation will prepare your people to get the full benefit from the inventory. Begin with a refreshment and conversation time (15–30 minutes). Sit in a circle or around a square of tables. Sing a song like "This Little Light of Mine," "We Are the Church," "'Tis a Gift to Be Simple," "Part of the Family," or "Amazing Grace." Pray for the fruitful presence of the Holy Spirit in your work together. Hand out a printed copy of one or both of the following scriptures for a brief Bible study:

- Deuteronomy 30:15–20. Ask: What are the alternatives Moses puts before the people and what are the alternatives before your people? Ask how it would be different if your people were to really "choose life." And what if they don't? Ask what changes would be required of them if they were truly open to choosing life.

- Luke 12:32–37. Ask your people to guess why Jesus taught this. Ask what fears exist among your people. Ask what Jesus is requiring of his hearers. Ask specifically what it would mean for your people to be "dressed for action," or what would they need to be doing differently.

Distribute the inventories. If tables aren't available, provide something for them to write on. Ask people to not confer while they're filling them out. Emphasize that there are no right or wrong answers and that they are to answer from their own point of view, not the way they believe others feel. Remind them to complete the two questions at the end of the sheet.

Once people have filled out the inventory and scored it, take a short break and then discuss it. If you have more than twenty people, divide into groups of about ten. Compare findings. Determine where there was unanimity and where you disagreed. Seek agreement on the four strongest and four weakest areas of church morale. Brainstorm one or two fairly simple strategies that would address each of the four areas of weakness and build on each of the four areas of strength.

If you've been working in two or more groups, come back together and share findings. Determine which one weakness particularly needs addressing and decide on at least one doable strategy for doing so—

what will be done, by whom, and when. From the other proposed strategies, pick at least three (related to weaknesses or strengths) that can be accomplished and determine what will be done, by whom, and when. Are there other appropriate groups in the church to whom other findings can be delegated? At the end of the session, invite the group to offer multiple prayers of thanksgiving, sing a song, finish the refreshments, and then go home.

There is no category in this inventory around which a church could not take some positive action. Any positive action, no matter how small or merely symbolic, can begin promoting a spirit of movement and hope. Don't commit to more than you can reasonably do. But don't commit to any less than you can reasonably do. Unless your church is in severe crisis, let the first strategies you pursue be ones that have a high probability of success.

A Twelve-Step Program for Church Renewal

You probably know one or more people who are involved in a twelve-step program that seeks to bring lasting change and healing, such as Alcoholics Anonymous or Narcotics Anonymous. The following is a twelve-step program that is guaranteed to renew a church that follows it "religiously." A church that commits to this program will soon have significantly higher morale. It will be more effective and faithful in what it does. There is a high probability that following these steps will attract new people to your church, provide more money for your ministry and mission, and cause the community to wonder what's come over your church. It could be used over a twelve-week period, but twelve months is more realistic and would have more substantive and longer-lasting results. A church or at least its leadership should commit to following this program and should designate a three-to-five member task group to implement and monitor the program.

Twelve Steps

1. Use the Church Morale Inventory with as many of your church members as possible and follow the process that accompanies it. Ask those present to do two things

throughout the next year. First, ask them to commit personally to work at one or two strategies for raising church morale.
Second, ask them to pray regularly for one another and for
their church.

2. Plan one sure-fire program, event, strategy, or change; make
   sure it succeeds; celebrate it; and then plan a second, then a
   third.

3. Ask someone from your denomination, a neighboring church,
   or a counseling agency to spend one or more sessions with
   your church doing some basic leadership training or development.

4. Since worship is or ought to be the heart and soul of your
   church, take steps to make your worship more spirited, more
   faithful, more meaningful, and more enjoyable. Sing more
   favorite hymns; make new, beautiful banners; have shorter,
   more involving sermons; introduce a worship innovation for
   a trial period; pray for the effectiveness of your worship; read
   and utilize the book, *Wonderful Worship in Smaller Churches.*

5. Take at least two concrete steps to make being together more
   pleasurable—such as having refreshments at every gathering,
   paint the room, get more comfortable furnishings, have a
   mandatory cut-off time for church meetings, or whatever else
   you can imagine.

6. Hold an all-church potluck dinner. For the program, ask
   people to list on newsprint every success from the last two
   years of church life and list twenty strengths of your church.
   Post these lists where others can see them for a few weeks and
   print them in your newsletter or bulletin.

7. Capitalize on one or more of the strengths on your list. For
   example, if you have charming children, celebrate them and
   involve them more in church life; if you have a beautiful
   building, have postcards made of it.

8. Identify one significant but solvable problem; brainstorm
   every conceivable strategy for addressing it; pick one or two
   strategies and get key persons to accept responsibility for

implementing the strategy; work the strategy; celebrate and evaluate what happened; and consider working on a second problem.

9. Pick one significant, new mission project (of the hands-on variety) that your church will enjoy doing together and do it.

10. Implement one interior and one exterior spruce-up or fix-it project as soon as you can schedule it. Encourage your people to do this together.

11. Over the time of this program, ask everyone in your church to give ten percent more money to the church. The money should not be used for paying routine bills. Rather, involve the church in identifying one or more uses of the extra money that they will feel good about. Some will make this additional ten percent a permanent increase.

12. At the end of the twelve weeks or months, plan an extravagant gala celebration of your twelve-step renewal program. Decorate the church. Ask people to dress up. Have a meal cooked by your best cooks or, even better, have it catered. Invite the whole church, including the kids. Invite the mayor and the news media. Show pictures that were taken throughout the process. Invite people to share memories and stories and learnings.

Beyond leading your church to work on measures to elevate their morale, what can you personally do if you are the pastoral or lay leader? G. Douglass Lewis, president of Wesley Theological Seminary and a former mentor of mine, in his book on leadership and ministry, names four simple rules for energizing or building the morale of others.[2]

1. Remember that every person wants to do something significant with his or her life and is constantly looking for ways to give expression to that desire. Take each person seriously and help him or her decide how to pursue that quest.

2. Focus on a person's strengths. It's usually easy to identify what we can't do or aren't good at. Focusing on these negatives is

debilitating for most people. Instead, help persons identify
and apply their strengths in the ministry and mission of the
church. This will release far more energy than one might
imagine.

3. Help people feel included. At some level, every person yearns
to be in community. Do what you need to do to make your
church more inclusive and less exclusive. Don't let anyone in
your midst feel that they don't matter.

4. Say thanks! Say thanks! Say thanks! Noticing and affirming
even the smallest and most insignificant of contributions will
energize and build the self-esteem and morale of your people.
As an example, in Shrewsbury, Emmetsburg, and San Rafael,
"Feather-in-the-Hat" awards were given at each annual
meeting to those who were unsung heroes or performed
exemplary service in the life of their church. Each recipient
got a crazy hat with a colorful feather, a flowery speech in
their honor, a round of applause, and their picture taken. One
of our "saints" in Emmetsburg was so proud of her hat that
her family placed it on her casket at her funeral.

No number of people or amount of money can compensate for a
church's collective lack of self-worth and self-confidence. However, a
church that feels it can climb any mountain and meet any challenge
will find a way to do so. I urge leaders of smaller churches to put
building church self-esteem and morale at the top of their "To Do"
list and keep it there.

This story illustrates the energizing power of high morale. A foreign traveler came to Chartres, France, to see the cathedral that was
under construction. He arrived at the end of the work day and entered the church as workers were preparing to leave. He asked one
dust-covered worker what his job was. The worker said he was a stone-
mason who spent his day carving stone. He spoke with a glassblower
who said he spent all day, every day, making slabs of colored glass. A
third workman wearily identified himself as a blacksmith who pounded
iron for a living. The traveler worked his way to the back of the new
cathedral and met an elderly woman who was sweeping up stone chips,

wood shavings, and glass shards from the day's work. He asked her what she was doing. She paused, leaned on her broom, looked up into the high arches, and replied, "Me? I'm building a cathedral for the Glory of Almighty God." When the people of smaller churches feel the same way, they will work with great pride and faithfulness and the result will be a spiritual cathedral that is beyond size.

Questions

1. How did you feel when you got up this morning and how did that affect the experience and productivity of your day?
2. How would you assess the self-esteem and morale of your congregation? What do you think accounts for it being high, or low, or in between?

Suggestions

1. Use the Church Morale Inventory with as many people as you can bring together.
2. Try to interest your church leadership in the Twelve-Step Program for Church Renewal or some variation of it.

chapter nine

Growth by Adoption

Welcome is one of the signs that a community is alive. . . . A community which refuses to welcome—whether through fear, weariness, insecurity, a desire to cling to comfort, or just because it is fed up with visitors—is dying spiritually.

—Jean Vanier, *Community and Growth*

The church is perhaps one of the few places left where we can meet people who are different than we are but with whom we can form a larger family.

—Henri J. M. Nouwen, *Reaching Out*

To GROW OR NOT TO GROW? That is the question, the issue, and the problem. Since it is almost impossible to maintain the status quo, churches inevitably decline or grow. If they decline without remission, they eventually die. If they grow without ceasing, they cease being a smaller church or community of faith and may become an ungainly religious institution. One who has read this far might think I am luke-warm to having smaller churches grow. After all, I published a book titled *Small Churches Are the Right Size*. Doesn't that imply that larger churches are not the right size? And I've made "church" and "community" synonymous and suggested that too many people make genuine community difficult, if not impossible. However, I believe the question is not whether, but how and why we seek growth.

Authorities don't agree with each other. C. Peter Wagner, a founder of the church-growth movement, wrote: "But whether a church is large or small, it should be a growing church. . . . If smaller churches are growing they eventually will become large churches."[1]

Carl Dudley wrote: "Most small churches have already grown much bigger than they 'ought to be.'"[2] For Dudley, the defining quality of smaller churches is the real relationships that exist between most or all the people, and too many people diminish the relational nature of the church.

Lyle Schaller, who has written more about congregational life than anyone, wrote: "The large congregation runs against the laws of nature . . . the small-membership church is consistent with the natural order of creation."[3] Nevertheless, he later wrote about how to grow smaller churches into larger churches.

Who's right? To grow or not to grow? If not, why not? If so, why and how?

There are many pressures on smaller churches to grow. Since society equates quality and quantity, a "good" church should be a growing church— shouldn't it? The rising costs of being a church necessitate more people to pay the bills. Pastors want their churches to grow in response to the gospel so that they can feel more successful and be better paid. Most members of smaller churches would like to grow so that there will be more people to share the work and financial burden, and they, too, would like to feel their church is being successful. Mainline denominations want their churches to grow to halt their denominational decline. All denominations want their churches to grow for reasons of viability, revenue, status, effectiveness, and faithfulness. More important than all of these reasons, Christ gave us good news to share and the marching orders to baptize and make disciples.

Some smaller churches are growing in size. Some are growing in ways other than in size. Some are trying to grow larger without obvious results. And some appear not to be trying. Of those not getting larger, some are not growing because of choices they've made and some because the odds against their growth are overwhelming. There are at least a baker's dozen of reasons why many smaller churches find numerical growth difficult, if not impossible:

1. A principal reason many smaller churches don't grow is their sense of inferiority. It's human nature to hide that about which we are embarrassed or ashamed. The object of

embarrassment or shame might be their paltry numbers, the shabbiness of the building, the quality of leadership, the absence of spirit, or something else.

2. For other smaller churches, their present size feels natural and "right" and works for them. They've found a way to cover the costs. They have no size-related inferiority complex. They have a sense of equilibrium and don't want to jeopardize that. There's nothing driving them to grow.

3. People fear loss of intimacy. Not only are they not motivated to grow, they resist it. With a strong sense of "family," the people feel growth would dilute or destroy their closeness.

4. Those who control the church fear new members would dilute their power and influence. Some smaller churches are more like fiefdoms than communities.

5. Some smaller churches don't grow because newcomers might be different and disrupt the homogeneity in class, culture, generation, or conviction. Newcomers might bring new ways and want a different kind of church. This will be particularly true if the church feels like a safe enclave in a hostile or alien context. A cold shoulder is an effective strategy to keep out the unwanted.

6. Many smaller churches don't grow because there are limited opportunities for growth. When some churches take a census of those who've died, gone into a nursing home, moved away, or dropped out in the last year, it's a monumental feat just to replace those who've been lost. Even if these churches aggressively and successfully reach out, it may appear they're standing still. Many smaller churches in rural areas, changing inner-city neighborhoods, and declining regions of the country have little chance of replacing a population that has migrated elsewhere. Some smaller churches are in heavily over-churched communities or in places where there are few or no prospects for their kind of church. Many smaller churches deserve commendation, not condemnation, for their efforts to stem the ebbing tide.

7. Some churches simply aren't offering what people are looking for—hospitality and community, spiritual nurturing, meaningful worship, an opportunity to make a difference in community and world, social opportunities, a place to belong. Some churches aren't speaking the cultural or lifestyle language that potential members speak. This is particularly true of churches populated mostly by older people who don't know how or can't talk the language and address the needs of younger people.

8. Many churches offer organizational membership rather than personal meaning. Few people want to join one more organization. Many are looking for lasting good news, light to light their living, and warmth in a cold world.

9. Some dynamic smaller churches haven't grown because many prospects are intrigued by their passionate commitment to social justice and serious discipleship but are afraid of the serious commitment that is expected.

10. Many don't know how to attract new people. No one has helped them identify the effective outreach strategies that would attract and hold new members for the church family.

11. Many have wanted to grow but haven't because they've desired growth for the wrong reasons. Their efforts to attract people to staff their committees, help pay the bills, teach Sunday school, and take out the garbage have repelled, not attracted, folks.

12. Some smaller churches attract many newcomers but fail to do the hard work of assimilating them while retaining their old-timers. The church of the open door is often the church of the revolving door.

13. Finally, their whole focus and energy has been poured into the struggle to simply survive.

Do any of these descriptions fit your congregation and context?

Each of the four churches I've pastored had been in decline for decades. Each stemmed the bleeding and grew slowly and steadily, attracting and incorporating a wide variety of people. Many, if not most, smaller churches could do the same. I believe in and practice helping churches grow but for the right reasons. My goals are not to help the church grow to a "respectable" size, not to lure hands to keep the ship afloat, and not to feather my own nest. Right and faithful reasons for reaching out to seekers and searchers are:

- To share the good news of the Christian faith and the hospitality of Christian community
- To provide love for the loveless, food for the hungry, home for the homeless, and wisdom for the clueless
- To enlist colleagues and disciples for the mission of building God's community
- After these first three, to keep the church body strong and healthy

Together, these comprise the purpose of evangelism. They are the only legitimate reasons for pursuing church growth. While the difference may appear subtle, I'm much more interested in "evangelism" (or sharing good news) and outreach (or one beggar telling others where food has been found) than I am in church growth (adding bodies) for the purpose of perpetuating or enlarging the institution. Evangelism and outreach strategies will bear more and longer-lasting fruit than church growth strategies.

Growth in numbers is only one form of church growth. Loren Mead, one of the wisest students of the church, says there are four ways churches grow, not just one. While these may be related they are different, with different emphases and different objectives. The first, most obvious, and most seductive is numerical growth. Many churches are working hard on this one. There are legitimate and illegitimate reasons for pursuing this kind of growth.

The second type of church growth is maturational growth. Some churches—for good reasons—cannot grow in size, but all can grow in maturity. We all can think of tragically immature persons, as we confess to a little immaturity of our own. Maturational growth means growth in spiritual sensitivity and mature faithfulness, growth in the ability to nurture faithfulness in others and to be nurtured. Living in a secular world, maturational growth is crucial and undergirds other kinds of growth.

Organic growth is growth in the ability of the church to function and sustain itself as a faith community. As human organizations, some churches are healthy, effective, and viable, and some aren't. Without attention to the church's organic growth, numerical growth will be sporadic, at best, maturational growth won't be sustained, growth in mission will founder.

The fourth type of church growth is incarnational or missional growth. This is growth in the church's capacity to apply what it believes out in the real world beyond the doors of the church. A church needs to attend to each of these four types of church-growth in order to be faithful and effective, in the same way that people need to eat from the four food groups in order to be healthy and vital. Sustained numerical growth results from and necessitates maturational, organic, and incarnational growth. Much of this book addresses maturational, organic, and incarnational growth. However, the focus in the next few pages is numerical. [4]

The Pentecost story, as illustrated in Acts 2:40–47, provides us with both a larger-church and a smaller-church model for how to help churches grow numerically. According to the text, on that day a vast crowd was attracted, Peter preached a spellbinding sermon, and three thousand people were converted and became the core of the fledgling Christian Church. This mass-appeal model is utilized by larger churches. The text then implies that these people were divided into smaller house churches in which "many wonders and signs" were done and people shared life in common and saw that no one was in need. While they still went to the temple, the heart of their life was in home gatherings where they broke bread together, experienced "glad and generous hearts," praised God, earned the "goodwill of those around," and grew "day by day." Smaller churches that grow in this way will do so by the quality of their common life and by the way those around them perceive them.

I referred in Chapter 3 to Arlin Rothauge's little booklet, *Sizing Up a Congregation for New Member Ministry*. He recognizes that churches will grow more naturally and effectively if they do so in

ways compatible with their size. Two of his size categories fit our focus. The family church has up to fifty active members or an average of
up to forty in worship. A pastoral church has fifty to 150 active members or forty to one hundred in worship.[5]

The family church is similar to Dudley's one-celled church. According to Rothauge, people will be attracted by the quality of life they
observe in the "family" and by the church's witness and service in the
community. New members tend to come through family and friendship
ties. Often the newcomer will be known by and vouched for by a church
member or "gatekeeper." Full inclusion or adoption will take some time.
Newcomers will need the same kind of orientation to family heritage
and ways that would be provided to a child being adopted into a nuclear
family. The adoption process will be facilitated if a "sponsor" is infor-
mally or formally assigned to nurture the new family member. True adoption will include being added to the "grapevine" and being treated as
"one of us" when encountered in the community. The adoptee will
need to be included in the organic life of the church and encouraged to
take appropriate leadership when she or he is ready. The role of the
pastoral leader is to be one more "aunt" or "uncle" for the adoptee and
to monitor the adoption process to prevent glitches and see that the
process is carried through until the adoptee is fully a member of the
family. The adoption will be sealed when the church family is "there
for" the adoptee in the first time of need or crisis.

In the pastoral church, the pastoral leader plays a more pivotal role.
The pastor's personality, style, gifts, and priorities will play a larger
part in the newcomer's decision about whether this is the appropriate
church. The pastor in this-sized church may be the one who extends
the first invitation and is usually the one who orchestrates or enables
the assimilation process for the newcomer. Even though a church is
in the pastoral-size category, the laity are just as crucial in extending
hospitality and welcome into the family. A formally appointed sponsor can help see that the newcomer doesn't get lost or fall through the
cracks. The church leadership circle needs to be intentional in seeing
that the new folks are invited to the planned functions, oriented to
the heritage and ways of the church, and encouraged to find their
place in the organic life of the church. This inclusion will include
helping the new person find his or her niche—the choir, mission group,

prayer chain, women's or men's fellowship, or new task group. It will likely fall to the pastor to make sure the practices of hospitality and inclusion are maintained and sharpened.

In both the family church and the pastoral church, growth is preferable when it is intentional, slow, and steady. It's difficult for a church to accommodate and assimilate more than ten percent growth a year. If there were to be a large influx of new people, I've even mused about the advisability of having a waiting list—not to be exclusive, but to be effective at assimilating so that the open door does not become a revolving door.

Beyond being concerned with how it attracts and includes, a smaller church (particularly the pastoral leader) will give continual attention to helping the church feel and act "small" while it grows. This is no easy or natural task. Attention must be given to keeping hospitality warm, welcoming, and inclusive of all; to keeping worship participatory; to seeing that newcomers are attended to and fully adopted; to never letting the new person fall into a spectator role or through a crack.

If a smaller church is effective at sharing its and God's good news and meeting people's needs and hopes, it may eventually grow beyond being a smaller church. It will then do one of three things: First, if it is not careful or if it is enamored with numbers, it will act like a larger church in which more and more people become spectators rather than involved players in the church's life. A second and wiser strategy would be to provide multiple, small-church experiences within the larger church—multiple and diverse small nurturing groups, a variety of worshiping opportunities, and multiple mission or discipleship endeavors.

The third, most radical, and perhaps most faithful and effective strategy for the significantly growing church is what churches commonly did before the middle of the twentieth century—cell division or breaking off a group to start a new church. The church might form two churches, which have a different geographic, style, or mission focus. This is what Gordon Cosby (the founding pastor) and the Church of the Savior in Washington, D.C., did. Church of the Savior was founded after World War II as a highly disciplined and mission-focused church. In order to join, prospective members were required to commit to intensive study, serious personal and financial commitment, and personal involvement in a mission group. In 1976, after the church grew to about 140 members, Gordon Cosby preached a sermon in which he announced that the church was much too large and proposed dividing the church into several smaller churches with different mission emphases. Church of the Savior formally disbanded and was reconstituted into nine, separate, little, dynamic churches. Imagine if more churches had this kind of faith, commitment, and creativity!

As of this writing, the San Rafael church is beginning to wrestle with this question. Several years ago, as the church was growing, we had to decide what to do with our long, narrow, dreary sanctuary. There was general agreement that the quality of worship decreases as the quantity increases beyond ninety or one hundred. Being more concerned with quality than quantity, the church chose to make its sanctuary smaller to better fit its growing congregation and understanding of worship. The result of our rebuilding was an extraordinary worship space for up to one hundred that facilitates a very personal and participatory worship experience.

More and more often, this sanctuary is comfortably full. My hope is that when we average eighty-five in worship (we now average about seventy, including children) we will have the courage and conviction to create two "churches" or communities within one, larger congregation. That might mean two separate and different worship services, perhaps one being on a day other than Sunday. It would also mean separate organizational structures to govern and enable each church's functional and missional life. Essentially, we would have two "yoked" churches. I imagine there would be frequent visiting back and forth between the two churches. We would have periodic worship and social gatherings of the whole congregation in borrowed or rented space and nurturing events and programs that would be supported by both churches. To me, a less satisfactory alternative would be to remain as one church with two worship services. The least satisfactory option would be to simply cram people in until people started staying home or going elsewhere.

Smaller churches grow numerically in five ways—by addition, multiplication, division, adoption, and assimilation.

Growth by addition is the least intentional and least effective way of growing. Like a person trying to fish, some churches try to snag new folks as they swim by or in. This can be effective when the church is located in a community to which people frequently move, or when it is a high status church, or has very winsome people, or occupies a lovely building, or has some other attracting quality. Churches that attempt to grow by addition often lose as many as they gain, because of their lack of intentionality.

Growth by multiplication has been promoted by Lyle Schaller and others. In his strategy for smaller church growth, Schaller envisions a new pastor in an established smaller church unilaterally starting a series of homogeneous interest groups that are adjunct to the ongoing life of the church and primarily oriented to those outside. If the strategy works, the church becomes the newcomers church, and the single cell church becomes a multicell or medium-sized church. This strategy, in which an outsider (the new pastor) unilaterally transforms the church by changing its nature, replacing its leadership, and making it what it never was, is artificial and lacks integrity.[6]

The third form of church growth is the most historical—growth by division. Like cell division, the church grows to the point where its qualities of intimacy, caring, and personal involvement are strained. The church intentionally divides and a new church is started. Many of our present churches got their start in this way. It has much to recommend it. However, with today's escalating costs and fixation on bigness, few churches are willing to split off good members.

The fourth type of growth is by adoption into the church family. Generally, this is the most appropriate strategy for smaller churches. It's preferable to topsy-turvy growth that transmutes a church from a rabbit into an elephant. It's slow but sure. People (perhaps already known and vouched for by some) are attracted and invited. They are welcomed with a genuine and generous spirit of hospitality. If they choose to come back, they are officially or unofficially sponsored by church folk with whom they are well matched. They're involved in church activity, responsibilities, and power-sharing as soon as they're ready and comfortable with church ways. Opportunities are provided to learn the family story and to experience the church's life and expectations. The newcomer's interests, style, and gifts are discerned and matched with the church. When the match doesn't take or isn't right, people will wonder, "What ever happened to what's his name?"

Usually when the adoption is ready to be finalized, there will be a personalized ritual to formalize the relationship between the adoptee and adopter (the church).

Another type of church growth is assimilation. Most churches lose a significant number of people who have never really connected with the church or who leave because they are angry, bored, or seduced by something else. A church that concentrates on thoroughly assimilating its people by making sure they fully identify with their church and are deeply committed to its shared ministry and mission will discover that it is growing simply because fewer people leave.

Many churches that are full of gray-haired people yearn for young people and young families, seeing them as the solution to their sense that "we're all dying off." I have two thoughts about this perceived need for young blood. I know of a little church that looked around one day and the members said to one another, "We're all old. Our church is going to die." Then they decided they would concentrate on having a really good time until the last one died. What they didn't count on was the fact that once they started having a really good time, they became a magnet for older people. Soon they were a thriving church of older people. It's certainly true that there will always be older people, and the church that has a superb seniors ministry will be a thriving church of seniors.

But I confess I love it when young people and young families visit, like what they see, and become deeply involved. It makes church life more interesting, dynamic, and diverse. The confluence of old and young enriches the lives of all. Too often, the gray-haired church wants younger people—as long as the younger people like things the way they are and don't ask for a different kind of music, a different style of worship, a say in what happens, or some of the power. Often, churches don't grow because they are too restrictive in who they let in and too rigid in what they allow.

If a church wants to attract younger people it must do tangible things to demonstrate its seriousness. In the Emmetsburg and San Rafael churches, we put in a new, accessible bathroom. Changing tables were installed in both, even though neither church had a baby in the congregation. As in the film *Field of Dreams* (dir. Phil Alden Robinson; Universal, 1989), in which an Iowa cornfield was turned into a baseball diamond and players came to play, when we put changing tables in each church, babies came. In addition to a changing table, get a new hymnal and be willing to sing new hymns and songs along with the oldies; repaint, recarpet, and refurnish the nursery (or establish one); provide child care during worship and for church functions; accept that there will be a little more noise in worship; and know that your church will have a lot more fun. If you really demonstrate you want them, families with children will come.

I don't believe in growth for growth's sake. I do believe in and practice evangelism and church development. Here are thirteen principles I believe in and practice:

1. A healthy, loving, hospitable church will have a passion to share what it has and be open to all who wish to enter. But it will not try to turn a Volkswagen into a Winnebago.
2. The church will do its theological homework so that it knows why it's reaching out, to whom it most needs to reach out, and how to do so in the most authentic ways. It will discern that Jesus and the early church were not attempting to build institutions or lead mass movements. Like them, it will be intent on meeting needs and building living communities of faith.
3. Before it goes looking for new people, it will reach out to those already in its sphere of influence—those who are dropping out or have dropped out, those who are on the perimeter who have never been fully assimilated, and those who are younger and at risk of dropping out.
4. It will understand that there are four ways to receive new people—addition, multiplication, division, and adoption. It will decide which of those is most faithful and natural for it. Then it will determine what strategies will be most effective, given the church's particular style and setting.
5. It will give serious attention to its level of self-esteem and morale. (See Chap. 8.) If those are not at a healthy level, any effort to reach out will be futile.
6. The church will be as serious and intentional about assimilating new people as it is about attracting them. It will utilize specific strategies for both.

7. It will think about and plan for how to "scratch where people itch." One list of what people are looking for in a church named these "itchy" places:

- Religious education for their children
- Opportunity to talk about their religious feelings and doubts
- Need for fellowship and community
- Desire to have personal interest shown in them
- An opportunity to help others
- Help at the crisis times in their lives

So, if these are places where people itch, what can a particular church do to scratch in those places?

8. It will compile an inventory of what is uniquely and particularly attractive about it and what it has to offer others. The content of this inventory will vary from church to church. Then, it will determine how to package or "market" those particular qualities and make them available.

9. It will remember that the God-given goal is new disciples and not new members, and it will know the difference. Attracted people will be involved in discipleship, not institutional support.

10. It will know it cannot be all things to all people. Without being exclusive, it will figure out what kinds of people are most likely to be attracted to and at home and ministered unto by their kind of church and figure out how to particularly reach out to these people.

11. It will understand what I've called the "moth principle of church attraction," which believes that people (like moths) will naturally seek out those places where they find light and warmth. Not only will the church understand that, but also it will work on generating more light and warmth and on projecting its light and spreading its warmth into dark and cold places. If it does not have both light and warmth, it is not a Christian church.

12. It will understand that there are particular times in people's lives when they are especially seeking or are open to church involvement and plan its outreach accordingly. These times are when people relocate and are desiring to meet new people, when people have young children and are seeking religious education, and when people are in crisis or life change.

13. It will work to grow "smaller" as it grows larger:

- By sharing the power widely and making everyone an "owner"
- By creating more opportunities for involvement
- By improving communication
- By expanding the cross-cultural and intergenerational sense of family
- By developing a more relational theology
- By creating a more hospitable environment
- By more effectively helping everyone know everyone else
- By nurturing greater intimacy
- By creating more participatory worship
- By seeking to involve everyone in the mission of the church

If growth came easily or naturally, you wouldn't be reading this chapter. Faithful, appropriate, continuing growth requires thoughtfulness, planning, follow-through, and some risk-taking. The following process for planning a smaller church's evangelism and growth strategy could be used by a leadership team, an appropriate board or committee, or the whole church. It begins with six crucial questions that require honest deliberation. Then there are five steps for creating and implementing an outreach plan.

Wrestle with these six fundamental questions:

1. Why do you want to grow? How many of your people want to grow? What price will you pay to grow? Are you and they willing to pay that price?

2. What's keeping you from growing? Attitudes? Demographics? Other reasons?

3. Specifically and concretely, what does your church have to offer? What's attractive about the congregation? What are its specific gifts?

4. What specific problem areas in your church do you need to address in order to be more attractive, ready, and equipped?

5. What particular kinds of individuals and groups might be naturally attracted to your church? What kinds of individuals and groups are unchurched or have unmet needs in your community or area?

6. Who are your warmest "gatekeepers" (those who let or usher people in) and "magnets" (those who attract)? How can these people be more effectively brought in contact with visitors and prospects?

Five steps in creating and implementing an outreach plan:

1. Based on your conclusions to these questions, use your imagination and identify at least six specific, concrete, appropriate outreach ideas or strategies for your church.

2. Pick the three most appealing and promising. Give a framework or blueprint to each, including:

- Its theological rationale
- How the strategy particularly fits your situation
- How it would work
- Who would do it
- Whom you would target
- Steps in developing and implementing the strategy

3. Select and commit yourselves to the strategies you will implement.

4. Implement the outreach strategies.

5. Celebrate and evaluate the results and continue or repeat the process.

God does not call the church to grow or be successful. God calls the church to be faithful and effective. A church that is faithful and effective will pursue fitting and intentional ways of sharing its and God's good news. Such a church will want to build the community of God. It will build that community by being disciples and by seeking to enlist new disciples. Most likely, its light and warmth will attract others.

Questions

1. What is your church's recent history of evangelism, outreach, and attempts at growth?
2. If your church is declining or merely stable, which of the thirteen factors given for churches not growing are true in your situation?
3. How would you answer the six questions that begin the outreach process above?

Suggestion

Call together the appropriate people and enlist them in the above process.

chapter ten

Affording to Be a Smaller Church

I think it's great that Jesus Christ is our sure foundation, but how are we going to fix the leak in our roof?

—Churchwoman to pastor's spouse

TWO WHIMSICAL AND PROFOUND STORIES . . .

After squeezing a lemon dry, the carnival strongman offered one hundred dollars to anyone who could extract another drop from it. Several macho men tried and failed. Then a little old woman asked if she could try. The strong man scoffed and handed her the squashed lemon. She took the lemon, squeezed hard, and extracted half a cup. Flabbergasted, the strong man asked the woman how she did it. "It's simple," she said, "I'm the treasurer of my little church."

And then a hen and a pig walked past the little Baptist church one Sunday morning and noticed a signboard that said: "Ham and egg breakfast this morning, public invited, $2.50." Henrietta Hen said to Peter Pig, "Hey, Peter, let's go in." Peter said, "No way. If we go in they'll ask you for a donation, but they'll ask me for a total commitment!"

The first story illustrates what I believe to be true. More often than not, when you look at the total budget of smaller churches, they are more cost effective or accomplish more per dollar than their larger cousins. Take the rather extreme example of the tiny Trinitarian Congregational Church of Warwick, Massachusetts, which had a 1971 total budget of $1585 (granted, those were 1971 dollars). From their paltry budget, they managed to squeeze fifty-two worship services, conducted a Sunday school for the children of the town, offered basic crisis coverage, were community for one another and others who happened by, and maintained, heated, and lit their building. A year later, when they doubled their budget to $3000, they added a youth group, greater pastoral care and crisis response for the whole community, a greatly expanded mission commitment, and a resident pastor. Or consider the Union Congregational Church of Bryant, South Dakota, which in 2001 squeezed a very effective comprehensive ministry and mission (including $2115 for denominational missions) out of a budget of $24,580. Smaller churches can be quite good at squeezing a lot of lemonade from just a few lemons. The theory and practices offered here can help even the smallest and poorest churches move from sour lemons to sweet oranges.

Smaller churches do what they do not just with donations but also with considerable commitment and often sacrifice. Start with the pastor who, by choosing to serve in a smaller church, forfeits the larger salary and greater pension benefits received by pastors of larger churches. Statistics have shown that, on average, people in smaller churches contribute more time, talent, and treasure than those in larger churches. People in smaller churches will identify more with Peter than Henrietta. Beyond donating, generally they are heavily committed.

Money, or the lack of it, is frequently perceived as a life-and-death squeeze in smaller churches—and frequently it is. It's around money matters more than anything else that people take issue with my belief that smaller churches are the right size. If it weren't for the financial crunch, more smaller churches would be happy with their size, more pastors would choose to pastor smaller churches, and fewer smaller churches would close. Due to the increasing costs of being a church—including the pastors' need to earn a living wage, escalating insurance costs, dealing with deferred building maintenance, rising utility costs, and luxuries (like photocopiers) that have become necessities—churches that aren't growing are getting poorer.

As a result, denominational officials often conclude that some of their smaller churches are no longer viable, pastors and laity despair, and those on the outside looking in consider smaller churches to be lost causes. All too often the plug is pulled—frequently unnecessarily and prematurely. I'm convinced that churches don't die from lack of money. Generally, the cause of death is lack of faith, vision, will, and awareness of alternatives—on the part of churches, pastors, and those on the outside who are responsible for helping them. Often these closures are unnecessary because there are viable alternatives—alternative understandings of faith and money, alternative ways of financing their church, and alternative ways of being a church.

Alternative Understandings of Faith, People, and Their Money

Experience shows that the following sixteen financial principles are true, even if unconventional:

1. Concern for stewardship precedes concern for money and the two are not synonymous. Pastors often speak the word "stewardship" and lay people hear the word "money." Stewardship relates to our way of understanding our relation to God and God's creation. While money is our culture's obsession, it is better understood as a useful resource for doing God's will as God's people. There are twenty-six explicit references to "steward" or "stewardship" in the Bible. The steward was the servant in a household but not an ordinary servant. The steward was the supervising servant, the one given responsibility for the caretaking and management of the household. In Luke 12:42, Jesus says: "Who then is the faithful and prudent manager whom his master will put in charge of his slaves, to give them their allowance of food at the proper time?" All those in the church are called to be faithful and prudent managers, working toward building the Community of God. Biblical stewardship is about being faithful and prudent managers of the whole of creation, including both the church and our own resources. Churches who ignore stewardship and are only concerned about money or the lack of it will find their financial resources drying up.

2. Money is a spiritual matter and its use is a statement of faith. Why is it that the richest nation in human history is, according to surveys, recording more and more unhappiness and disillusionment and a widening gap between rich and poor?

While people prefer to separate matters of the spirit from matters of the wallet, Jesus would have none of that. He said: "Where your treasure is, there your heart will be also" (Luke 12:34). Where your checkbook is, there you will find your heart. Our checkbook register and credit card balance sheet registers our spiritual priorities. Our church budget is our church's mission statement.

I preach three things that allow us to take a low key approach to church finances. First, I preach gratitude. Sick or well, rich or poor, we all have so much for which to be grateful. A man's first response after his wife died was: "Why me?" His second response was, "Why not me?" He was well aware that his life was filled with far more graces than his goodness warranted. I encourage our people to, as the old gospel hymn said, "Count your blessings, name them one by one," and tell them that their largest gifts are only small returns on what they've been given. Second, I preach generosity. People are encouraged to be generous for their own sakes as well as for the good that they do, because it's obvious that generous people enjoy being generous and are happier and healthier people. A smaller church of grateful and generous stewards will contribute far more than a larger church of parsimonious people. The third thing I preach is community. We are created for community. We are most fully human in community. An inclusive community is God's vision and intention. We are responsible not just for ourselves but for the whole of God's community, which has no borders.

3. Churches should budget, pledge, and talk openly about money. People now talk openly about sex, are learning to talk about death, but still hate to talk about their money. If money is primarily a spiritual matter, people will not be spiritually open until they are free to talk openly about their money. This revolution—and it is a revolution—will not happen quickly or easily. But people will not grow much spiritually until their financial attitudes and practices become part of the church community's business. One of the biggest struggles in San Rafael was moving away from having the treasurer

draw up a budget (always pretty much the same as the previous one), which the church adopted with little thought or adjustment. We now have a more open and deliberative process.

4. People will pay for what they value and value what they pay for. It's a no-brainer to observe that people somehow find the money for the things they really want, which is what they really value. Some churches are worth a fortune; others aren't worth more than a dollar or two in the plate. Our people in San Rafael have come to be exceptionally generous because we've worked together to have their church personify and underwrite their highest values. Church leaders have a dual task. First, we have to work to have a church that is valuable and worth valuing. So we keep working on the quality of our worship, improving our educational ministry, deepening the level of care and community our people experience, expanding our mission involvements and commitments. Second, we have to help our people see and experience how valuable and worthy of support their church really is. We do that through written and oral communication.

   Our Every Dollar Feeds Kids project illustrates this principle. By finding a way to eliminate graft, overhead, and administrative costs so that people's money buys nothing but economical food for hungry kids, we have developed a program our people and others value greatly and support generously. And part of what our people value and are willing to pay for is a church small enough to provide them with a richer, more intimate church experience. A Lutheran pastor in Cincinnati was courageous and correct when he said: "Congregations don't need to do fund-raising. Do the ministry consistently well and the money will be there."[1]

5. Most churches are what *Consumer Report* calls a "Best Buy." Consider the cumulative value of what your church provides. It offers twenty-four-hour-a-day, seven-day-a-week, 365-days-a-year support. It cares for body, mind, and spirit, from birth to death. It cares for our needs and the needs of people

throughout the community and around the world. In contrast to the TV evangelists, who appear so sincere, our local churches are far, far more responsible and cost-effective. Our churches build a pretty decent community out of all ages, both genders, different classes and cultures, and varying political and philosophical persuasions. Not only does it do all this, but also its people have a direct say in shaping what does and does not happen—particularly in smaller churches.

6. People will not give beyond their level of trust. Why do people resent sending tax dollars to the Internal Revenue Service while they give generously to their favorite charity? They don't trust the IRS to not squander their tax money, but they trust the charity they've grown to believe in. One church finance book counseled against printing the specific staff salaries in the budget and annual report. It said we shouldn't provide people with budget figures to argue with. This is wrong, particularly in smaller churches. The community has a right to know. If they have a say in setting the church's priorities, building the budget, and evaluating its work they will trust that their church is using their money wisely. Our people are channeling more of their charitable giving through their church because they trust their church to be more cost effective. People's giving will be commensurate with their assessment of the pastor's and church's credibility. Your church's credibility unlocks your church's generosity.

7. People will only give as much as they can imagine or visualize. Henri Nouwen wrote: "One finding is that all people committed to large humanitarian causes had at some point had a significant encounter with someone outside their own circles who was able to widen the boundaries of their lives and show them larger perspectives."[2] This is why I take people to meet the poor of Mexico and why our Board of Mission recruits church members to help prepare and serve meals at our nearby homeless program. Have your church photographer make a photographic display of your church budget—pictures of what your church money makes happen.

If you're the pastor, write a newsletter article or letter illustrating the ways you and your church have touched people's lives in the last month—being careful to not violate confidences. The wider your people's horizons, the more committed and generous they will be.

8. People would rather invest in people than maintain an institution. The Catch-22 for smaller churches that are struggling to survive is that they increasingly communicate their institutional needs to their people who, particularly in smaller churches, care more about people than institutions. I learned from Epiphany Church in St. Louis that by keeping its focus on its mission, the institutional needs managed to get met. But what about all the money churches pour into their buildings? Actually, churches that successfully raise large sums of money for building costs, have usually emphasized the people who are served by the building and the difference the building makes for the people who use it. If the church's heart is with the people the people's time and treasure will be there too.

9. People want to make a difference and will act to make a difference. Why did someone named Kilroy write "Kilroy was here" on a wall during World War II? Why does graffiti appear in public places? People don't want to die without making a difference and having someone notice they were there. This is one of the primary reasons people come to and stay in smaller churches. There, they are known and make a difference. Churches that go about business as usual will have fewer resources for their business. Churches that are making a tangible difference in people's lives, in the community and world, will have the money to make that difference. By giving our people a way to invest themselves, they then invest their resources.

10. Churches never believe they have enough money. I never heard a church of any size say, "We're not taking an offering today because we have enough money." We could all be more candid in determining our need. It's all relative.

11. All churches have more than enough money. Assuming someone has a Bible, it costs absolutely nothing to be a church! Let's be honest. You don't need a building. You could meet in someone's house or, if you're too large, you could divide into house-sized churches. You don't need a paid pastor. You're all gifted people and could divide the pastoral tasks among yourselves and donate your services. If you've got a Bible, your own faith experience, and a love of children, you don't need a Sunday school curriculum. You could simply be together, share what Jesus means to you, and practice Christian love in your daily living. Your denomination wants and needs your support, but even that is a choice. Yet most of us want these things in our churches. We believe we can be more faithful and effective by sprinkling a little money on our ministry and mission, so we choose to allocate money for them. But it's a matter of choice.

12. Therefore, churches can choose between giving and making more money or living on less money. People will give more when they have a choice and know the alternatives. Paint a scenario of how it will be with and without the money, and trust your people to be faithful in their giving.

13. Raising and making money should not be all that a church talks about and does. Another Catch-22 for smaller churches in a money squeeze is that they talk more and more about their need for money and work harder and harder on generating the money they believe they need. This is dis-spiriting and exhausting! One reason churches with bi-vocational or part-time pastors often do better is that they have time and energy to do something other than generate income. Some churches have done better by asking people to donate the money they would have spent on a bake sale rather than having the bake sale. Do whatever you have to do to not spend all of your time and energy on money-raising. Spend more of your time together doing the things that are more rewarding. You will probably have more money in the long run.

14. A church should put some fat into its budget. Dying people are often put on life support systems. Churches sometimes do this to themselves. They go on a subsistence diet by deferring maintenance, reusing curriculum, and cutting their mission-giving and pastor's compensation. They turn back the thermostat five degrees and eliminate the church newsletter to save money. The best treasurer is seen as the one with the sharpest pencil. This all makes church less enjoyable, less rewarding, and less of a difference-maker. As a result, people often give less because they get less for their giving.

    Put some fat in the budget and get off life supports. If you're going to die, well then, live well until you do. Turn up the heat. Serve refreshments and good coffee instead of cheap coffee. Fund a new, difference-making mission project. Paint the building—inside and out. Give the pastor a love gift. Make being together more pleasurable. Have your annual meeting dinner catered. Appear to the outside world like your church is a going concern. People will give more when they're off life supports and relishing life.

15. People who feel deeply loved will sacrifice for the one who loves them. The more impersonal our society becomes, the more love-starved people are. People know when they are being loved and when they are merely needed or, worse, being taken for granted. Carl Dudley said smaller churches want their pastors to be "lovers." He was one hundred percent right. It would be profitable for a church's lay and pastoral leadership to survey how loved the people in the pews who pay the bills really feel. If they don't know how to better express love, they could ask, "How can we more genuinely help you feel loved?

16. A church will not know what it's financially capable of until it tests itself. This is extremely important. You cannot accurately estimate what your people are capable of giving or what they will choose to give. All the principles above come into play. If churches want or need something, they can generally find the means. If they value their church, they will sacrifice for it in

order to pay for it. People like to make a difference and enjoy feeling generous. They want to enjoy their church. If they trust their lay and pastoral leadership, the leadership says they can do it, and they are helped to visualize the need or opportunity, they will come up with what's needed. I've seen this demonstrated over and over again in smaller churches—for big ticket capital funds campaigns, special projects, and annual budgets. The necessary money is usually there.

Faithfully follow these principles and your people will surprise, even shock you.

Most of the stewardship and church-finance books give brief lip service to theory and theology and jump right to methods and techniques for extracting money from people who are assumed to be reluctant to part with it. Methods and techniques are the easy and less important part. What's important are the principles just identified. Churches that aggressively and continually adhere to them will have far more money than they ever dreamed.

Even in the smallest church where the people know each other well, no one really knows who has what invested in blue chip stocks and CDs, in real estate, in bank accounts, or has already put the church in their wills. In most of the churches of the people reading this book, there is one or more persons who could give a $100,000 gift to their church and many who could double what they give annually—if they were asked to or wanted to. Never, ever assume that you or anyone in your church knows the limits of your people.

Alternative Ways of Financing a Smaller Church

There are at least nine ways to finance a church. A wise and faithful church can utilize most, if not all, of them. Smaller churches are often poorer churches because they are timid about asking for financial support, neglectful of potential sources of funding, and often not very creative in pursuing them. If we believe the church's work is God's work and important work and if additional money would help get the work done, then we should not be shy or hesitant in pursuing it. In

Jesus' parable of the talents (Matt. 25:14–30), the difference between the two servants who invested wisely and were rewarded and the one who buried his resources and was punished, was that the five talent and the two talent servants or stewards were aggressive in getting the most from their resources, while the one talent servant was lazy, shy, or neglectful. How many of the following does your church employ in funding its life-giving ministry and mission?

1. **Pledged, regular giving.** This is basic and almost universal, even though it seems to contradict the smaller church characteristic of preferring to give what's needed when needed. Pledged, regular giving is basic because almost all churches have regular expenses requiring payment—salaries, building expenses, utilities, and so on. Churches need to know that the money will be there when the bills come due. It's at least as important for every member of the church family to annually put a price tag on where their church ranks in the priorities of their lives and what portion of the support of the church they are willing to be responsible for. Their willingness and generosity in doing this is more a measure of their gratitude for the blessings of life and their love of their church and its work and less of an indication of their financial means.

For their sake and the church's, we ask our people to do four things:

- Annually evaluate their financial situation and what their church means to them
- Determine what percentage of their income they now invest in their church's ministry and mission and whether they can and will increase that by at least one percent of their income
- Pledge that amount with the understanding they can raise or lower their pledge if their situation changes
- Follow through on their pledge

There's nothing exceptional or unusual in this. Almost all of our people make pledges and follow through on them. In fact, we now receive more money from our pledgers than what they've pledged.

What is unique about our pledging process in San Rafael is when and how we do it. Because the level of trust and morale is so high in this church and because our people believe strongly in their ministry and mission, we are quite low-key and often tardy in our annual appeal. We separate the budget from the pledges and don't ask our people to cover the budget. We trust they will and would prefer that they focus on their sense of gratitude, growing generosity, and desire to be part of the important things happening at First Congregational. Generally, a lay leader and I cowrite a letter, which goes to every active person or family, with a percentage-giving chart and a pledge form to return. The letter thanks them for their generosity in the past, talks about the extraordinary difference our church is making, asks them to count their blessings, and invites their generous response. When necessary and without any arm-twisting, someone follows up with a phone call or after-worship conversation. My unorthodox conclusion is that the more aggressively the financial appeal is ratcheted-up, the more resistant people become. So we stay low-key and concentrate on being a church worthy of generous support.

There's also nothing too unusual about how our budget is devised. Our treasurer develops a first draft based on past performance and expenses and future projections and needs. I, as pastor, prepare some proposals based on the needs and opportunities before us and where I think God may be leading us. Each of the boards and committees are asked for their requirements and suggestions. We always increase our mission budget, both in dollars and in percentage of the budget. We encourage our congregation's budget suggestions. This all results in a budget that will enable us to be the church we want and need to be in the coming year. Then this is measured against the pledges we've received. Sometimes the pledges are higher, sometimes the budget is. I can't recall a major discrepancy. If anticipated income is less than the budget, we usually commit to finding a way to fund the difference and always do.

2. Rents and Donations for Building Use. While the cost of having a church building just north of San Francisco is very high, having a facility here is essential to both our mission and our income. Since rents are astronomical and meeting places are at a premium, about two-fifths of our income comes from facility rental. We receive rent for the space we make available for Head Start (while retaining the right to use the space on Sunday), from a Fijian church that worships before we do and a Korean church that worships afterward, from a rented office, for use of our parking lot, and for a variety of other uses. In addition, four twelve-step programs use space and cover their utility and building-upkeep costs. We have a stepped rental schedule that has one fee for profit groups, one for nonprofit groups, one for church groups, and free use for groups from our denomination. We adjust the rates when necessary. Our facilities are used seven days a week in several ways, and we see this as both mission and income and an opportunity for hospitality.

In Warwick, we made our building available to any community group at no charge. The resulting goodwill resulted in donations of various kinds from nonchurch members. Urban or rural, your facility is an expense to you, but it is generally a source of potential income. Have at least one room that's attractive and comfortably furnished, and communicate to the community that it's available for either a donation or a specific rental. A neighboring church receives fifteen hundred dollars a month for allowing a cellular phone antenna in its bell tower. Have your business-minded people and your mission-minded people look at your buildings and grounds to determine what income potential is there. If there is potential, then you can decide whether that would contribute to or detract from your understanding of being a church. If you receive rental income, talk with your city or county about whether you have some tax liability.

3. In-Kind or Donated Services. I worked with a small town church in Rock Rapids, Iowa, that could no longer afford custodial services. A group of its retired folks volunteered to be the "Dust Busters." They met one morning a week to clean their church, drink coffee, and have a great time. In San Rafael, we figure that we received at least a hundred thousand dollars worth of donated labor from our busy laity during our renovation. In Warwick, we hired one good carpenter to lead our volunteers in renovating and adding on to our building. Most churches receive a significant amount of donated labor, which saves a considerable amount of money. Not only is money saved but also community is built and people feel more useful. Inviting volunteer help can even be a form of evangelism as people agree to help the neighborhood church and discover the good things and good times that happen there. Thousands of churches receive many millions of dollars in donated janitorial, secretarial, and musical services, and building maintenance and improvements.

4. Memorial Gifts. The pastor of the Presbyterian church in Storm Lake, Iowa, was called by the funeral director and asked to do a funeral for a nonchurch member. He agreed and did the service. Several days later, the funeral director told the pastor that the husband of the deceased wished to talk to him. Suspecting the intention was to make a memorial contribution, the pastor went armed with a sliding scale of possibilities. The husband said he wanted to make a gift in memory of his wife and asked for suggestions. The pastor began with the lesser possibilities and ascended to the greater. Finally, he said what the church really wanted was a new pipe organ. The husband asked what that would cost, and the pastor said two hundred thousand dollars. The husband said that that was about what he had in mind. He also paid the twenty-five thousand dollars to remodel the church chancel to house the organ.

A wise church will have, post, and remind people of its "Wish List," ranging from the inexpensive to expensive needs and wants that would enhance the ministry and mission of the church and be fitting gifts in honor of or memory of others. A wise church will not put memorial gifts into an account but use them for specific, concrete uses. And it will let people know about the gift. My preference is to have a memorial book where gifts are recorded with appreciation rather than memorial plaques. When we've invited people to donate money for things like new hymnals and pew Bibles in honor of or in memory of special people, our only problem was shutting off the gifts when enough money was received. People find meaning in remembering others and being remembered themselves through memorial gifts.

5. Estate Bequests and Endowments. Harry Emerson Fosdick, renowned pastor at Riverside Church in New York, insisted that every letter going out from the church include the question: "Have you remembered Riverside Church in your will?" An older woman volunteered at her United Church of Christ church in Nebraska at least five days a week. When she died, she left a huge bequest to the Girl Scouts and nothing to her church. Someone from the church asked one of her adult children why she had left nothing to the church. The answer: The church never asked.

All of our churches are populated by people who have given dearly, even sacrificed for the church they loved and been served by. These people would prefer that their church not die when they do. Most of our churches don't bother to educate their people about end-of-life medical and financial decisions including wills, gift annuities, charitable remainder trusts, gifts of life insurance and property, and so on. Only about a third of the people who die have made a will. Our pledge form asks our members if they have remembered their church in their will. There are resources and people available to your church that could conduct a helpful educational program on end-of-life decisions. Your people will be open to supporting their church in death as they have in life.

I've seen endowments give life and drain life from churches. In Warwick, the unexpected generous bequest from Alice Anderson enabled the building renovation and expansion that we could not have done ourselves—or so we thought. We used her gift to pay for the work we did. We should have used it to guarantee a loan and then invited the rest of the church to help repay it. The Shrewsbury Church had received a considerable amount of money in bequests, which they invested in the stock market. The earnings were used to underwrite the church budget, which allowed the church to not be responsible for a majority of its budget, which weakened rather than strengthened it.

Learning from that experience, in San Rafael we adapted and adopted an endowment policy from another church. The policy invites bequests from wills, gift annuities, charitable remainder trusts and annuities, life insurance, transfer of property, and memorial gifts. The church created an endowment committee. The policy requires that the principle not be used. The genius of the policy is that most of the interest must be used in the following ways: ten percent used outside the church but in the county for benevolent purposes, ten percent used outside the church and county for benevolent purposes, ten to fifty percent used for innovative ministries which cannot be financed within the church budget, and no more than twenty-five percent of the operating budget of the church can be underwritten by the endowment fund. This endowment policy guarantees new ministries and prevents the church from living off of its endowment.

Beyond this endowment policy, our Pilgrim Hill Foundation encourages bequest gifts that will create new mission ventures in perpetuity. Through our endowment policy, the Pilgrim Hill Foundation, and Every Dollar Feeds Kids we have created three different opportunities for the people of our smaller church to tailor their bequests to fit their values and priorities and ways to channel them through the church they have been loving, trusting, and investing in for years.

6. Fund-raisers. I enjoy fund-raisers and endorse them—within reason. They can be profitable, fun, community-builders, opportunities for evangelism, and even faith-nurturing. An example of the last is a talent project, modeled on the parable of the talents in Matthew 25. Money is borrowed from the church and made available in twenty-, ten-, five-, and one-dollar bills. A sermon is preached about the parable and the challenge of investing whatever gifts, skills, or talents we might have for the greater good. Then everyone is invited to come to the front of the church where the treasurer is seated, ready to give out money. People can take up to twenty dollars. They may work independently, with a friend, or as a family. They have six months to try to grow the money into a larger amount. We've had people buy yarn and knit mittens and socks to sell; someone bought pea seeds and raised and sold them; another bought sap pails, made maple syrup, and sold it; others have used the money to put on a dinner or party. We've done this four times in four churches, and each time people returned at least five times the total amount that was taken.

Fund-raisers aren't businesslike. They don't look like serious stewardship. But they are a way for a church to generate needed funds, often in a way that allows the outside community to support the church, while they have a good time and introduce others to their church. The purpose of the church is not to raise funds, but fund-raisers can be one means of fulfilling some of its purposes.

7. Special Appeals. This is often the easiest way of generating needed income. Epiphany church in St. Louis needed a new, twenty-five-thousand-dollar boiler or they would have to close the church. The twenty-five thousand dollars appeared in a church that didn't know where its next nickel was coming from. Emmetsburg needed a hundred thousand dollars for its building with a drooping roof and spreading walls. That much was pledged by a church that was very hard-pressed. Kate Scott needed a ramp so that she could get in and out of her mobile home. More money and donated help was offered than was needed. Stories are legion of churches that are always in the red in August and in the black by the end of December. Smaller church folks will give what's needed when needed. It's the ongoing needs that are difficult to cover.

8. Capital-Funds Campaigns. "I have been warmed by fires I did not build; I have drunk from wells I did not dig." That ancient maxim became the motto for Emmetsburg and San Rafael as each church—with trepidation—embarked on capital-funds campaigns to raise more money than they thought possible. Such campaigns are once-in-a-generation efforts to build on what has been received in order to give a gift to those who will come after. These campaigns must address a genuine, felt need, be led by people who are trusted, and be presented in a way that people can see the difference that will be made.

Most denominations have professional fund-raisers who are trained and capable of helping a church conduct a successful capital-funds campaign. That's the safest and most assured way to go. In Emmetsburg, we conducted our own but did it in conjunction with our state Conference's capital-funds campaign that was led by a professional. In San Rafael, we conducted our own. Both were very successful. Here's some of the wisdom I've learned and believe to be true and applicable anywhere.

The rule of thumb in the capital funds "business" is that a well-run capital-funds campaign can raise three to five times a church's annual budget. The well-run part is the hard part. You need a committee of people trusted by the church who genuinely believe in what you are trying to do. The more input your people have in developing what you want, the more support they will give. Have at least one part of your project be an obvious visual need that will please people. It's a hard sell to raise money to replace the sewer lines and drainage ditches.

The first phase is defining the project, getting accurate financial projections, and preparing a clear and compelling case for your people. The second phase is having two or three people who know your congregation go through your membership list to determine how much support you realistically believe your individuals can give. Then develop a "standard of gifts" chart that shows how many gifts you need at different levels, ranging from one or two very large gifts to several gifts of modest amounts. Most churches have one or more persons who could give fifty to a hundred thousand dollars—if they wanted to. Then callers are recruited to be trained to call (usually in pairs) in each home in the church. The callers need to make their pledge before they make their calls. The hardest part is helping callers not be afraid to ask their friends for money. Have a few, large pledges in and announced before the calling begins. It's better to ask people for gifts spread over three to five years, rather than one-time gifts.

In San Rafael, we did it a little differently. We had two people who thoroughly understood the project and were highly respected by the congregation. Bob and Joan volunteered to make all the calls. They made some calls together and some separately. They were well received everywhere and people were highly interested. People were asked to make pledges of money to be paid over five years. The results were more than we expected. After four years, our project grew larger and more expensive, and we had several new families in the church. So we did a second mini-campaign in which new pledges were received, and many people who were finishing their pledge either increased their pledge or added additional years. We had one hundred thousand dollar gift, one thirty-five thousand dollar gift, and several other large gifts. The project that cost six hundred thousand dollars required only a hundred thousand dollar loan that is close to being retired. We have successfully built a fire and dug a well for the next generation, and your church can, too.

9. Grants. To many churches, this is a new concept; to others, it's old hat. As this book is being written, Congress and the president are working on legislation to make it easier for faith-based groups to get federal money for social-service programs sponsored by religious organizations. It's assumed that something will be passed that will make it more feasible for groups, including churches like yours, to get government dollars for nonsectarian mission or social-service ventures. There are more and more foundations, and more and more of them are going to be willing to grant money to churches that can document the social benefits of what they propose to do. In San Rafael, we've had two, small foundation grants for church projects and four for Pilgrim Park.

These are nine sources of funding for supporting the essential ministry and mission of your church. If yours is a cat or collie church (see Chap. 3) these nine sources can be the same as nine lives for churches wondering how they can afford to be a smaller church.

Alternative Ways of Being a Church

Of the fifty-two churches I served as an area minister in Iowa, a majority either had a part-time pastor, were yoked with a church of another denomination, were federated with a church of another denomination, or were being served by a lay pastor. (A minority were independent, one-denomination churches served by a full-time, ordained pastor.) It was projected in the early 1990s that by the year 2000, of the 196 churches in the Iowa United Church of Christ Conference, only eighty-three would be able to afford a full-time pastor. And that's not just Iowa's problem. Today, more than one-third of churches in America are being served by pastors with some kind of supplemental income. In several denominations, a majority of their pastors will be retired within ten years, which means the growing clergy shortage will be increasingly severe. Many churches are finding it takes years, not months, to call a suitable pastor. In most cases, the problem is financial. We must find ways to help our smaller churches find additional and adequate ways of affording to be a church.

Ironically, many of the alternatives for tomorrow's churches were commonplace in yesterday's churches. None of them make a church inferior or less than a "real" church. Following are alternatives that offer creative possibilities that can make churches more faithful and effective. See what may fit your church:

- Bi-vocational or "tent-making" ministry, in which a pastor has some kind of supplemental income
- Part-time ministry in situations where pastors can afford a part-time salary (because they also receive a pension or have support from a spouse, etc.)
- Yoking, in which two or more churches share a pastor
- Ecumenical shared-ministry, in which two or more churches of different denominations share a pastor, buildings, and so forth.
- Two or more churches sharing a building
- House or storefront churches
- Team ministry, in which two or more pastors serve three or more churches
- Lay ministry, usually in which the lay pastor has a second job
- Lay shared-ministry, in which a team of people share the leadership of their church
- Church clusters, in which several churches are led by local lay or apprentice pastors who are supervised by one itinerant "circuit riding" pastor
- Partner richer and poorer churches together, in which the richer church assumes some of the cost and responsibility for pastoral leadership in the smaller church
- Recruit, call, and train committed, gifted laypeople to ministry who have been laid off, retired early, or are simply fed up with their secular job
- Churches don't have to meet weekly or Sunday to be a church
- Find a way to equalize clergy salaries and retirement benefits, regardless of size of church
- When everything else fails, merge or close churches that are too tired or discouraged to keep trying

There are alternative ways to understand churches and money, alternative ways to finance smaller churches, and alternative ways to be Christian churches. No church needs to close for lack of money. That's the truth.

Questions

1. Which of the ideas about faith, church, and money could be included in your church's deliberations about affording to be a church?

2. How many of the nine ways of funding smaller churches is your church utilizing? What about the others?

3. What promising ideas have you found in this chapter?

Suggestion

Offer each of your lay leaders or all the people in your church one thousand dollars in play money to come spend a day talking about what money means to them and explore new visions of how your church can afford being a church for the foreseeable future.

chapter eleven

Leading Smaller Churches to 2030

We are at the front edges of the greatest transformation of the church that has occurred for 1,600 years. It is by far the greatest change that the church has ever experienced in America; it may eventually make the transformation of the Reformation look like a ripple in a pond.

—Loren Mead, *The Once and Future Church*

Social systems cannot work for more than an instant without leadership. Someone will always have to step up and call others to move together in some direction. Whether it's a herd of horses, a pod of seals, a team of oxen or of athletes, all will sit around and look at each other, and look out for themselves, unless someone says, "Let's go there" or "Let's stay here," "Let's do that" or "Let's not do this."

—William Chris Hobgood, *The Once and Future Pastor*

Thomas Merton, spiritual mentor to many, was teaching in an obscure little college in upstate New York. A friend asked: "Thomas, why do you waste yourself in a place like this?"

Merton thought carefully and said, "It is my vocation."

It has been my vocation to serve as a pastor, observer, and leader of smaller churches for over thirty years. This book has provided the opportunity to reflect on thirty years of experience, study, and discovery with this unique genre of churches. Up to now in this book, we've been introduced to a variety of smaller churches and have theologized, theorized, and explored the most important aspects and issues of smaller-church life. Now let's envision the next thirty years.

Why 2030? I hope to be around to participate in and observe the next thirty years. It will be one-third of the new century. Thirty years is short enough to envision and plan for and long enough to test what we think and do. It's even long enough to accomplish the improbable. This is crisis time in every area of life—economic, the environment, health care, international relations, as well as religious. What happens in the next thirty years will go a long way toward determining whether and how we have learned to live together and how habitable the earth will be. The world has changed dramatically in the last thirty years. Imagine what is likely in the next thirty. For example, the United Nations is serious about ending chronic world-hunger by 2030. In thirty years, the church as a viable and meaningful societal influence will either reform and be relevant for a rapidly changing world, or it will be a useless relic.

Some church futurists believe that the future of the Christian church is with very small and small churches and large and very large churches. Churches in the middle that are too big to offer the intimacy and community of smaller churches and too small to offer the abundance of programs and the image of success of larger churches may struggle most for viability. Kennon L. Callahan, who has written about all sizes of churches, concludes, "The twenty-first century is the century of small, strong congregations. More people will be drawn to small, strong congregations than any other kind of congregation . . . around the planet, the vast majority of congregations will be small and strong, and the vast majority of people will be in those congregations."[1]

I had planned to conclude this book with two chapters—one about pastoral leadership in smaller churches and one about lay leadership. Then, realizing how interdependent each is on the other, I decided to merge both into one chapter on leadership for the future. Great pastoral leaders without a committed laity will simply charge up steep hills alone. With the best of intentions, committed laity without good pastoral leaders are likely to wander all over the hills and have difficulty agreeing on the right direction and the right approach. They may live today with meaning and effectiveness, but will struggle to get to tomorrow without gifted pastoral leadership. The pastoral leader and the faithful community are incomplete without each other.

The subject of leadership has long intrigued me. Warren Bennis, who has studied and practiced leadership for over thirty years, wrote:

> Roosevelt, who challenged a nation to overcome its fear; Winston Churchill, who demanded and got blood, sweat, and tears from his people; Albert Schweitzer, who from the jungles of Lambaréné inspired a reverence for life; Albert Einstein, who gave us a sense of unity in infinity; Gandhi, David Ben-Gurion, Golda Meir, and Anwar Sadat, who rallied their people to great and human causes; Jack and Bobby Kennedy and Martin Luther King Jr., who said we could do better— are all gone now. Where are their successors? . . . *Where, for God's sake, have all the leaders gone?*[2]

In my earlier list of twenty-six characteristics of a small church, I said, "Lay people are more important than the pastor." In the expanded list of thirty characteristics of smaller churches in Chapter 4, I added a new characteristic: "Capable, compassionate pastoral leadership is usually required to lead a smaller church from simply surviving to really thriving." I now believe both statements are equally true, complementary, and interdependent. When I consider the faithful and effective smaller churches I know, and specifically the ones I visited during my cross-country odyssey, they all have a capable, compassionate pastoral leader, and they all have a gifted, committed core of lay leaders. Furthermore, these churches involve all the people in the ministry and mission of the church. Salt and pepper, ham and eggs, left and right, lay and pastor—without both pastoral and lay leaders and followers, churches will be one-dimensional.

Lay people who passively wait for a Rev. Moses to save them and lead them to the promised land will have a long wait. Few quality pastors feel called to save and lead a passive herd of sheep. Pastors who think they can take a church to the ecclesiastical promised land as Lone Rangers who rely mostly on their own instincts and gifts are living a fantasy.

In the ideal world, the pastoral leader will come with a palpable call to ministry that cannot be resisted; biblical and theological wisdom; effective strategies, practices, and ideas; a vision of what God intends for the community of God; and the requisite gifts for loving and leading a diverse, even balky, people. It is hoped that this pastor will be met by a community of laity who understand that supporting the pastor means being equally yoked with the pastor in a mutual ministry, rather than merely being financially responsible for the care of the pastor. The laity need to have a vision of the church thriving as it risks itself and gives itself to those God calls them to serve, rather than merely surviving as an organization. They must be willing to be an oasis for those lost in the desert, a M.A.S.H. unit for those caught in various cultural cross fires, an open sanctuary for those seeking the safety of belonging to God's community, and a staging ground for those willing to experience the cost and joy of discipleship.

Think about terminology. I have intentionally not used the word "clergy" or assumed that the pastor is ordained. I have not used the word "minister" to refer to the pastoral leader. I've used the pronouns him and her, she and he, equally. Smaller churches through the next thirty years will be led by ordained, licensed, and "raised up" lay pastoral leaders. Rather than interpreting that list as a qualitative hierarchy—with ordained as most desirable and raised up from within the congregation as the least—new, more equitable, and mutually respected ways of acknowledging and authorizing pastoral leadership are needed. Smaller churches will be led, at least, as often by women as by men, and the church will be better for it.

For a decade, the masthead of the San Rafael bulletin has identified the church's "ministers" as "The Whole Congregation." Each and every one of us is called to Christian ministry in and through our baptism. I have long referred to myself as a "bi-vocational pastor," which I am. But in reality, all of us in the church are bi-vocational ministers—people who spend part of our lives earning our keep and the rest of our lives living and serving as ministers in every place we live, work, play, and invest ourselves.

One of the exciting and promising changes in the next thirty years, particularly for smaller churches, will be a further blending of the distinction between minister and layperson. This blending will lead us back to the biblical church where there was no clear distinction. Then, a role in the church was determined not by what kind of theological education one had, but by one's spiritual gifts. The old-fashioned distinction between the minister or pastor as the professional Christian and the laity as amateur Christians has never been accurate and will no longer work. In the Greek, the closest word for "ministry" is *diaconos*, which means "one who serves," and the word "laity" comes from *laos*, which means "the whole people of God." In truth, all those who are baptized are one, whole people of God, who serve God and the people of God (which is the whole of humanity). Distinctions between lay and ordained are neat and handy but theologically confusing. So this chapter is both about those whom the gathered community calls to lead them in the pastoral role and about the gathered community who work alongside the pastoral leader.

Leadership

I don't define the leader as the one who makes the rules or cracks the whip. I don't mean the outsider or dictator or power monger who tells people what to do. A true leader does not just keep a seat warm, or thinks that where we are is where we ought to be, or merely does what some or even all want him or her to do. A genuine leader accepts responsibility for being a moral (do the right thing) leader. A good leader always listens to others and doesn't communicate "my way or no way." Particularly in smaller churches, the mantle of leadership is earned and not given automatically. In smaller churches, one becomes a leader by caring, by being present, by setting an example, by being a man or woman of God, by working hard, and by being called and accepted by the people.

Not all smaller churches know that they need a pastor who is a leader, but all do. Smaller churches need caring, capable leadership when they struggle to feel valuable, when they lose their place in a society that demeans them, when there are too few resources, when they forget that faithfulness and survival are not synonymous, when people in need are going unserved, and when they know they're being called but aren't sure where. It has been reported that in 1790, during the infancy of the United States, Abigail Adams wrote to Thomas Jefferson: "These are the hard times in which a genius would wish to live. Great necessities call forth great leaders." Great necessities in smaller churches are calling out for great leaders there, too.

Church leaders are those who have and exercise the gifts for lovingly keeping the people of God moving faithfully and effectively toward a specific manifestation of God's community, just as Moses led the people of God from slavery to freedom. Daniel Biles, in *Pursuing Excellence in Ministry*, examines the difference between churches that are really faithful and effective with those that are going through the motions or barely hanging on. He says, "Mission, pastoral leadership, lay commitment: these are the basic foundations of excellence in parish ministry."[3] Following is his list of the seven things an "excellent" pastoral leader does with my interpretation:

1. Plan to stick around. Others including Lyle Schaller have said a pastor doesn't really become effective for at least five or six years and increasingly so after that. In general, don't see your smaller church as a stepping stone, but as the place where God has called you on an open-ended basis. The people won't follow you until they trust you and they won't trust you until you've proven to be trustworthy and willing to stay.

2. Focus on the basics of ministry and avoid distractions. Those basics are worship and nurture of the congregation, caretaking and community-building, mission beyond the doors, and building a viable organization.

3. Practice "ministry by wandering around." Get to know your people—well. Be out among them. Work alongside them. Make sure they know they come first with you. Be there at the important times of their lives.

4. Promote mission, not "bodies and bucks." Help them practice mission as the raison d'être of the church. Help them make a difference where God planted them.

5. Constantly seek new ways to improve what you and the congregation do in your ministry and mission. It's not change smaller churches resist, it's folly. Most people in smaller churches know change is necessary, even desirable. They expect it to be sensible and respectful of who and where they are.

6. Do things that will cause people to sit up, take notice, and climb on board. Once they have been helped to elevate their

self-esteem and shake off their doldrums, they will be ready to move and act.

7. Enlist the whole church's involvement in its ministry and mission. Say "we" more and "I" less. Elicit and encourage members' ideas. Create the kind of church that is a higher priority in their lives. From youngest to oldest, work on changing people from spectators into ministers, and critics into participants. [4]

The Bible provides a model for leadership in the church—the servant leader. The prophet Isaiah describes the servant leadership Israel will need to lead it out of exile: "Surely he has borne our griefs and carried our sorrows" (Isa. 53:4). In the Gospel of Mark, Jesus voluntarily and pointedly models servant leadership as he washes the feet of his disciples and tells his followers to do the same. When the disciples bicker over which of them is greatest, Jesus draws a contrast between the way the world works and the way the faith community works: "In the world the recognized rulers lord it over their subjects . . . [but] among you, whoever wants to be great must be your servant" (Mark 10:42–43). Paul prescribes this quality of leadership for the early church as he reminds the little church in Galatia, "Through love become slaves [servants] to one another" (Gal. 5:13). Robert K. Greenleaf, in his classic book *Servant Leadership: A Journey into the Nature of Legitimate Power and Greatness*, says it simply: "The great leader is seen as servant first, and that simple fact is the key to his greatness."[5] While servanthood is not trendy and may not be attractive to those in the leader role, it is biblical and it is effective.

For many years I've been influenced and shaped by the cumulative leadership theory found in ecclesiastical, corporate, and management books by people like Daniel Biles, Robert Greenleaf, Warren Bennis and Burt Nanus, Tom Peters and Nancy Austin, Stephan Dobbs, and Lin Bothwell. As in the Moses-led Exodus, every church leader (pastoral and lay) is called to lead his or her people from one place and time and way of being the church to where and what God calls the church to be. Being a people on a pilgrimage is God's continuing call to all faithful people.

In order for the church's pilgrimage to be God's pilgrimage, its leadership needs to focus on vision, trust and love, morale, and faithfulness. All the leadership literature agree and emphasize that vision is fundamental. As the ancient Chinese proverb says: "If we don't change our direction, we're likely to end up where we're headed." It's the vision that inspires, guides, and shapes the change of direction. The visions that have guided my ministry have emerged from a careful study of scripture and culture, listening to the hopes and needs of my people, discerning the issues and opportunities that are present, and utilizing the resources and energies that are available. The leader doesn't impose a unilateral vision but works with the people to fashion a common vision. Leaders help the people understand that the vision is only a pipedream until they begin bringing it to pass.

The vision won't be realized if the people don't trust that the leader is telling the truth, is not going to abandon them midstream, and loves them. Leaders with character and integrity will always lead further than those who rely on glitz and manipulation. And it is mutual love that carries the people through the hard places and seasons the good times. The more the people know the leader loves them (and vice versa) the more likely they are to forgive her or his mistakes.

I've learned from experience that a leader can only lead a people as far as their morale can carry them. Many smaller churches believe they're too small, poor, old, and weak to do any more than to hold on. By carefully leading step-by-step from little to larger victories, effective leaders enable their people to discover how able and gifted they are and that they really can change the world—in little and not so little ways. The effective leader is something like a personal trainer who carefully and systematically stretches the people and builds their emotional and spiritual muscle.

Finally, the smaller church leader must be a faithful person and understand that being successful and faithful are not the same thing. Success is a secular concept. Being faithful is a sacred term. The latter is what God expects of us. The faithful leader will use worship, biblical reflection, prayer, and a thoughtful reading of the signs of the times to lead the people toward their faithful vision.

The Future Smaller Church Pastor

How times change! Here was the ideal pastor a few decades ago.

> At nine o'clock on a bright March morning a young man in his first
> thirties walked slowly along High Street. He was tall with the shoul-
> ders and waist of an athlete. . . . His clothes were distinctly well-tai-
> lored and he wore them with an easy nonchalance. A stranger inter-
> ested enough to hazard a guess might have set him down as a hand-
> some young lawyer, or a business man with his feet well set upon the
> ladder of success. They would probably not have surmised that he was
> a clergyman . . . [6]

More likely than not, the new pastoral leader of the smaller church
between now and 2030 will not be in the "first thirties," will not have
a chiseled, athletic appearance, will not be wearing well-tailored clothing, may well not be a he, and will not be a rung up on the ladder of
success.

The pastors of the next thirty years will reflect the diversity of the
times and places in which we live. The savvy and faithful church will
have very, very few preconceptions of its next pastor. Two prerequi-
sites are enough. The preliminary requirement should be a person of
faith who can talk the language or is willing to learn to talk the faith
language of the people he is intending to serve. Secondly, the appropriate pastor should have those intangible qualities that would allow
her to grow into being at home with the particular people she's being
called to serve and lead. These two requirements are intentionally
subjective.

Over the last decade, as a part-time denominational placement officer, I've helped almost fifty churches search for and find a pastor.
More often than not, the person called has not fit the ideal of what
the church thought it wanted. The final choice may have been a
woman when the majority was expecting a man or an older person
when the hope was for a younger person or vice-versa. The pastor
finally called may have had a physical disability, or a history of emotional difficulty, or was in some other way different from what the
church was idealizing. More than once, he or she was gay or lesbian.

Yet, when the matchmaking process has been conducted carefully and creatively, the match has usually proven to be a good and healthy one. When both sides of the equation are searching faithfully, it is the Holy Spirit who makes the match. And the Holy Spirit has a long history of illogical and wonderful matches. The most important question is this: will she or he love us, lead us, and be Christian with us?

The following assumptions and expectations were common when I entered seminary in 1965:

- Beginning pastors would be under thirty and straight out of college and seminary. Today, the average beginning pastor is almost forty and entering a second or third career. In the United Church of Christ, sixty-five percent of pastors are over fifty, and twenty-five percent are over sixty.
- Generally pastors are male. Today, in the United Church of Christ, probably fifty percent of pastors of smaller churches are women.
- Pastors normally serve a church on a full-time basis. Today, about one-third of all pastors and considerably more pastors of smaller churches have supplemental income or serve less than full time.
- Pastors serve one church. Today, an increasing number of pastors serve more than one church, sometimes three or more.
- Pastors serve a church of one denomination. Today, more and more serve churches aligned with more than one denomination.
- Pastors will be ordained. Today, with a growing clergy shortage, we will be relying on and recruiting more lay pastors.
- Pastors will move after three to six years and maintain that pattern. Today, more pastors are staying longer, which contributes to happier and more productive pastorates.
- Pastors are expected to be called to (or climb the ladder to) a medium-sized church or larger after serving a smaller church "apprenticeship." Today, more pastors in smaller churches are choosing to remain in smaller churches—if they can afford to.

The very faithful and effective pastors and churches I visited on my cross-country odyssey exemplify the emerging, varied face of pastoral ministry in smaller churches for the coming decades:

- David Popham, Vernal, Utah. David is serving an ecumenical congregation full-time on an inadequate salary and stretching the congregation with his creativity.

- Larry Pray, Big Timber, Montana. Larry is committed to town-and-country ministry. He conducts a very personal, pastoral ministry, while he uses his gifts in and is compensated by a secondary form of ministry.

- Marjie Brewton, Bryant and Erwin, South Dakota. Marjie is a woman pastor who serves two churches. She first chose where she wanted or needed to live and then found a way to do ministry there. She created her own tent-making ministry (running a retreat center) and expects to stay for the long haul. Living where and how she wants to live helps make up for her inadequate level of compensation.

- Atanasio Osphaldo, Sioux Falls, South Dakota. Atanasio is an immigrant pastor serving an immigrant church. He organized the church and then established a denominational connection and was credentialed after forming the church. The church rents space in another church. His wife's income helps make this ministry possible.

- Steve Jewett, Westfield, Iowa. Steve is a bi-vocational, licensed, lay pastor. He talks the language of his people and is extremely effective. He does what needs to be done in about twenty hours a week.

- Karen Hendke, Oto, Rodney, Smithland, Iowa. Karen was called by one of her churches to be their pastor. She was given lay-ministry training, was licensed, and now serves three churches from two denominations. Her husband's farm income supplements her own. Hers is a long-term ministry, and she's exceptionally well-matched with her churches.

- Mac McHarg, Red Oak, Iowa. Mac began serving the church when he was seventy and served for eight years as a semi-retired and part-time pastor who created a challenging and secure environment in which the laity form and realize their vision.

- (<u>Vacant</u>), Indianola, Iowa. This church is like a ship that pretty well sails itself but needs a pastor to be at the helm and chart the course. They have little preconceived notions of who the next pastor will be.

- Deborah Pope, Chamois, Missouri. Deborah is a second-career pastor serving two churches of two denominations. She sounds like she's been there forever but hasn't and is very much a part of the lives of her people.

- Michael Vosler, St. Louis, Missouri. Michael is over fifty and thrives on the challenge of and opportunity for a creative community ministry. He is a visionary who has the knack of calling forth the ministry of others and keeping it organized just enough so that it works. He and his spouse combine their efforts and earn a livable income.

- Ray Strickland, Pensacola, North Carolina. Ray has been the bi-vocational pastor of this church for twenty-two years. He's a drywall contractor for money and pastor for love.

- Charles Walton, Littleton, North Carolina. Charles is an African American pastor serving an African American church. He's a social worker by day and a pastor by night and week-ends. He led the church back from the loss of their building to an arsonist's match and is leading the church toward an ex-panding mission.

- Michelle Wiley-Arey, Vinalhaven, Maine. As Michelle sinks her roots deeper and deeper into the rocky island soil, she is helping her church of mostly gray-haired folks grow younger. This is another church in which it takes the salary of both pastor and spouse to make a living. She may be here for a long time, which is just what this church needs.

None of these pastors fits the stereotype portrayed in the "young man in his first thirties" quote. Each of their ministries is uncon-ventional in one way or another. Each pastoral leader is gifted, accomplished, providing effective leadership, and finding satisfaction in a smaller church. Of these thirteen pastoral positions, women hold four, two are multiple churches, seven are bi-vocational or part-time, lay pastors are effectively filling two.

I have taught as an adjunct in five seminaries and served on the regional staff of three denominational judicatories. Unfortunately, I believe theological schools and denominational judicatories are likely to be less helpful in the future to smaller churches than they have been in the past. Whereas many seminaries once had departments of town-and-country ministry, most are now doing well to have even one course aimed at the majority of settings into which students will go as pastors. In the academic setting, there is little recognition of the importance of size in shaping the nature of congregations and little understanding of the uniqueness of ministry in those settings. Given the sheer number of smaller churches, there ought to be basic courses in smaller-church ministry, worship in smaller churches, mission out of smaller churches, pastoring the rural church and inner-city churches, and bi-vocational ministry, to name a few. However, courses like these are hard to find.

Most seminarians are second-career people who come to seminary after pursuing other vocations. These students could be challenged by the seminary to see their first career as an option for one piece of a bi-vocational ministry, but that seldom happens. Every seminary, either unilaterally or cooperatively, ought to offer a track for those pursuing lay ministry, with classes held evenings, weekends, on location, by computer networking, and television down-link or distance learning. Three effective seminary-related programs for smaller church ministry are the Center for Theology and Land: Rural Ministry Program at Wartburg Theological Seminary in Dubuque, Iowa, the Appalachian Ministries Educational Resource Center in Berea, Kentucky, and the Certificate in Small Church Leadership program at Bangor Theological Seminary.

Mainline denominations at all levels are retreating and retrenching as their funding and, perhaps, vision wither. There are fewer staff to work with more churches in need or crisis. At the national and regional level, there is little functional understanding that most of their churches are smaller and therefore in need of different and specialized intervention and assistance. Volunteers who staff denominational boards, committees, and structures are mostly from larger and denominationally oriented churches. Their experience prevents them from grasping that most churches aren't like and don't think like the ones from which they come. Training events—especially for rural and inner city churches—that will really address smaller church realities are not likely to be available.

Denominational polity and credentialing practices still assume that most churches have and will have full-time, ordained pastors serving one church of one denomination. New ways of naming, describing, and honoring alternative types of ministry that are not hierarchical and discriminatory are needed. The early church looked for spiritual gifts in determining a person's fitness for ministry. Smaller churches would be better served if this practice was reclaimed rather than judging solely by whether enough academic and denominational hurdles have been jumped. Ordained and lay ministries need to be recognized as two viable approaches to parish ministry rather than seeing ordination as the ideal standard for "real" ministry and lay ministry as a "make do" or second fiddle option for those pastors and churches that don't measure up to the preferred standard. While it's been understood for decades that compensation practices, insurance coverage, and pension plans discriminate against smaller-church pastors in most denominations, very little is being done to rectify this inequity and injustice.

In the near future, most of the equipping and support for smaller churches and their leaders will probably have to be of the self-help variety and will be found in the following and other locations:

- Books like this and those in the bibliography
- Journals like *The Five Stones* and newsletters that are produced at the grass-roots level
- Colleagues in ministry who commit to support, challenge, and act as resources to one another
- Neighboring congregations (from the same and differing denominations) who choose to forge informal and formal alliances

- County agents, community colleges, departments in universities
- People within individual congregations who commit to working together toward greater faithfulness and effectiveness
- Computer Web sites and chat rooms

What are some of the changes I expect to see in the next thirty years?

First, I expect to see more ecumenical cooperation, particularly on the local level. I expect to see more churches crossing lines to share facilities, programs, pastoral leadership, resources, and training events. Karl Barth unequivocally claimed that, "There is no justification, theological, spiritual, or biblical for the existence of a plurality of churches genuinely separated in this way and mutually excluding one another internally and therefore externally. A plurality of churches . . . means a plurality of lords . . . . every division as such is a deep riddle, a scandal."[7] Barth is not condemning the plurality of churches but the degree of their separation. There's a Lutheran church and Roman Catholic church in Mankato, Minnesota, that built individual sanctuaries with a common fellowship hall between them. These churches discovered that they were a magnet for Catholic-Protestant families, where they could worship in their accustomed way and still fellowship together. Expect to see much more sharing of facilities. For example, the San Rafael church shares its facility with a Fijian church before its worship and a Korean Presbyterian church afterward. Expect to see more sharing of pastoral leadership, such as a Baptist and Methodist church in the same community sharing a pastor or a lay religious educator. Expect to see churches in a small community sharing one inter-church office among some or all the churches in the community. Expect to see more combined youth groups, educational programs, mission ventures.

There will be vastly more electronic sharing. Communication by e-mail is only scratching the surface. Already there are electronic sermon preparation and Christian education sharing groups. Seminaries will be conducting much more theological education in virtual reality. Pastors in remote settings will be connected by chat room support groups. There will be much more theological education on-line. Denominations may be providing much of their training and resourcing through electronic networks. Pastors looking for the right church and churches looking for the right pastor will find each other on-line. Much pastoral care is already being supplemented via e-mail. The electronic revolution has great possibilities for smaller churches.

Bi-vocational or tent-making or part-time ministry will become much more common. As people move from vocation to vocation, they will less frequently leave the secular one behind as they become pastors. In addition to my career as a pastor, I have also directed two social-service agencies, been a pastoral counselor, worked for three regional denominational conferences, and have been an at-home father, an author, a consultant, a student, and have built two houses. I thrive on the synergy of doing multiple tasks simultaneously. I expect there will be more and more pastors and potential pastors who, for a variety of reasons, will want to engage in parish ministry but who will need to supplement the income they can receive from a smaller congregation with other income. Others will want to serve congregations while they reserve a significant part of their time and energy for other pursuits. As more churches struggle to make-do financially, they will be seeking sources of quality pastoral leadership when they can't afford a full-time salary. Bi-vocational ministry can provide this.

Tent-making ministry has a rich history. At the beginning of the Christian tradition, the Apostle Paul made and sold tents at the same time he was planting churches. Tent-making has been practiced throughout church history. It has several virtues and advantages. Combining a pastoral salary with compensation from another source can provide an adequate income. Bi-vocational ministry allows a person to pursue more than one area of interest. If a pastor is working outside the ecclesial realm, she or he has the opportunity to experience more of the world that her or his laypeople experience. By having more than one work experience, there should be more vocational satisfaction. Working in the secular realm allows a pastor to be a faithful presence in that setting. My experience has been that the essential work gets done in the available time and the laity, by necessity, have to pick up more of the leadership and administrative responsibility. Finally, it's been my experience that everything I've done in addition to pastoring has enhanced my ministry in one way or another.

A four-pronged approach could make bi-vocational ministry a more viable and useful option for many churches and pastors. Seminaries should be preparing their students for the possibility of bi-vocational ministry. Denominations should be counseling smaller churches about the advantages of this alternative and helping them consider other potential employment opportunities in their communities. Those who are discerning a call to parish ministry ought to be envisioning what it would be like to be a pastor while they use time and talents in other pursuits. Congregations should be discerning what other forms of productive endeavor exist in their area as they contemplate calling the next pastor.

The number of churches being served by lay pastors will certainly increase—perhaps dramatically. The ministries of Karen Handke and Steve Jewett demonstrate that lay ministry is not second class or inadequate ministry. It's a powerful witness to the rest of the laity when the pastor has been raised up from among her own people. Such an occurrence helps the church see that the gifts of ministry can be present throughout the congregation and not just in the seminary-trained person who comes from elsewhere.

Two things are necessary to fully equip and validate lay pastors. First, more and better educational programs are needed that are designed for and focused on the lay pastor. It's not realistic or necessary for many potential lay pastors to take up residency in a seminary to participate in the full Master of Divinity degree program. Adequate education can be received evenings, weekends, in intensive weeks, during the summer, and on-line. The United Church of Christ Iowa Conference has created one of the many superb lay ministry training programs that are effectively training lay pastors. Second, we have to find a way to validate or credential lay ministry so that it's not a second-class ministry. My denomination has two hierarchical levels of pastoral ministry—ordained and licensed. Why not put the emphasis on spiritual gifts more than academics and then ordain both the seminary-educated and the life-educated persons who are suitably gifted for ministry?

We will need more parish pastors. In most parts of the country, the clergy shortage is growing quickly. When the supply of pastors is limited, the smaller, poorer, more remote churches are left without. To expand the pool of parish pastors, current church leaders need to help more young people discover the satisfactions of ministry. And every arm of the church will need to be more intentional in interesting, calling, and equipping more middle-aged and older persons for ministry. Lay people like Handke, who are already doing ministry of one kind or another in their congregation, need someone to say, "You have the gifts for being our pastor. Will you accept our call?" There are many gifted people like Jewett who are experiencing insufficient satisfaction in their secular job. We will need to smooth the way and straighten the road so more of these people can become pastoral leaders. The lay pastor often speaks the people's language and relates to their world in a way that's difficult for someone who has spent most of her or his life in the church.

Another source of leadership is people who retire early and discover themselves unfulfilled. These folks are ideal because they already have a lifetime of lay leadership. Many of them already have their retirement income and can afford to do ministry on a part-time basis. We will need more pastors like Mac McHarg, who want to stay in pastoral ministry past the conventional retirement age. Finally, people who are being largely supported by another person, like a spouse, may be free to invest themselves in a vocation for love more than money.

More new forms of smaller churches will emerge. In the North American Catholic world, there is a growing phenomenon of what are called "small Christian communities," meeting in homes and offices and benefiting from the intimacy that is possible in such a gathering. Influenced by the base Christian communities of Latin America, it's estimated there are 37,000 of these small, Catholic Christian communities with about a million participants nationwide.[8]

There will be more groups of colleagues from secular work settings who gather in offices, homes, and banquet rooms in restaurants for worship, study, and the experience of Christian community. Small groups who gather around a mission concern or project will discover in the gathering the best of a parish experience. Persons from a variety of ethnic groups will feel God's call and gather in small groups in living rooms and storefronts where they will discover that what they are is a smaller church. More and more people will come to realize that the gnawing hunger in their soul is a hunger for God and for community and will search out like-minded persons or existing groups where that hunger can be satisfied. People who feel left out or alienated in existing churches will gather with others like them and discover themselves to be the church they never knew before.

While through merger and closure there may be fewer ecclesiastical institutions on street corners thirty years from now, I'm confident there will be many more smaller communities of faith that gather in the name and service of Jesus. Depending on how receptive and responsive existing denominations are, they may carry a denominational label or they may follow their own independent and idiosyncratic path. The next thirty years will be surprising, intriguing, and rewarding for those who are interested in smaller faith communities.

Affording to Be a Smaller-Church Pastor

Pastors have to live and have a right to adequate compensation. In my denomination, the average compensation for fifty-seven percent of full-time pastors in 1999 was over fifty thousand dollars (sixty-three percent of men and thirty-five percent of women). Most churches do not have enough people and resources to pay that level of compensation, particularly if they want to have something left for the rest of the church's ministry and mission. Faced with this shortfall, churches do one of three things. They partner with one or more other churches in paying for a full-time pastor. They prorate the compensation and pay the pastor for part-time ministry. Or, they underpay the pastor. The first two can work; the last is unjust. What's a pastor and church to do?

Throughout my ministry, churches have struggled to get my compensation to a reasonable, just, and adequate level. Nevertheless, our family has always relied on the combined income of wife and husband. I have been a bi-vocational pastor all but four years of my time as a parish minister. This arrangement enabled the churches to pay me fairly for the time for which I contracted, even if the salary they paid wasn't enough to live on. I was free to seek other employment for the time not being compensated for by the church. The satisfactions

I experienced as a pastor of those churches was another form of payment that helped compensate for what they could not pay me. Having grown up in a pastor's home, I knew from the outset that one should never be a pastor if one is seeking wealth or probably even an upper-middle-class lifestyle.

The problem of just and adequate compensation for smaller church pastors will not go away. It is unlikely denominations will have the means to equalize pastoral salaries and retirement benefits. Most smaller churches in the future are not going to be able to pay their pastors a full-time, livable salary. While their financial future is difficult, it's not hopeless. Here are options for pastors and churches:

- Test whether the church that thinks it can't pay a fair salary can, in fact, do so. A church that utilizes all of its available methods of generating income will be able to afford more ministry and mission, including compensating its pastoral leadership, than one that doesn't. (See Chap. 10.)

- Consider bi-vocational ministry as an interesting challenge and promising opportunity. Make it work if it fits your situation.

- Judicatories can provide gifted, smaller-church pastors part-time employment and, thereby, receive the benefits of their talents while supplementing their incomes. I was brought to Iowa by a Conference minister who wanted to have four half-time area ministers in the four quadrants of the state who would also serve smaller churches. I've also been employed part-time at the Conference level in Massachusetts and Northern California. This is a promising model.

- For those with an employed spouse or partner, develop a mindset that calculates total income, not each individual income.

- Consider a yoked or shared ministry so more than one church shares the benefits of the pastor's gifts while sharing responsibility for compensation.

- The church and pastor can try to find a way to "pay" the pastor in ways other than money. My three-quarter-time arrangement with the San Rafael church is described as almost full-time most of the year with twelve weeks when I'm free to do other things—vacation, travel, write, teach, consult, build boats. This works for both the church and for me. A church might grant its pastor free office space for a tent-making counseling practice. A rural church might provide its pastor with a side of beef and a truckload of vegetables. Another church might provide the pastor with free child care. The solution can often be found through creative problem-solving.

- There are some pastors who don't require full-time income, thanks to a pension, independent income, a spouse, or other income. They are and will be a blessing to smaller churches that are conscientious but unsuccessful in adequately compensating their pastor.

- Some smaller churches, particularly house churches and Christian-affinity groups, will solve the compensation problem by voluntarily sharing all the leadership functions and not paying anyone. Everyone then becomes a "worker priest" who works at a job for money while living out the call to minister. With people hungering for community, the number of these groups will grow.

Compensation and personal self-esteem will remain as the two most difficult issues for pastors of smaller churches. Those who can find a way to afford carrying out their vocation in a smaller place, who can find their ego-satisfaction in making a large difference in a smaller arena, and who have their spirit fed in such a place, will discover they are in a "place just right" as the "Simple Gifts" song says. Mother Theresa once said, "We can do no great things; only small things with great love." Smaller churches can be great places for those who understand Mother Theresa's wise insight.

The Lay Half of the Equation

A young man came into some money and bought a beautiful, fast, red sports car. He drove his new car out of the dealership and into the countryside to see what it would do. Driving too fast, he approached a bend in the dirt road. Another car careened around the bend toward him, swerving from side to side, as the driver tried to regain control. As the oncoming car passed him, the woman driving screamed out the window, "PIG!" The young man screamed an epithet back, roared around the curve . . . and ran head-on into a very large sow occupying the center of the road. Too often and in too many settings, this is how pastors and laity have related. Each reacts out of his or her own perspective, failing to understand the worldview of the other. Size and assumed differences have had much to do with creating two different worldviews and clashes along the way.

The larger the church, the greater the distinction between lay and pastoral leadership. The larger the church, the more time, attention, and energy that needs to be given to organizational matters and the more likely it is that laity and pastors will play their separate and, often, unequal roles. The smaller the church, the more all the people can connect with one another and focus together on their mutual ministry and mission. The root of the word "ligament," is *ligare*, which means "to bind together." In smaller churches, there is greater potential for pastor and lay people being bound together.

James Fenhagen's *Mutual Ministry: New Vitality for the Local Church* has fed me throughout most of my ministry. He wrote, "The greatest single obstacle to the genuine renewal of the church is the lack of mutuality that exists between the clergy and the laity."[9]

A summary statement by Henrick Kraemer has sustained efforts at church renewal for several decades:

> Everything in the Church and the world (from the point of view of the Gospel) revolves around the so-called "ordinary member of the church."
> . . . The apparatus of the Church has to be directed towards that end, not towards the maintenance of historical institutions and formulations as if they are sacrosanct and invisible. The total activity of the Church in its worship, its preaching, its teaching, its pastoral care, should have the purpose of helping the "ordinary membership of the Church" to become what they are in Christ.[10]

While every church tries to do that, the evidence suggests that mutuality doesn't happen easily and size is a determining factor. Smaller churches are the right size for greater mutuality. So, how can they further the mutuality between pastoral leaders and the laypeople with whom they are yoked?

Rather than viewing the laypeople as the ones who do the institutional work and pay the bills while the pastoral leaders do the real ministry, all must see themselves equally and mutually called to ministry and mission. Claiming that vision is the hard part. Once it is owned and internalized, then we build mutuality (or strong ligaments) through everything we do. Things that will grow mutuality include worship that is participatory, in which all the people are actors doing the work of the liturgy, in which the people interact with one another and the Word of God, in which the people help baptize the initiate and all share around the Family Table. Education and nurture that identify people's gifts and equip them for their Monday-to-Saturday lives build mutuality and make disciples. Pastoral care develops mutuality when the whole church is committed to caring for one another so that people grow more whole and healthy. Building a spirit of community is crucial so that all the people know they're not living without support in a difficult world. Most important is the conviction that what each person does from Monday through Saturday is part and parcel of the church's mission.

The goal of mutuality begins to be realized as people participate in the organizational life of the church. I work to see that everyone does something and no one does everything in the organized life of the church. People are only asked to do work that's essential (much church work isn't really essential), tasks are simplified, and power is shared broadly throughout the congregation. At each place I've pastored, there have been great benefits by asking everyone annually to fill out a questionnaire that does the following:

- Reminds all of us that each of us is a gifted person, whose gifts are needed and valued by the rest of the faith community
- Defines the task of every office and committee responsibility
- Asks people to circle a "1" beside each office or committee role that they would like to do; a "2" beside the ones they are willing to do; and a "3" beside those they do not want to do
- Lists the other volunteer possibilities in the church such as choir, bringing flowers, praying for persons in need, doing fix-it

work, helping with Sunday school, or being a lay reader in worship

- Thanks them for all that they are already doing to enhance our common life

Every year our nominating committee is surprised by what people volunteer for. People are not asked to do the things they mark as a "3." The work of the nominating committee is simplified and made much more enjoyable. People don't get stuck in or hang on to roles they've been fulfilling in the past. Almost all people have some role in the life of the church and experience making a difference.

Three other things we do foster mutuality. Sustaining and building church morale is a constant concern, people are shielded from receiving undeserved criticism (and even some earned criticism), and people are continually affirmed and thanked. I accept that, as the paid pastor, it is part of my job to deflect criticism away from others. Volunteers have a right to not be the object of destructive criticism. One simple little ritual that has paid huge dividends is our annual Feather-in-the-Hat Awards. This tradition is a delightful way of thanking people for special contributions to our ministry and mission.

One other mutuality issue is friendship. Conventional wisdom says that pastors should not have personal friends in the churches they serve. I have not lived by that axiom. I share common values and many common interests with people in my congregations. In rural areas, there is not an abundance of people from whom to build a network of friends. I do observe some boundaries: A few, very personal, matters are not brought into the friendships; I am careful about what church "business" I discuss with my church friends; I don't ask church friends for special support or favors. There are risks to friendships in the church, but the rewards have been greater. Finally, church friends do not replace the value of a network of friends that are not part of the church.

There's much more that could be written about the role of laity and mutuality between pastor and laity. The point here is that, in smaller churches, the lines are blending and will blend further. With some cautions, this blending is good and will be advantageous for the emerging community of God.

The world and the church are changing, and a whole new world is emerging as the new century unfolds. Smaller communities of faith are key components of the evolving ecclesiastical reality. As leaders in these communities, we are needed and called to a ministry and mission that offers intimacy, builds community, and makes a difference. God calls us to be the church where we are, as we are, without excuse or complaint. Together, we are the right size to do and be all that God needs of us in order to receive all that God offers us. Thanks be to God!

Questions

1. How do you define "leader"? How do you function as a leader in your congregation?
2. Do you foresee additional or differing expectations of pastoral leaders between now and 2030?
3. As you peer into your crystal ball, how do you picture your congregation in 2030? In order to have a viable presence then, what steps does your congregation need to take now?
4. How does your church deal with the challenge of adequate compensation for its pastoral leader?

Suggestion

Call your church leadership together for a leadership day of envisioning and leadership training. Use this book as a study guide with your best, brightest, and most committed.

chapter twelve

Conclusion

IN THE TIME AHEAD, many new smaller churches will be born. Some will not last and some will prove to be very vital. Some older, smaller churches will wither and die. Many will manage to keep on keeping on. Many more will discover themselves to be indispensable and will thrive. The poignant story of the Rabbi's Gift points to the alternative futures that are before smaller churches.

A monastery flourished in Europe throughout the seventeenth and eighteenth centuries. It had several branch houses and many monks. A wave of secularism swept the land during the nineteenth century, and the monastery fell on hard times. One by one, the branch houses closed. One after another, the monks, enamored with other things, dropped away until there were five monks left in the decaying motherhouse. The abbot and four others, all over seventy years of age, were the remnant. The future seemed bleak.

There was a little hut deep in the woods surrounding the monastery. It was a hermitage or retreat house used by the rabbi from a nearby village. After many years of prayer and contemplation, the monks had an uncanny sense of when the rabbi was at his hermitage. One monk would whisper to another, "The rabbi is in the woods." As the abbot agonized over the fate of his dying order, it occurred to him that the rabbi might have some wisdom that might help save the monastery.

The abbot found his way to the rabbi's door and was cordially invited in. After an exchange of pleasantries, the abbot shared the tragic story of the monastery's decline. The rabbi could only commiserate. "I know how it is," he lamented. "The spirit has gone out of the people. It is the same in my town. Almost no one comes to the synagogue anymore. They're too busy with other matters." Then the rabbi and abbot wept together, read the Torah together, and spoke of deep things. When it was time to leave, the abbot thanked the rabbi for the opportunity to meet and visit. At the door, the abbot again asked in desperation, "Don't you have any advice that might help save my dying order?"

The rabbi responded, "No, I'm so sorry. I have no useful advice to offer. The only thing I can tell you is that the Messiah is one of you."

When the abbot returned to the monastery, the other monks gathered around and asked, "Well, what did the rabbi say?"

"He couldn't help," the abbot answered. "We just wept and read the Torah together. However, just as I was leaving he did say something mysterious. He said the Messiah is one of us. I have no idea what that means."

In the days, weeks, and months that followed, the old monks pondered this cryptic message and wondered whether it held any possible significance. The Messiah is one of us? Could he possibly have meant one of us old monks here at the monastery? It seems impossible. But if he is one of us, which one of us? Could he have meant the abbot? Why, of course, if he meant anyone, it would have to be Father Abbot. He's been our leader for so long. On the other hand, he might have meant Brother Thomas. Brother Thomas is certainly a holy man. Everyone knows he's a holy man.

You know he couldn't have meant Brother Elred! Elred gets crotchety at times. But when you think about it, even though he's a thorn in the side of all of us, Elred is virtually always right. Surely he couldn't have meant Brother Phillip. Phillip is so quiet and passive. But then, without fail, Phillip has a gift for somehow always being there when you need him. He just magically appears at your side. Maybe Phillip is the Messiah. One thing we do know, the rabbi did not mean me! That's certainly not possible. I'm just an ordinary person. But, what if he did mean me? Suppose I am the Messiah?

As they each contemplated in this manner—over weeks and months—the old monks began treating each other with extraordinary respect and affection, on the off chance that one among them might be the Messiah. And on the off, off chance that each monk himself might be the Messiah, they began to treat themselves with extraordinary respect and appreciation.

Because the monastery was situated in a beautiful forest, people occasionally came to visit the monastery to picnic on its lawn, to wander along the paths in the surrounding woods, and now and then to meditate in its dilapidated chapel. As they did so, even without being conscious of it, they sensed the aura of extraordinary respect and affection that now began to surround the five old monks. That same extraordinary respect and affection seemed to permeate the atmosphere of the place. There was something strangely attractive, even compelling, about it—there was something at the monastery that was missing in wider society. People came more and more frequently to the monastery and they brought their friends to picnic, play, and pray. Friends brought other friends.

Some of the visitors talked more and more with the old monks. After a while one asked to join the order, then another, and another. Within a few years, the monastery was once again a thriving order, radiating faith, respect, and affection for all, which spread into the region around.[1]

This is a marvelous parable that smaller churches and those who love and serve them can chew on, savor, and digest. There is increasing need for communities of faith where contemporary wayfarers and pilgrims can find meaning, purpose, respect, and affection. Some of today's smaller churches are tired and discouraged remnants like that old, diminished monastery. Hope is gone, morale has plummeted, mission is missing, their *raison d'être* forgotten. Even respect and affection for one another is missing. Many newer and more vital smaller churches are not fully realizing their God-given gift. In a mega-world, we've lost the vision of how to be and why to be a micro-church. We've not fully incorporated what Carl Dudley observed almost twenty-five years ago:

> In a big world, the small church has remained intimate. In a fast world, the small church has been steady. In an expensive world, the small church has remained plain. In a complex world, the small church has remained simple. In a rational world, the small church has kept feelings. In a mobile world, the small church has been an anchor. In an anonymous world, the small church calls us by name.[2]

Dudley recognizes what many have forgotten or ignored—smaller churches can offer an alternative in a world that has grown beyond a livable and viable scale and pace. Throughout all of church history, there has never been a time when healthy, faithful, effective smaller churches have been more needed and necessary. Therefore, they have a very promising future—if their people believe to the core of their being that they are the right size to be faithful and effective communities of faith. Then they must practice the appropriate approaches and strategies that will fulfill their potential and meet the world's need.

I pray you, the reader, have found hopeful and helpful material here. I hope you understand that you cannot be too little to be faithful and effective. What does determine your faithfulness and effectiveness is whether and how you fulfill these ten characteristics of a Spirited church. Such a church will:

1. Love God and love to worship God with constancy, commitment, and contagious passion

2. Love each other, care for one another, and have a barrel of fun together

3. Be naturally generous and know that God will provide enough to do what God asks it to do

4. Recognize, honor, and utilize the special gifts of every one of its people

5. Really believe it can do anything it wants to do that God is calling it to do

6. Make a tangible difference in the local to global world

7. Be a community that treats every stranger and visitor as if she or he is the Christ, thus incorporating that person into the community of God

8. Know that even if there are only a few people, there are enough to be a thriving community of faith

9. Care little about survival and greatly about faithfulness

10. Have no fear, make no excuses, and exhibit bushels of faith, hope, and love

Be well, do good, carry on, Godspeed, gracias, and shalom.

Resources for Smaller Churches

Thirty Common Characteristics of Smaller Churches

Directions: Apply the following common characteristics of smaller churches to your church. If the statement is very true of your church, circle ONE. If it is kind of true, circle TWO. If it is not characteristic of your church, circle THREE.

1. A smaller church fulfills the common expectations of its people.

    ONE   TWO   THREE

2. Almost everyone knows almost everyone else in a smaller church.

    ONE   TWO   THREE

3. Beyond knowing one another, the smaller church acts and feels like "family."

    ONE   TWO   THREE

4. Almost everyone feels and is important and needed.

    ONE   TWO   THREE

5. Organizational functioning is simple, rather than complex, and sometimes immediate, not delayed.

    ONE   TWO   THREE

6. Communication is rapid and usually effective.

    ONE   TWO   THREE

7. Smaller churches are known more by their distinctive personalities and less by their programs or even their names.

    ONE   TWO   THREE

8. A smaller church is likely to be rooted in its history and nervous about its future.

    ONE   TWO   THREE

9. A smaller church's theology is relational, horizontal, and historical.

    ONE   TWO   THREE

10. Smaller churches understand and respond to mission in personal and immediate terms.

ONE   TWO   THREE

11. A smaller church prefers its minister be a pastor, friend, generalist, and lover and not a professional, specialist, administrator, or chief executive officer.

ONE   TWO   THREE

12. Smaller churches will look and feel like the churches described by the New Testament writers.

ONE   TWO   THREE

13. Smaller churches are people centered and oriented.

ONE   TWO   THREE

14. Smaller-church members are more likely to laugh and cry than larger-church members.

ONE   TWO   THREE

15. Worship is their primary activity.

ONE   TWO   THREE

16. Eating together is their favorite activity.

ONE   TWO   THREE

17. The children in smaller churches belong to the whole church.

ONE   TWO   THREE

18. Smaller churches are more intergenerational and integrated than larger churches.

ONE   TWO   THREE

19. Smaller churches are very good at celebrating the various stages of life.

ONE   TWO   THREE

20. Smaller churches are more story than treatise, more mythology than systematic theology.

ONE   TWO   THREE

21. Smaller churches operate on fluid, "people" time.

ONE   TWO   THREE

22. Most smaller church people would prefer, on the one hand, to give what is needed and when it's needed and, on the other hand, to underwrite what they value as a gesture of gratitude for God's goodness.

ONE   TWO   THREE

23. Lay people are more important than the pastor.

ONE   TWO   THREE

24. Capable, compassionate pastoral leadership is usually required to lead a smaller church from simply surviving to really thriving.

ONE   TWO   THREE

25. Smaller churches are often hard to get into and harder to get out of.

ONE   TWO   THREE

26. Smaller churches are tough and tenacious!

ONE   TWO   THREE

27. Smaller churches would rather do it "our way" because they're locally owned and operated.

ONE   TWO   THREE

28. Smaller churches are more effective than efficient.

ONE   TWO   THREE

29. Smaller churches are better at events than programs.

ONE   TWO   THREE

30. Smaller churches are better at meeting immediate needs than long-range planning.

ONE   TWO   THREE

Scoring: Count how many ONEs you have, then TWOs, then THREEs. The more ONEs you have, the smaller your church is (in terms of style and behavior). The more THREEs you have, the larger your church is. If you have more ONEs than THREEs, that is not bad. If you have more THREEs than ONEs, that is not necessarily good. It simply describes how your church lives its life.

Church Morale Inventory

Directions: Circle the number that is closest to your own assessment of how things are in your church within each category. The numbers toward each margin indicate that the statement is very true; numbers toward the center indicate one alternative or the other is somewhat true.

LOW MORALE	HIGH MORALE
1. Our church feels under siege in the surrounding community. 1 2 3 4 5	People trust the community to be friendly toward the church. 6 7 8 9 10
2. People fear red ink; financial failure. 1 2 3 4 5	People believe there's enough money to meet church's needs. 6 7 8 9 10
3. People are generally negative and pessimistic. 1 2 3 4 5	People are generally positive and optimistic. 6 7 8 9 10
4. Recalling the past, people remember loss and defeats 1 2 3 4 5	Thinking back, people recall wins and successes. 6 7 8 9 10
5. Our people feel abused and forgotten. 1 2 3 4 5	Our people feel cared about. 6 7 8 9 10
6. We think mostly about our own church and its needs. 1 2 3 4 5	We have a strong commitment to mission beyond our church. 6 7 8 9 10
7. Our church leadership is uncaring and incompetent. 1 2 3 4 5	Our leadership is caring and able. 6 7 8 9 10
8. Our people resist new ideas and change. 1 2 3 4 5	We welcome new ideas, change. 6 7 8 9 10
9. People attend out of duty and habit. 1 2 3 4 5	Our people look forward to and enjoy being present. 6 7 8 9 10
10. We aren't very friendly to visitors. 1 2 3 4 5	Visitors are warmly welcomed. 6 7 8 9 10

LOW MORALE	HIGH MORALE

11. Worship is routine and boring.

1   2   3   4   5   6   7   8   9   10

Worship is alive, touches us.

12. Our church preaches and practices a theology of sin and judgment.

1   2   3   4   5   6   7   8   9   10

We preach and practice a theology of love and grace.

13. Faith is defined as duty performed.

1   2   3   4   5   6   7   8   9   10

Faith is experienced as joyous living.

14. People's motives are suspect here.

1   2   3   4   5   6   7   8   9   10

People are fully trusted here.

15. Pastors look to leave soon after they arrive at our church.

1   2   3   4   5   6   7   8   9   10

Pastors feel at home and desire to stay here.

16. People give sparingly and reluctantly.

1   2   3   4   5   6   7   8   9   10

We give generously and gladly.

17. Church building looks and feels cold, drab, uncared for.

1   2   3   4   5   6   7   8   9   10

Church building looks and feels warm and attractive.

18. We avoid responsibility with excuses.

1   2   3   4   5   6   7   8   9   10

Most volunteer and do their part.

19. New people must wait their turn to become church leaders.

1   2   3   4   5   6   7   8   9   10

New people are welcomed into leadership and power.

20. Attendance is poor at worship, meetings, events.

1   2   3   4   5   6   7   8   9   10

Most people come to everything.

21. Conflict is frequent, divisive, and cancerous.

1   2   3   4   5   6   7   8   9   10

Conflict happens occasionally but is dealt with and resolved.

22. Children or youth wish they were somewhere else.

1   2   3   4   5   6   7   8   9   10

Children and youth feel at home and enjoy being here.

23. Church work is thankless here.

1   2   3   4   5   6   7   8   9   10

People are showered with thanks.

24. Church is business-like and somber.

1   2   3   4   5   6   7   8   9   10

Church loves to party, has fun.

25. We're spiritually lifeless.   We're growing spiritually.

   1   2   3   4   5   6   7   8   9   10

26. We have a bleak vision of the future.   We see the future with optimism.

   1   2   3   4   5   6   7   8   9   10

Now that you're finished, which four categories most need strengthening?

1.

2.

3.

4.

Which four categories show the greatest strength?

1.

2.

3.

4.

Scoring: Add the numbers you circled. A score of 80 or less suggests that your church's morale is in need of a transfusion and intensive care. A score around 110 means that you are alive but church health is somewhat precarious. A score of 140 or more suggests your church has solid self-esteem and a healthy morale. Churches that score low should begin by picking two key areas and strategize promising ways of addressing those areas, then move to others. Churches scoring 120 or higher should pay attention to those areas where they scored low and strategize to build on those areas that are strong. Churches scoring over 140 should strategize how to enhance their high self-esteem.

Worship Survey

Directions to survey takers: Have as many of your worshipers as possible fill out this survey. It will give the one or ones who plan your church's worship much valuable information concerning how your current worship is being received and how it might be customized to better fit the congregation. I have had good experience streamlining a worship service to make it shorter and then asking people to fill out the survey before they leave. Be sure and share the results of the survey with your congregation.

Introduction: Please help us rethink and improve our worship by taking up to twenty minutes to fill out this survey. So that we can take your views seriously as we plan our worship services, we need to know what you do and do not find helpful. Your thoughtfulness in offering information, affirmation, and suggestions for improvement will be appreciated.

Survey

How often do you attend worship here?
❏ Four times a month   ❏ Three   ❏ Two   ❏ One
❏ Occasionally

Your age: ❏ Child/youth   ❏ 20 – 40   ❏ 41–65   ❏ 66 or older

What is your denominational or religious background?

What sizes of churches do you have significant experience in besides this one?
❏ None   ❏ Very small   ❏ Small   ❏ Medium   ❏ Large

Would you prefer to worship with:
❏ Less than 50 people?   ❏ 51–100?   ❏ 101–200?
❏ 200–500?   ❏ More?

Why do you prefer the size you indicated?

Why do you worship here rather than staying home or doing other things?

Are your hopes and expectations for worship generally met?
❏ Yes   ❏ No   ❏ Why or why not?

Do you prefer our current worship time?   ❏ Yes   ❏ No   If not, what day and time would you prefer to worship? _____

Do you like the usual length of our worship?   ❏ Yes   ❏ No

Does it bother you if worship runs 10–15 minutes long?

❏ Yes ❏ No

15 –30 minutes long?   ❏ Yes   ❏ No

Our present order of worship/bulletin is:
❏ Interesting and helpful   ❏ It's O.K.   ❏ Doesn't work for me

Why or why not?

Is our order of worship/bulletin:
❏ User friendly?   ❏ Confusing? Suggestions:

Listed below are the elements of our worship experience. Please use the following 5–1 scale to evaluate each:

5=Very meaningful; 4=Helpful; 3=O. K.; 2=Fair; 1=Doesn't work

_____   Prelude music

_____   Welcome and Announcements

_____   Greeting each other

_____   Call to Worship

_____   Hymn choices/selection/way we sing them

_____   Time of Confession: Unison Prayer, Silent Prayer, Lord's Prayer, Assurance

_____   Children's Time

_____   Anthem(s)

_____   Scripture(s)

Do we use too much or too little scripture?
❏ Too much   ❏ Too little

_____   Sermon

Are sermons too long or too short?

❏ Too long   ❏ Too short

Are they usually relevant?   ❏ Yes   ❏ No

❏ Interesting?   ❏ Yes   ❏ No

Suggestions for our preacher:

_____   Joys and Concerns and Pastoral Prayer

_____   Offering of Gifts

_____   Commission or Benediction

_____   Passing of the Peace

We celebrate two sacraments in our worship: Baptism and Communion. Please evaluate again using the 5–1 scale:

_____   The way we do baptisms in this church

_____   The way we practice communion/the Lord's Supper/ Eucharist here

Suggestions for either:

Do you have feedback or suggestions about our celebration of the church year (Advent, Christmas, Lent, Easter, Pentecost)?

Would you like more or less lay participation in worship?

❑ More   ❑ Less Why?

Please note kudos and suggestions for those who plan and lead worship:

Please note any hymns you'd like to sing more often:

Please note hymns you'd like to sing less often:

Please note kudos and suggestions for those who plan and/or lead our music:

Please note any changes or improvements that would make our worship space work better for you or others:

Note how we could make our Sunday gathering and worship more welcoming to visitors and new folks:

Please note any other suggestions on the back of this sheet. Sign your name if you're interested in talking to someone about our worship. THANK YOU for helping with this survey. Results will be shared. Please return by _____.

Notes

Preface

1. Walker Percy, *The Moviegoer* (New York: Knopf, 1961), 13.
2. T. S. Eliot, excerpts from "Little Gidding - V" in *Four Quartets* (New York: Harcourt, Inc., 1970).

Introduction

1. Anne Lamott, *Traveling Mercies: Some Thoughts on Faith* (New York: Pantheon Books, 1999), 46–48, 54–55.
2. Carl S. Dudley, *Making the Small Church Effective* (Nashville, Tenn.: Abingdon, 1978), 48.
3. Robert W. Lynn and James W. Fraser, "Images of the Small Church in American History," *Small Churches Are Beautiful*, ed. Jackson W. Carroll (San Francisco: Harper & Row, 1997), 7.
4. Lyman Beecher, *Autobiography*, 2 vol., ed. Barbara M. Cross (Cambridge: Belknap Press of Harvard University Press, 1961), 1:70.
5. Lynn and Fraser, "Images of the Small Church in American History," 9–10.
6. E. Franklin Frazier, *The Negro Church in America* (New York: Schocken Books, 1964), 53.

7. Clarence Seidenspinner, "Church for Tomorrow," *The Christian Century* 61 (1944): 1132.
8. Kennon L. Callahan, *Small Strong Congregations: Creating Strengths and Health for Your Congregation* (San Francisco: Jossey-Bass, 2000), vii.

Chapter 1

1. Marjie Brewton, *Heart of the Earth* (Chamberlain, S. D.: Register-Lakota Printing, 1989), 9–10.

Chapter 2

1. Robert N. Bellah, et al., *Habits of the Heart: Individualism and Commitment in American Life* (New York: Harper & Row, 1985), 221.
2. Theodore H. Erickson, "New Expectations: Denominational Collaboration with Small Churches," *Small Churches Are Beautiful*, ed. Jackson W. Carroll (San Francisco: Harper & Row, 1977), 160.
3. T. S. Eliot, excerpt from "Choruses from 'The Rock,'" in *Collected Poems 1909–1962* (New York: Harcourt, Inc., 1936).
4. Diectrich Bonhoeffer, *Life Together* (New York: Harper & Row, 1954), 21.

5. John Macquarrie, *Principles of Christian Theology* (New York: Scribner, 1966), vii.

6. Bernie S. Siegel, *Love, Medicine, and Miracles: Lessons Learned about Self-healing from a Surgeon's Experience with Exceptional Patients* (New York: Harper & Row, 1986), 22–24.

7. Georg Simmel, *The Sociology of Georg Simmel*, ed. and trans. with an introduction by Kurt H. Wolff (New York: Free Press of Glencoe, 1950), 115.

8. Aldous Huxley, *The Devils of Loudon* (New York: Carroll & Graf, 1986), 317.

9. Robert Putnam, "Bowling Alone: America's Declining Social Capital," *Journal of Democracy* 6, no. 1 (Jan. 1995): 65–78.

10. ——— *Bowling Alone: The Collapse and Revival of American Community* (New York: Simon & Schuster, 2000), 111–12.

11. Ibid., 66.

12. Ibid., 283.

13. Ibid., 409, (italics mine).

14. Paul D. Hanson, *The People Called: The Growth of Community in the Bible* (San Francisco: Harper & Row, 1986), 5–6.

15. Ibid., 467.

16. Eliot, "Choruses from 'The Rock,'" 101–02.

17. A. Paul Hare, *Handbook of Small Group Research* (New York: Free Press, 1976), 216.

18. Lyle E. Schaller, *The Small Church Is Different!* (Nashville, Tenn.: Abingdon, 1982), 10–12.

19. Carl S. Dudley, *Making the Small Church Effective* (Nashville, Tenn.: Abingdon, 1978), 16.

20. Ibid., 35.

21. Reinhold Niebuhr, *Moral Man and Immoral Society* (New York: Scribner's Sons, 1932), particularly the introduction and chapter 1.

22. Paul Tillich, *The Shaking of the Foundations* (New York: Scribner's Sons, 1948), 153–163.

Chapter 3

1. David R. Ray, *Wonderful Worship in Smaller Churches* (Cleveland: The Pilgrim Press, 2000), 9–11.

2. Charles H. Cooley, "Primary Groups," *Small Groups: Studies in Social Interaction*, ed. A. Paul Hare, Edgar F. Borgatta, and Robert F. Bales (New York: Knopf, 1955), 15.

3. Carl S. Dudley, *Making the Small Church Effective* (Nashville, Tenn.: Abingdon, 1978), 33.

4. Malcolm Gladwell, *The Tipping Point: How Little Things Can Make a Big Difference* (Boston: Little & Brown, 2000), 179.

5. Ibid., 181.

6. Lyle E. Schaller, *Looking in the Mirror: Self-appraisal in the Local Church* (Nashville, Tenn.: Abingdon, 1984), 15–23.

7. Arlin J. Rothauge, *Sizing Up the Congregation for New Member Ministry* (New York: Episcopal Church Center, [1982]), 5–36.

8. Douglas A. Walrath, "Types of Small Congregations and Their Implications for Planning," *Small Churches Are Beautiful*, ed. Jackson W. Carroll (San Francisco: Harper & Row, 1977), 36–42. This material is also discussed by Walrath in Carl S. Dudley and Walrath, *Developing Your Small Church's Potential* (Valley Forge, Penn.: Judson Press, 1988), 10–30.

9. Walrath, "Types of Small Congregations and Their Implications for Planning," 43–44, and Dudley and Walrath, *Developing Your Small Church's Potential*, 34–38.

10. Walrath, "Types of Small Congregations and Their Implications for Planning, 44–46.

11. Dudley and Walrath, *Developing Your Small Church's Potential*, 38–45.

12. Robert Redfield, "The Folk Society," *American Journal of Sociology* 52, no. 4 (Jan. 1947): 293–303.

13. Anthony G. Pappas, *Entering the World of the Small Church* (Bethesda, Md.: Alban Institute, 2000), 14.

14. Nancy Foltz, ed. *Religious Education in the Small Membership Church* (Birmingham, Ala.: Religious Education Press, 1990), 38–41.

15. Martin F. Saarinen, *The Life Cycle of a Congregation* (Washington, D.C.: Alban Institute, 1986).

16. Alice Mann, *Can Our Church Live? Redeveloping Congregations in Decline* (Bethesda, Md.: Alban Institute, 1999), 1–12.

17. Foltz, *Religious Education in the Small Membership Church*, 98–99.

18. A. Paul Hare, *Handbook of Small Group Research*, (New York: Free Press, 1976), 16.

19. Dietrich Bonhoeffer, *Life Together* (New York: Harper & Row, 1954), 94.

20. Dudley, "Small Churches Are Special," *JED Share* 8, no. 1 (spring 1979): 5.

21. Dudley, *Unique Dynamics of the Small Church* (Washington, D.C.: Alban Institute, 1977), 20–21.

22. Dudley, *Making the Small Church Effective*, 71–72.

23. Garrison Keillor, *Lake Wobegon Days* (New York: Viking Penguin, 1985), 7.

24. Robert Frost, "The Death of the Hired Man," *Complete Poems of Robert Frost* (New York: Holt, Rinehart & Winston, 1963), 53.

Chapter 4

1. David R. Ray, *Wonderful Worship in Smaller Churches*, (Cleveland: The Pilgrim Press, 2000),135–37.

2. Henri J. M. Nouwen, *Sabbatical Journey: The Diary of His Final Year* (New York: Crossroad, 1998), 84.

3. ———, *Reaching Out: The Three Movements of the Spiritual Life* (Garden City, N.Y.: Doubleday, 1975), 46.

4. Gilbert Frederick Cope, ed., *Making the Building Serve the Liturgy: Studies in the Reordering of Churches* (London: A. R. Mowbray, 1962), 5.

5. Cris Williamson, "Song of the Soul," (Marcola, Oreg.: Bird Ankles Music, 1973).

6. Miriam Therese Winter, *Preparing the Way of the Lord* (Nashville, Tenn.: Abingdon, 1978), 78.

7. Dietrich Bonhoeffer, *Life Together* (New York: Harper & Row, 1954), 61.

8. James F. White, *Introduction to Christian Worship* (Nashville, Tenn.: Abingdon, 1980), 157.

9. John H. Westerhoff III, *Will Our Children Have Faith?* (Harrisburg, Penn.: Morehouse, 2000), 76.

Chapter 5

1. John Westerhoff III, *Will Our Children Have Faith?* (Harrisburg, Penn.: Morehouse, 2000), 20.

2. Peter L. Benson and Carolyn H. Eklin, *Effective Christian Education: A*

National Study of Protestant Congrega-tions—A Summary Report on Faith, Loyalty, and Congregational Life (Minneapolis, Minn.: Search Institute, 1990), 14–16.

3. Westerhoff III, *Will Our Children Have Faith?*, 9.

4. Ibid., 82.

5. Ibid., 81–82.

6. Ibid., 141.

Chapter 6

1. Henri J. M. Nouwen, *Reaching Out: The Three Movements of the Spiritual Life* (Garden City, N.Y.: Doubleday, 1975), 46.

2. Carl S. Dudley, *Unique Dynamics of the Small Church* (Washington, D.C.: Alban Institute, 1977), 8.

3. Elizabeth O'Connor, *The New Community* (New York: Harper & Row, 1976), 9.

4. Abraham Maslow, "A Theory of Human Motivation," *Psychological Review* 50 (1943): 370–96.

5. David L. Ostendorf, "Toward Wholeness and Community: Strategies for Pastoral and Political Response to the American Rural Crisis," *Word and World: Theology for Christian Ministry* 6, no. 1 (winter 1986): 58.

6. One of the best sources of information regarding the healing properties of religious faith is Larry Dossey's book *Healing Words: The Power of Prayer and the Practice of Medicine* (San Francisco: Harper SanFrancisco, 1993). See also Claudia Wallis, "Healing: A Growing and Surprising Body of Scientific Evidence Says They Can," *Time*, 24 June 1996, 59–62.

7. Rachel Naomi Remen, *Kitchen Table Wisdom: Stories That Heal* (New York: Riverhead Books, 1996), 245–46.

Chapter 7

1. Emil Brunner, *The Word and the World* (London: SCM, 1931), 108.

2. Kennon L. Callahan, *Small, Strong Congregations: Creating Strengths and Health for Your Congregation* (San Francisco: Jossey-Bass, 2000), 39.

3. Ibid., 32.

4. Anthony Pappas and Scott Planting, *Mission: The Small Church Reaches Out* (Valley Forge, Penn.: Judson Press, 1993), 22.

5. Carl Dudley, *Making the Small Church Effective* (Nashville, Tenn.: Abingdon, 1978), 85–86.

6. Victor N. Claman and David E. Butler with Jessica A. Boyatt, *Acting on Your Faith: Congregations Making a Difference* (Boston: Insights, 1994).

7. Bill Briggs, *Faith through Works: Church Renewal through Mission* (Franconia, N.H.: Thorn Books, 1983), 86.

Chapter 8

1. Kirkpatrick Sale, *Human Scale* (New York: Coward, McCann & Geoghegan, 1980), 64–65.

2. G. Douglass Lewis, *Meeting the Moment: Leadership and Well-Being in Ministry* (Nashville, Tenn.: Abingdon, 1997), 22–23.

Chapter 9

1. C. Peter Wagner, *Your Church Can Grow* (Ventura, Calif.: Regal Books, 1984), 97.

2. Carl S. Dudley, *Making the Small Church Effective* (Nashville, Tenn.: Abingdon, 1978) 47.

3. Lyle E. Schaller, *The Small Church Is Different!* (Nashville, Tenn.: Abingdon, 1982), 11–12.

4. Loren B. Mead, *More Than Numbers: The Ways Churches Grow* (Washington, D.C.: Alban Institute, 1993).

5. Arlin J. Rothauge, *Sizing Up the Congregation for New Member Ministry* (New York: Episcopal Church Center, 1989), 7–21.

6. Schaller, *Growing Plans* (Nashville, Tenn.: Abingdon, 1983), 15–49.

Chapter 10

1. Daniel V. Biles, *Pursuing Excellence in Ministry* (Washington, D.C.: Alban Institute, 1988), 18.

2. Henri J. M. Nouwen, *Sabbatical Journey: The Diary of His Final Year* (New York: Crossroad, 1998), 69.

Chapter 11

1. Kennon L. Callahan, *Small, Strong Congregations: Creating Strengths and Health for Your Congregation* (San Francisco: Jossey-Bass, 2000), 12–13.

2. Warren Bennis, *Why Leaders Can't Lead: The Unconscious Conspiracy Continues* (San Francisco: Jossey-Bass Publishers, 1989), 59. Italics mine

3. Daniel V. Biles, *Pursuing Excellence in Ministry* (Washington, D.C.: Alban Institute, 1988), 53.

4. Ibid., 79–81.

5. Robert K. Greenleaf, *Servant Leadership: A Journey into the Nature of Legitimate Power and Greatness* (New York: Paulist Press, 1977), 7.

6. Agnes Sigh Turnbull, *The Bishop's Mantle* (New York: Macmillan, 1947). Qtd. in Robert W. Lynn and James W. Fraser, "Images of the Small Church in American History," *Small Churches Are Beautiful*, ed. Jackson Carroll (San Francisco: Harper & Row, 1997), 6.

7. Karl Barth, *Church Dogmatics*, vol. 4, no. 1, ed. G. W. Bromiley and T. F. Torrance, trans. G. T. Thomson, (New York: Scribner's Sons, 1956), 675.

8. Bernard J. Lee with William V. D'Antonio and Virgilio Elizondo et al., *The Catholic Experience of Small Christian Communities* (New York: Paulist Press, 2000), 10.

9. James C. Fenhagen, *Mutual Ministry: New Vitality for the Local Church* (New York: Seabury Press, 1977), 22.

10. Hendrick Kraemer, *A Theology of the Laity* (London: Lutterworth Press, 1958), 132.

Chapter 12

1. M. Scott Peck, *The Different Drum: Community Making and Peace* (New York: Simon and Schuster, 1987), 13–15.

2. Carl S. Dudley, *Making the Small Church Effective* (Nashville, Tenn.: Abingdon, 1978), 176.

Bibliography

Books

Ammerman, Nancy T., et al. *Studying Congregations: A New Handbook*. Nashville, Tenn.: Abingdon Press, 1998.

Beecher, Lyman. *Autobiography*. 2 vols. Ed. Barbara M. Cross. Cambridge: Belknap Press of Harvard University Press, 1961.

Bellah, Robert N., et al. *Habits of the Heart: Individualism and Commitment in American Life*. New York: Harper & Row, 1985.

Bennis, Warren. *Why Leaders Can't Lead: The Unconscious Conspiracy Continues*. San Francisco: Jossey-Bass, 1990.

————, and Bert Nanus. *Leaders: The Strategies for Taking Charge*. New York: Harper & Row, 1985.

Bernanos, Georges. *The Diary of a Country Priest*. Trans. Pamela Morris. New York: Macmillan, 1937.

Biles, Daniel V. *Pursuing Excellence in Ministry*. Washington, D.C.: Alban Institute, 988.

Bonhoeffer, Dietrich. *Life Together*. Trans. John W. Doberstein. New York: Harper, 1954.

Brewton, Marjie. *Heart of the Earth*. Chamberlain, S.D.: Register-Lakota Printing, 1989.

Briggs, Bill. *Faith through Works: Church Renewal through Mission*. Franconia, N.H.: Thorn Books, 1983.

Brueggemann, Walter. *The Land: Place as Gift, Promise, and Challenge in Biblical Faith*. Philadelphia: Fortress Press, 1977.

Brunner, Emil. *The Word and the World*. London: SCM, 1931.

Burt, Steve, and Douglas Alan Walrath, ed. *Activating Leadership in the Small Church: Clergy and Laity Working Together*. Valley Forge, Penn.: Judson Press, 1988.

Burt, Steven E., and Hazel Ann Roper. *The Little Church That Could: Raising Small Church Esteem*. Valley Forge, Penn: Judson Press, 2000.

Callahan, Kennon L. *Small, Strong Congregations: Creating Strengths and Health for Your Congregation*. San Francisco: Jossey-Bass, 2000.

Carroll, Jackson W., ed. *Small Churches Are Beautiful*. San Francisco: Harper & Row, 1977.

Chromey, Rick. *Children's Ministry Guide for Smaller Churches*. Loveland, Col.: Group, 1995.

Claman, Victor N., and David E. Butler. *Acting On Your Faith: Congregations Making a Difference*. Boston: Insights, 1994.

Cooley, Charles H. "Primary Groups." *Small Groups: Studies in Social Interaction*. Ed. A. Paul Hare, Edgar F. Borgotta, and Robert F. Bales. New York: Knopf, 1955.

Coote, Robert B., ed. *Mustard-Seed Churches: Ministries in Small Churches*. Minneapolis: Fortress Press, 1990.

Cope, Gilbert Frederick, ed. *Making the Building Serve the Liturgy: Studies in the Reordering of Churches*. London: A. R. Mowbray, 1962.

Crandall, Ron. *Turnaround Strategies for the Small Church*. Nashville, Tenn.: Abingdon, 1995.

Dudley, Carl S. *Making the Small Church Effective*. Nashville, Tenn.: Abingdon, 1978.

———. *Unique Dynamics of the Small Church*. Washington, D.C.: Alban Institute, 1977.

———, and Douglas Alan Walrath. *Developing Your Small Church's Potential*. Valley Forge, Penn.: Judson Press, 1988.

Eliot, T. S. *Collected Poems 1909–1962*. New York: Harcourt, Inc., 1936.

———. *Four Quartets*. New York: Harcourt, Inc., 1970.

Farley, Gary, and D. G. McCoury. *We're Family: Help for the Smaller Membership Church*. Nashville, Tenn.: Convention Press, 1992.

Farris, Lawrence W. *Dynamics of Small Town Ministry*. Bethesda, Md.: The Alban Institute, 2000.

Fenhagen, James C. *Mutual Ministry: New Vitality for the Local Church*. New York: Seabury Press, 1977.

Foltz, Nancy T. *Caring for the Small Church: Insights from Women in Ministry*. Valley Forge, Penn.: Judson Press, 1994.

———, ed. *Religious Education in the Small Membership Church*. Birmingham, Ala.: Religious Education Press, 1990.

Frazier, Edward Franklin. *The Negro Church in America*. New York: Schocken Books, 1964.

Friedman, Edwin H. *Generation to Generation: Family Process in Church and Synagogue*. New York: Guilford Press, 1985.

Gladwell, Malcolm. *The Tipping Point: How Little Things Can Make a Big Difference*. Boston: Little, Brown & Co., 2000.

Greenleaf, Robert K. *Servant Leadership: A Journey into the Nature of Legitimate Power and Greatness*. New York: Paulist Press, 1977.

Griggs, Donald L. and Judy McKay Walther. *Christian Education in the Small Church*. Valley Forge, Penn.: Judson Press, 1988.

Huxley, Aldous. *The Devils of Loudon*. New York: Carroll & Graf, 1986.

Jung, L. Shannon, and Mary A. Agria. *Rural Congregational Studies: A Guide for Good Shepherds*. Nashville, Tenn.: Abingdon, 1997.

————, et. al. *Rural Ministry: The Shape of the Renewal to Come*. Nashville, Tenn.: Abingdon, 1998.

Hanson, Paul D. *The People Called: The Growth of Community in the Bible*. San Francisco: Harper & Row, 1986.

Hare, A. Paul. *Handbook of Small Group Research*. New York: Free Press, 1976.

Hobgood, William Chris. *The Once and Future Pastor: The Changing Role of Religious Leaders*. Bethesda, Md.: Alban Institute, 1998.

Keizer, Garret. *A Dresser of Sycamore Trees: The Finding of a Ministry*. San Francisco: HarperSanFrancisco, 1993.

Keillor, Garrison. *Lake Wobegon Days*. New York: Viking, 1985.

Kraemer, Hendrick. *A Theology of the Laity*. London: Lutterworth, 1958.

Lamott, Anne. *Tender Mercies: Some Thoughts on Faith*. New York: Pantheon Books, 1999.

Lee, Bernard J. *The Catholic Experience of Small Christian Communities*. New York: Paulist Press, 2000.

Lewis, G. Douglass. *Meeting the Moment: Leadership and Well-Being in Ministry*. Nashville, Tenn.: Abingdon, 1997.

Macquarrie, John. *Principles of Christian Theology*. New York: Scribner, 1966.

Mann, Alice. *Can Our Church Live? Redeveloping Congregations in Decline*. Washington, D.C.: Alban Institute, 1999.

Mead, Loren B. *More Than Numbers: The Ways Churches Grow*. Washington, D.C.: Alban Institute, 1993.

————. *The Once and Future Church: Reinventing the Congregation for a New Mission Frontier*. Washington, D.C.: Alban Institute, 1991.

Norris, Kathleen. *Dakota: A Spiritual Geography*. New York: Ticknor & Fields, 1993.

————. *The Cloister Walk*. New York: Riverhead Books, 1996.

Nouwen, Henri J. M. *Creative Ministry*. Garden City, N.Y.: Doubleday, 1971.

————. *Reaching Out: The Three Movements of the Spiritual Life*. Garden City, N.Y.: Doubleday, 1966.

———. *Sabbatical Journey: The Diary of His Final Year.* New York: Crossroad, 1998.

O'Connor, Elizabeth. *The New Community.* New York: Harper & Row, 1976.

Pappas, Anthony. *Money, Motivation, and Mission in the Small Church.* Valley Forge, Penn.: Judson Press, 1989.

———, and Scott Planting. *Mission: The Small Church Reaches Out.* Valley Forge, Penn.: Judson Press, 1993.

Pappas, Anthony G. *Entering the World of the Small Church.* Bethesda, Md.: Alban Institute, 2000.

Percy, Walker. *The Moviegoer.* New York: Knopf, 1961.

Putnam, Robert D. *Bowling Alone: The Collapse and Revival of American Community.* New York: Simon & Schuster, 2000.

Ray, David R. *The Big Small Church Book.* Cleveland: The Pilgrim Press, 1992.

———. *Small Churches Are the Right Size.* New York: The Pilgrim Press, 1982.

———. *Wonderful Worship in Smaller Churches.* Cleveland: The Pilgrim Press, 2000.

Remen, Rachel Naomi. *Kitchen Table Wisdom: Stories That Heal.* New York: Riverhead Books, 1996.

Rothauge, Arlin J. *Sizing Up the Congregation for New Member Ministry.* New York: Episcopal Church Center, 1989.

Sale, Kirkpatrick. *Human Scale.* New York: Coward, McCann & Geoghegan, 1980.

Schaller, Lyle E. *Growing Plans.* Nashville, Tenn.: Abingdon, 1983.

———. *Looking in the Mirror: Self-appraisal in the Local Church.* Nashville, Tenn.: Abingdon, 1984.

———. *The Small Church Is Different!* Nashville, Tenn.: Abingdon, 1982.

———. *The Small Membership Church: Scenarios for Tomorrow.* Nashville, Tenn.: Abingdon, 1994.

Siegel, Bernie S. *Love, Medicine, and Miracles: Lessons Learned about Self-healing from a Surgeon's Experience with Exceptional Patients.* New York: Harper & Row, 1986.

Simmel, Georg. *The Sociology of Georg Simmel.* Trans., ed. and introd. Kurt H. Wolff. New York: Free Press of Glencoe, 1950.

Vanier, Jean. *Community and Growth.* Rev. ed. New York: Paulist Press, 1989.

Wagley, Laurence A. *Preaching with the Small Congregation.* Nashville, Tenn.: Abingdon, 1989.

Wagner, C. Peter. *Your Church Can Grow*. Ventura, Calif.: Regal Books, 1984.

Waldkoenig, Gilson A. C., and William O. Avery. *Cooperating Congregations: Portraits of Mission Strategies*. Bethesda, Md.: Alban Institute, 1999.

Walrath, Douglas Alan. *Leading Churches through Change*. Nashville, Tenn.: Abingdon, 1979.

———. *Making It Work: Effective Administration in the Small Church*. Valley Forge, Penn.: Judson Press, 1994.

———, ed. *New Possibilities for Small Churches*. New York: The Pilgrim Press, 1983.

Westerhoff, John H., III. *Will Our Children Have Faith?* Rev. and exp. Harrisburg, Penn.: Morehouse, 2000.

White, James F. *Introduction to Christian Worship*. Nashville, Tenn.: Abingdon, 1980.

Wiesel, Elie. *Souls on Fire: Portraits and Legends of Hasidic Masters*. Trans. Marion Wiesel. New York: Random House, 1972.

Willimon, William H., and Robert L. Wilson. *Preaching and Worship in the Small Church*. Nashville, Tenn.: Abingdon, 1980.

Wilson, Robert L. *The Multi-church Parish*. Nashville, Tenn.: Abingdon, 1989.

Winter, Miriam Therese. *Preparing the Way of the Lord*. Nashville, Tenn.: Abingdon, 1978.

Journals

Dudley, Carl S. "Small Churches Are Special." *JED Share* 8, no. 1 (spring 1979).

Ostendorf, David L. "Toward Wholeness and Community: Strategies for Pastoral and Political Response to the American Rural Crisis." *Word and World: Theology for Christian Ministry* 6, no. 1 (winter 1986).

Redfield, Robert. "The Folk Society." *American Journal of Sociology* 52, no. 4 (Jan. 1947).

Subject Index

Appalachian Ministries Educational Resource Center, 251
Area minister, 15, 16, 18–19, 80
Austin, Nancy, 245

Bailey, Pearl, 152
Bangor Theological Seminary, 76; Certification in Small Church Leadership, 251
Baptism, 58, 96, 97, 124–26, 138. See also Sacraments
Barth, Karl, 253
Beecher, Lyman, xvii
Bellah, Robert, 41
Bennis, Warren, 241, 245
Biblical community, 48–49; smaller churches' resemblance to, 56–60
The Big Small Church Book, x, 88
Biles, Daniel. 244, 245
Bi-vocational ministry, 7, 31, 80, 237, 242, 249, 250, 251, 254–255, 257, 258
Bonhoeffer, Dietrich, 41, 42, 90, 122, 150
Bothwell, Lin, 248
Brewton, Marjie, 12
Briggs, Bill, 180, 187–88
Bruner, Emil, 169
Buber, Martin, 61
Buildings, 4; additions to, 7–8, 16; alternative meeting spaces, 23, 24; congregations sharing, 4, 14, 230, 237, 249, 253; growth and, 212–13; investment in people not institutions, 224; morale and, 199; projects that build personal relationships, 33, 230–31; renovation of, 4, 17, 29, 38, 117–19; rents and donations, 229–230; use by other organizations, 4, 29–31, 38, 175–76, 230. See also Finances; Worship
Butler, David E., 183

Callahan, Kennon L., xxii, 169, 240
Call to ministry, 241, 243
Caring, 39, 59–60, 88, 152–68; caring communities, 154–56, 159–61; examples of, 156–58; pastoral leadership and, 155, 242–45; Seventy-Nine Caring Strategies, 159–67. See also Hospitality
Carroll, Jackson, xix
Celebrations, 97, 102; morale and, 198–99; seasonal celebrations and worship, 115, 127–28
Change, 239–40, 244
Children in smaller churches, 96; worship and, 111. See also Christian education

Christian education, 129–51; adults and, 130, 133, 149–50; biblical basis and foundation, 59, 142–44; curriculum and materials, 148–49; denominational resources, 146, 148; ecological, 141–42; experiential, 133, 145; familial, 139–41; goals of, 131, 144; hospitality, 135–36, 153; in history, 134–35; individualized, 138–39; intergenerational, 139–40, 146–47, 150; leaders and teachers, 147–48; mature Christian faith and, 131–34, 137; methods, 146–47; public school model and, 131, 134; space for, 145–146; worship and, 137; youth, 141, 149. See also Discipleship
Chromey, Rick, 148
Church; as community, 46–51; biblical expectations, 58–60; criteria for, 46; defined, x–xi; family systems, 85
Church and social context; 76–77; U.S. Census Web site, 76
Church Morale Inventory; 195–98, 201, 272–274. See also Morale
Claman, Victor N., 183
Closing churches, xxii–xxiii, 17–19, 28, 79, 85; effect on community, 19, 101; finances perceived as cause, 219–20, 237
Communication, 91, 247
Communion, 58, 124, 126–27, 140. See also Sacraments
Community, 60, 71; church as community, 46–51, 58–61, 107, 111, 202; community building strategies, 159–61; importance of church to, 101
Community of faith, vii, 25, 30, 34–36, 39, 41–42, 44, 80, 47–51, 58, 81, 106, 110, 132, 145, 244, 256–57, 261; biblical community, 48–50, 56–60; importance of for society, 47–48; size and, 51–58; theology of small, x. See also Remnant; Worship
Compensation. See pastoral compensation
Confirmation, 8–9, 97, 126, 139. See also Christian education; Sacraments
Conflict, 23–24
Congregational Life Cycle theory, 83–85. See also Theory
Cooley, Charles, 70–71
Copastors, 28, 31, 78. See also Shared ministry
Cosby, Gordon, 209–10

Damon, Daniel, 104
Dante, 153

Smaller Churches—an Odyssey

Scripture Index